TEARS
OVER
RUSSIA

TEARS OVER RUSSIA

A SEARCH FOR FAMILY AND THE
LEGACY OF UKRAINE'S POGROMS

LISA BRAHIN

PEGASUS BOOKS
NEW YORK LONDON

TEARS OVER RUSSIA

Pegasus Books, Ltd.
148 West 37th Street, 13th Floor
New York, NY 10018

First Pegasus Books cloth edition June 2022

Interior design by Maria Fernandez

Library of Congress Cataloging-in-Publication Data is available.

ISBN: 978-1-63936-167-0

10 9 8 7 6 5 4 3 2 1

Printed in the United States of America
Distributed by Simon & Schuster
www.pegasusbooks.com

To Grandma Anne "Channa"
In loving memory
August 11, 1912–February 27, 2003

CONTENTS

PART III: EXODUS TO THE GOLDENE MEDINA, 1920–1925

PART IV: REBECCA AND ISAAC'S CHILDREN: SELECT STORIES IN PHILADELPHIA, 1926–1941

PART V: RABBIS AND REUNIONS 1941–1950 RAINBOWS 1925 AND 2003

APPENDICES

A GRANDDAUGHTER'S MEMORIES

As a child, I was drawn to an old sepia-toned photograph taken in Russia that stood proudly on my great-grandmother's shelf. The Cabinet Portrait showed her as a stunning young brunette propping up her infant daughter on a four-legged stand. It was my first clue that another world preceded mine, and the image of my great-grandmother and grandmother living a different reality ignited within me a lifetime desire to learn every detail of their past.

When Great-Grandma died in July 1972, I was nine years old and visiting my grandparents in the Adirondack Mountains in upstate New York, as I did every summer vacation. During that visit, it occurred to me that many of our family's secrets died with the passing of my oldest relative. I regretted not tapping her on the shoulder and asking her, "What was your grandmother's name?" or "What was your wedding like?" or "Who else in our family missed the boat to America?" I know that she would have been moved and happy had I expressed interest in the family's past.

So, I did the next best thing. I directed my questions to her daughter, my grandmother Anne. One night I couldn't sleep, and Grandma came into my room and started humming and patting my shoulder.

"Grandma," I asked her in the wee hours of the morning, "Why did your mother call you Channa?"

"It's my Jewish name from Russia," she answered.

"Please, Grandma," I begged her, "tell me about when you met the bandits in Russia."

At first, she didn't take my interest seriously.

"Honey," she answered, "wouldn't you rather I make you a cup of hot chocolate?"

I already knew that my grandmother's happiest childhood memories, in the years just preceding the Revolution, were of playing and picking flowers on Count Branicki's estate. As a young girl, I watched as Grandma planted lilac bushes on the property line of my mother's home in New Jersey. She said that this reminded her of the purple lilacs in bloom that formed a hedge in the count's botanical gardens, a constant attribute to springtime in her native town, Stavishche, Russia, located today in Ukraine.*

Now I was delving into memories that she would rather forget. Faced with the dilemma of how to entertain a young insomniac, Grandma eventually came to learn that the only way I would fall asleep was by listening to the soft sound of her voice as she described in detail her early childhood in Russia. I was barely old enough then to understand the implication and weight of her words, but I sensed that my mother's mother had lived through turbulent times that continued to plague her throughout her life.

After hearing my grandmother Anne's secrets and stories, it became clear to me why she battled with nervous phobias. There were too many "episodes" to count, but her one brave attempt to ride an elevator with me when I was a child made the most lasting impression. On our way to a department store fashion show, wearing matching spring hats, we were unexpectedly directed to an upper floor. When the elevator doors closed, absolute panic set in. Grandma couldn't catch her breath and anxiously pressed every button to get out.

My grandmother was so fearful of enclosed spaces that even as an elderly lady, she opted to take the stairs. Her claustrophobia was an unwelcome result of the trauma she endured during the anti-Jewish pogroms of 1918–1920,† when she spent her days hiding in crawlspaces. As a little girl, she was caught in

---

* At the time of Channa's birth, Stavishche was located in Tarashcha Uyezd (district) and Kiev Guberniya (province) in the Russian Empire, with her official passport stating she was born in Russia. During her childhood in Stavishche, her hometown became a part of Ukrainian People's Republic/ Ukrainian National Republic, and has since endured a long history. Today it is in Ukraine.

† I believe that the full scope of this wave of pogroms was between 1917–1921, but my grandmother's personal experiences of violence in the region were mostly between 1918–1920. There were also pogroms that extended outside of Ukraine, but the focus of this story is what happened in Ukraine where my grandmother lived.

pandemonium as her village evacuated, and people ran for their lives. The chaos that she survived shaped fears that haunted her for nearly ninety years.

Grandma Anne's story is not about the Holocaust but rather a prelude, twenty years earlier, of the horror that was to come. She was a young Jewish girl born into a world that refused to tolerate or accept Jews and their way of life. In fact, she lived in a world that did not want Jews at all.

As a young teenager, I decided that the intelligent thing to do was to tape-record Grandma's stories so that, in years to come, I could write a biography of the events leading up to my ancestors' voyage to America. Unfortunately, because of my grandmother's nervousness, the stories flowed better when the cassette wasn't turned on. The minute she saw the tape recorder in front of her, she froze.

Grandma Anne finally relaxed after I suggested that she should pretend I was the only one who would ever hear what she said. She began recounting her miraculous tales, and, after dozens of hours of successful storytelling, I was proud of myself for having recorded them for posterity. However, posterity didn't last as long as I had expected. Late one evening, when I decided to listen to the many recordings, I realized that the machine had malfunctioned; the tapes were blank.

My grandmother, disappointed that so many hours of her storytelling were all in vain, agreed to redo the many taping sessions while waiting for the bus to arrive at her new condominium in Florida to take her to nightly bridge games. During my many visits with Grandma in the late seventies, I followed her, with a microphone in hand, and we bonded at that bus stop.

Grandma Anne's vivid accounts of her family's survival during Russia's deadliest wave of pogroms—when estimates ranging from well over one hundred thousand to nearly a quarter of a million Jews were annihilated during scores of riots that swept across the country—left me searching for answers. I craved more information about this historical nightmare that befell my family in Grandma's childhood town of Stavishche.

My curiosity only heightened when I discovered that there was almost nothing published about this time period. As a young newlywed contemplating my own future, I could not help but wonder: Where was this mysterious place on the other side of the earth, where my grandmother's world began and then so abruptly fell apart?

It was upstairs, in a back room of the historic Free Library of Philadelphia, where I first experienced the exhilaration of pinpointing Stavishche on a map. I stood over an old photocopier with a pile of change and printed out sections of the magnified page from a large atlas that covered a thirty-mile radius. I then carefully matched the pages and Scotch-taped them all together. With absolute delight, I circled all the obscure villages near Kiev* whose names I had heard over and over again during my own childhood: Stavishche, Skibin, Zhashkov, Tarashcha, Sokolovka, and Belaya Tserkov.

I tucked the map in an envelope, sent it off to Grandma in Florida, and eagerly awaited her reaction. In a letter dated May 25, 1984, I received a thrilling answer. "Dear Lisa," Grandma wrote. "I'm getting a big kick reading the map you sent. Where were you able to find a blown-up map from the area? I finally saw the town in print, where I was born. Now I can confirm that I was really born somewhere."

Throughout the years, my thirst for information never ceased. My unyielding determination to piece together the puzzle of the past set me on a path to pursue what has become my lifelong passion—Jewish genealogy. I began by writing to curators around the world, who combed their archives for unpublished, mostly handwritten, documents and manuscripts about the pogroms in her area. Many of these elusive sources had been collecting dust for decades while sitting on shelves in New York City; Washington, DC; Kiev; Warsaw; Jerusalem; and Tel Aviv. With the assistance of a number of talented linguists, mostly volunteers, who pored over the Yiddish, Hebrew, Russian, Ukrainian, and Polish pages, my grandmother's tales were at last historically validated.

Many years after conducting interviews with my grandmother and the last generation of Jews to live in the town, I was determined to tap one last wealth of unpublished sources—family histories. With doors now opened by the Internet, families with ties to Stavishche living in seven countries around the world shared their personal stories with me. What I didn't expect during this fascinating journey were the many exciting anecdotes that would emerge of colorful person-alities of the day. Their accounts painted a portrait of the town, bringing light to an entire group of people who lived so long ago.

In the end, despite her hesitation and constant battle with nerves, Grandma was at peace with having entrusted me with the details of her most private experiences, knowing that I intended to thoroughly research and chronicle her saga. Scholarly materials and eloquent testimonies from her childhood neighbors that I gathered in the years following our taping sessions are woven

---

* The modern name for Kiev is Kyiv.

into this narrative, enhancing my grandmother's viewpoint, which remains the fulcrum of the book.

In February 2003, Grandma Anne succumbed to pneumonia and was buried alongside my grandfather—her husband of sixty-six years—at my synagogue's cemetery in Neptune, New Jersey. The week of her death coincided with a major snowstorm, and the ground was both frozen and muddy. At her grave-side, a handful of family members and friends gathered together, shivering under umbrellas, sharing their memories of this wonderful woman. During the eulogy, while a sleet-like rain pummeled us, I stood there thinking that although Grandma finally "went to sleep" (a phrase that she often used referring to death), I would see to it that her stories would never die.

Many thanks, Grandma.

A BRIEF CHRONOLOGY
OF HISTORICAL EVENTS
1881–1921

1881

Tsar Alexander II is assassinated and is succeeded by Alexander III.

Following unsubstantiated rumors that Jews were behind the tsar's murder, the first of three waves of anti-Jewish pogroms sweeps across Russia. In 1881 alone, 250 attacks are committed against the Jews. The attacks continue until 1884.

1882

Tsar Alexander III passes the May Laws, anti-Jewish regulations that severely restrict the freedom of Russia's Jewish population.

1892

The anti-Semitic work *The Talmud Unmasked: The Secret Rabbinical Teachings Concerning Christians* is published in St. Petersburg, Russia.

1894

Tsar Alexander III dies and is succeeded by Nicholas II.

1897

5,200,000 Jews appear in the first census of the Russian Empire.

1903

The newspaper of St. Petersburg, Russia's *Znamya* (*The Banner*), publishes a fraudulent document, *The Protocols of Zion*, the most notorious work of modern anti-Semitism.

In Kishinev, a three-day pogrom breaks out over Easter, killing nearly fifty Jews. The massacre receives worldwide attention.

A second wave of bloody anti-Jewish pogroms hits Russia from 1903–1906, leaving an estimated two thousand Jews dead.

1904

Russia and Japan fight in the Russo-Japanese War.

1905

In January, the Imperial Guard fires at one thousand peaceful demonstrators who arrive with a priest at the Winter Palace to petition the tsar for better working conditions. During this incident, which becomes known as "Bloody Sunday," two hundred people are killed and eight hundred are wounded.

Russia's defeat in the Russo-Japanese War is followed by a revolution in that year, leading to the institution of the Duma.

During the two weeks following the October Manifesto, an estimated three hundred to seven hundred anti-Jewish riots break out during the second wave of pogroms.

The Black Hundredists provoke anti-Semitic sentiments, resulting in numerous pogroms against Russia's Jews.

1911

Dimitry Bogrov, an agent of Okhrana and the son of a Jewish lawyer in Kiev, assassinates Prime Minister Pyotr Stolypin at the Kiev Opera House while the tsar is in attendance.

1913

The Beilis Trial, a blood libel accusation falsely made against Menaham Mendel Beilis, a Jew from Kiev, causes an international storm of public opinion. It becomes apparent during the murder trial that the evidence was fabricated against him because he is Jewish.

1914

After the assassination of Archduke Franz Ferdinand of Austria in Serbia, World War I breaks out in Europe. Germany declares war on Russia.

1915

German troops invade and occupy the area of Ukraine, where large Jewish populations live in what is known as the Pale of Settlement.

1916

The war continues to go badly for Russia. Tsar Nicholas refuses to make the needed reforms in the government.

The royal adviser Rasputin is murdered by a group of nobles.

1917

The February Revolution is followed by the abdication of Tsar Nicholas II.

The Pale of Settlement is abolished by the Provisional Government.

Alexander Kerensky succeeds Prince George L'vov as prime minister of the Provisional Government. During the October Revolution, the Bolsheviks replace Kerensky with Vladimir Lenin.

1918

The Rada (Parliament) refuses to give up control of Ukraine to the Bolsheviks. They declare the independence of the Ukrainian National Republic. Stavishche, Russia, the hometown of the author's grandmother, becomes a part of the Ukrainian National Republic.

Bolshevik troops invade Ukraine, but the Germans drive them out.

Russia and Germany sign the Treaty of Brest-Litovsk, marking Russia's exit from WWI.

A third wave of anti-Jewish pogroms picks up momentum and sweeps across Russia and Ukraine. During the period of civil unrest (1917–1921), it is estimated that anywhere from well over 100,000 to nearly 250,000 civilian Jews are murdered; many thousands of Jews are left homeless, and many thousands of Jewish children are left orphaned.

Tsar Nicholas II, his wife, and their children are murdered by the Bolsheviks.

Germany is defeated by the Allies.

1919–1920
Symon Petliura becomes head of Army and State in Ukraine. His soldiers begin to carry out brutal massacres against the Jews.

Poland and Russia are at war.

Ukraine is caught up in a bloody civil war. The three forces struggling for power are the White Army (who are against the Bolsheviks), the Ukrainian Army (the Nationalists), and the Bolshevik Red Army.

While fighting against the Bolsheviks, both the Whites and Ukrainian forces are responsible for the majority of pogrom massacres being committed against the Jews of Russia. In 1919 and 1920, the greatest concentration of anti-Jewish violence is in Kiev Province and is carried out by various bands controlled by leaders such as (but not limited to) Nikifor Grigoriev and Danylo Zeleny. Petliura and Anton Denikin lead armies that commit massacres against Jewish civilians.

Bessarabia, once an integral part of the Russian Empire, unites with Romania. Jews fleeing from Russia and Ukraine must now cross over a new border, the Dniester River.

1921

The Bolshevik Red Army defeats the Whites and Ukrainian forces.

Famines in both Ukraine and Russia kill millions of people.

The United States enacts an immigration quota that limits the annual number of immigrants admitted into the country. As a result, tens of thousands of Jewish pogrom victims from Russia and Ukraine are stranded in Europe.

As a combined result of the three violent waves of anti-Jewish pogroms in Russia and Ukraine (1881–1884, 1903–1906, 1917–1921) more than two million Jews flee Russia and Ukraine (over the thirty-year period) and emigrate to other lands.

STAVISHCHE
JUNE 15–16, 1919

As dusk fell, a near full moon shone over Stavishche. Isaac and his wife, Rebecca, enjoyed a break from a long workweek, relaxing and celebrating with friends under the moonlight in a courtyard garden. Suddenly, the air erupted with nearby gunshots: Rebecca was panic-stricken. A man ran by and yelled, "Zhelezniak's thugs! They're back! There's more of them—hide!" before dashing away. At almost the same moment, a woman screamed, "Please, no!" A child cried; a plate-glass window crashed. Thugs were bashing in doors and destroying the Jewish shops and homes. Many, like theirs, were attached to both sides of the Stavishcha Inn, behind which they now sat frozen in fear.

"The girls!" Rebecca yelled. The thought of her daughters unfroze her, and she bolted toward the house. Another woman screamed, this time just across the courtyard wall. They were too close. Isaac grabbed his wife's arm hard, pulling her to her knees. "There's no time! Root cellar!"

They were just steps from the inn's cellar, a half-dugout, musty hole under the crumbling corner of the old stables. Here, in the dark, they kept potatoes, bins of dried beans, hanging herbs. The cellar was cool and black. It felt dank and smelled slightly rotten, a hundred years of cobwebs, termite-infested rafters, manure, spilled pickle juice, and mildew. Isaac climbed down and wiggled to the back on his stomach; his wife did more of a crawl, protecting her growing belly from scraping the ground. Their hearts thumped as they lay with their arms around each other. A body thudded against Rebecca: it was her friend Rachel, followed by Rachel's new husband, Elias.

The shots were more muffled now but still clearly nearby. The never-ending sounds jostled them: crashes of window glass, smashed liquor bottles, boots stomping, splintering of wood as doors were axed open, and then more gunshots. They heard the wild laughter of a group of drunken men.

"Our babies," Isaac said in her ear. "I have to go get them."

"It's too late," Rebecca whispered back.

Her hand tightened on his arm. "No!" she cried to him, knowing it was the cruelest word. "They'll see us. They'll follow us to the children. We'll all die."

From outside, more crashes, screams, laughter.

What have I done? Isaac thought, regretting his decision to leave the girls alone in the house.

Rebecca feared the worst. *We've lost them forever*, she thought. The dank root cellar would surely be their own grave; she knew it.

Just minutes earlier, the couple's evening had begun peacefully. The near full moon meant that the night's sky would never get completely dark. Yet this longer day of sunlight meant that Rebecca's sewing continued well into the evening. It was Sunday, just before eight, when the pretty seamstress finally tucked her girls into their small bed in the back room, telling them, "Go to sleep now." Slightly plump little Sunny, nearly three, snuggled her back against her six-year-old sister, Channa.

Rebecca moved quickly through the tiny living quarters, finishing her chores before heading out of the house. She took only a moment to fix her long, dark hair. Isaac was just arriving from the front room, set up as his shoe factory, where all day long he'd nailed soles onto boots. Sundays were especially long since the day before was Sabbath. Rebecca exchanged a weary smile with her handsome, dark-haired husband.

"The children are asleep?" he asked.

"On their way."

The couple headed to the courtyard garden out back, near the stables that housed the horses for the guests at the nearby establishment. In a far corner, their neighbors Rachel and Elias, just married, sat and held hands on a bench. Isaac and Rebecca greeted their new friends with a bottle of wine. "Mazel tov!" they wished them, as the foursome raised and clinked together Rebecca's silver shot glasses in a celebratory toast. Rebecca, resting her hand on her pregnant belly, did not raise the cup to her lips.

The courtyard was still and warm; a late spring dusk appeared. From the street they heard the clop-clop of horse-drawn wagons. They drank and laughed until most of the daylight disappeared after nine.

Inside, in the dark back bedroom, Channa snuggled her sister's warm body until Sunny stopped wiggling. Then, feeling warm in the June evening, Channa kicked off the blanket and stared at the ceiling. Finally, she, too, dozed off: first fitfully, then so deeply that she didn't hear the initial gunshots in front of the Stavishcha Inn.

The explosion had their parents sitting bolt upright: Rebecca's round blue eyes widening, Isaac's clean-shaven chin jutting from his face. Rachel screamed; Elias covered her mouth.

They waited in the root cellar. Hours of it; it would never end.

As daylight approached, the noises changed. First the commotion stopped. Rebecca and Isaac still lay in place, breathing lightly in rhythm, too afraid to move. Then the screams began again, but these were different: wails by the injured, wails for the dead.

The foursome crawled and then climbed out of the cellar and into the early June sun. From every corner, the neighborhood was coming out of hiding, hugging and crying or screaming next to the victims of the pogrom.[*] Rebecca and Isaac ran quickly to their house. They opened the back door, which was still closed and intact, and rushed to their daughters' bed.

Their legs froze in place, preparing for the worst. Rebecca felt an awful pit in her stomach, afraid of what horrible scene they might find. Instead, Channa lay peacefully on her back, and, as usual, her arms were outstretched. Sunny lay in a fetal position, her face pressed into the goose-feathered pillow. But they were breathing. They were sleeping, untouched. They'd slept through it all!

The violent mob had passed over their house!

Rebecca looked at her husband. His cheeks had gone white. Hands shaking, he picked up Sunny, who stretched and smiled. Rebecca broke down and sobbed uncontrollably into Channa's long, brown hair. Confused, the girls looked around with wide eyes. Everything was exactly as Rebecca had left it: a soaking pot

---

[*]   Note: A violent riot or organized massacre aimed at the persecution of a particular ethnic or religious group, often aimed at Jews in Russia, Ukraine or eastern Europe.

still stood upright on its stand, sewing needles and a small jewel case left on a nightstand remained undisturbed. The girls were oblivious to what had happened.

"Nothing—nothing touched," Isaac said; wondering, "Why did they spare us?"

"Isaac!" a howl came from outside the front door, followed by loud banging. "Isaac! Isaac Caprove! Your peasant Vasyl has murdered my wife!"

TEARS
OVER
RUSSIA

PART I

CALM BEFORE THE STORM
1876–1918

CHAPTER ONE

FAMILY FOLKLORE

The *Get*: 1876

I t was a matchmaker's worst nightmare.

Rebecca's mother, Fay, and her bewildered husband, Samuel, both appeared before the rabbinical court, also known as the *beit din*, in 1876, for a legal hearing. According to Jewish law, there was a "special rule regarding the *get*, or bill of divorcement."[*] Since the marriage could only be dissolved after her husband handed Fay the get,[†] young Samuel stood before a rabbi and asked, "Rabbi, in front of my witnesses, I ask you for a divorce from my wife, Fay Berkova, the *feldsher* Kohen's daughter."

The beautiful fourteen-year-old redhead was instructed to remove her engagement and wedding rings. She accepted her divorce decree as her husband had and recited the obligatory words, "Behold, this is your get; thou art divorced by it from me and thou art (hereby) permitted to marry any man.[‡]"

Fay was finally free to marry the man that she loved—Carl Cutler. However, the first man in her life, her father the feldsher, would never forgive her.

---

[*] ChaeRan Y. Freeze. *Jewish Marriage and Divorce in Imperial Russia*. Waltham, MA: Brandeis University Press, 2002, page 144.

[†] For more details of the laws involved with obtaining a get, see Freeze's scholarly work, *Jewish Marriage and Divorce in Imperial Russia*.

[‡] Freeze, *Jewish Marriage and Divorce in Imperial Russia*, page 144.

Her matchmaker, an important woman in the *shtetl*, struggled to rebound from such a professional disaster. Just a few years earlier, there were less than five hundred divorces reported among Jewish couples living in the vast area of Kiev Guberniya.* Divorce was so rare that it never occurred to Fay or her father, Kohen,† that his young daughter with a gorgeous crown of red hair would ever be included in such a statistic. Now the matchmaker's own unblemished success record was on the line.

Kohen was a talented and successful feldsher, who provided the only medical care for the entire village and its environs.‡ The more formally educated doctors treated the wealthy, while feldshers were used by the vast peasant population. As a feldsher, Fay's father had spent many years away from home in the service of Tsar Alexander II. It had been his professional duty, along with the draft board, to travel from village to village performing medical examinations on those unfortunate young men of age who were being drafted into the tsar's army.§ When he returned home, he was finally able to enjoy his substantial estate in the rural *dorf* of Skibin. The gorgeous lilac bushes that he instructed to be planted surrounding his home bore a slight resemblance to those that lined the botanical gardens of Count Wladyslaw Branicki's palace in nearby Stavishche.

As was common in those days, the newly wed Fay and Samuel were residing for the first year of their marriage with the bride's family, which was a part of her father's obligation known as *kest*.¶ Although Fay was not lacking in material comforts, she was trapped in a loveless marriage and suffered enormously.

The inner turmoil she felt over her unhappy marital predicament began to take both a physical and emotional toll on the young woman. The marriage forced upon Fay by her father and the matchmaker was destroying her. In short, her

---

* The general Jewish population in the province that year was 267,867. (Freeze, *Jewish Marriage and Divorce in Imperial Russia*, page 302.

† While he was known as the feldsher Kohen, the proper name of Fay's father was most likely Berko or Ber Braunstein HaKohen. He was a *Kohanim*. Kohanim, or *Kohen* (Hebrew for priest), are considered to be of direct patrilineal descent from the biblical Aaron, brother of Moses.

‡ The term *feldsher* was actually borrowed from the German word *feldscherer*, which means "field barber" or "barber surgeon." In the 1700s, Peter the Great of Russia used feldshers for medical and surgical treatment of his soldiers. See article by L. M. Rousselot, MD, in Notes.

§ In such a day, when entrance into the tsar's army meant no exit for years, Russian men were desperate to find any means to avoid conscription. It would often be the feldsher who witnessed the self-mutilating wounds that these young men would inflict upon themselves to be saved from such a fate.

¶ *Kest* is an agreement in the marital contract when one set of parents agree to provide room and board for the newlyweds as they adjust to their first year of marriage.

appetite for life had disappeared; she derived no pleasure from her food, and she could find no comfort in sleep. Fay was so wrapped up in her own emotional pain that when she arrived on foot one Tuesday morning at the bustling marketplace in nearby Stavishche, she collapsed. The noise of the peasants and peddlers bargaining and closing deals around her went silent as she fainted at the feet of two young brothers, Carl and Hertz Cutler, wheat sellers from Skvira and Zhashkov.*

As her dizziness began to subside, Fay opened her eyes for a closer look at Carl, the tall, blond peddler who had rushed to save her from hitting the ground. Her heart was racing, a sensation that she had never felt before. Fay was not the only one to be instantly lovestruck; Carl immediately felt the exchange of electricity between them. From that day on, Tuesdays were days that the couple met and disappeared from his booth at the market, holding hands during long walks away from the prying eyes of the shtetl. After her shocking divorce, the couple married in a small ceremony under the stars, standing beneath a flower-laden *chuppah*.

Despite being disowned and cut off from her family's great resources, Fay and Carl Cutler raised their seven children in Skibin, the same rural dorf where she grew up, whose border with the larger shtetl Stavishche was lined with tall wheat fields. The couple lived off Carl's meager income as a wheat seller at the fairs in Stavishche and in other nearby markets held on different days in Zhashkov, Tarashcha, and Pyatigory.

Skibin: 1900–1911

A peek into a crystal ball would reveal disasters in 20th-century Russia that would cause devastation to all its subjects, including Fay and Carl Cutler's growing family. The tsar's family and other nobles would eventually be murdered, and a revolution, preceded by starvation, violence, and hopelessness, would soon erupt. Estimates ranging from over one hundred thousand to nearly a quarter of a million of Russia's Jews, many who lived in the region of Kiev, where the Cutler family resided, would be murdered in pogrom massacres that incited peasants to "Kill the Jews and Save Russia!" Many Jews would soon find themselves dreaming of a life across the ocean in the *Goldene Medina*, the "golden land" where the streets were rumored to be paved with gold.

---

* The brothers, sons of Shimon Kotlyar of Skvira, were referred to as Kelman and Gertz in the 19th-century Russian Revision lists.

Fay and Carl's seven children (in the order of their birth, Shalum, Yunkel, Hiya, Rebecca, Molly, Avrum, and Bessie) would not be immune to that dream as adults.* However, as children, they mostly enjoyed a happy and carefree existence in Skibin, blissfully sheltered from the worries of the world and ignorant of the impending doom that would soon loom over Russia. The few Jewish families who resided in this mostly impoverished countryside village in Tarashcha Uyezd assimilated with their Christian neighbors. Jewish children learned to speak Russian fluently without an accent, thanks to the many hours they spent playing with the local peasant children.

During warm summer evenings, the Cutler siblings intermingled with young peasants their age, setting out in wagons to the forest to congregate by firelight. A peasant boy taught the third youngest, Molly, how to pluck songs on his bala- laika, a triangular folk lute popular in Ukraine. Molly played the balalaika as her younger brother and sister sat by her side in the woods singing Russian folk songs.

The four oldest children would come of age and marry before the onset of the Revolution. However, matters of the heart would soon bring two of the couple's children, son Yunkel and daughter Rebecca (Channa's mother), to plant roots in the same neighboring town, Stavishche, where both would meet their future spouses under scandalous circumstances.

Yunkel

Yunkel, the couple's second son, a dashing young man who was slightly shorter and huskier than his two brothers, Shalum and Avrum, bore a handsome face with expressive and kind eyes. Yunkel fell madly in love with Esther Moser, the pretty and feisty daughter of the world-famous cantor of Stavishche, David-Yosel Moser. His love life became complicated, though, after learning that Esther had already been promised to another man.

Esther's intended groom was a member of another well-known family in her town. In the decade preceding the Revolution, there were two prominent Jewish families in Stavishche. One family was Esther's, named Moser; the

---

* In the list of the Jews living in the countryside in Taraschansky Uyezd in 1882, and updated in 1893, a daughter named Sarah, who probably died during childhood, was born before Rebecca. The two youngest children, Avrum and Bessie, were born after the list was compiled. The family appears on the list as living in Skibin illegally due to the tsar's edicts restricting where Jews lived.

other prominent clan was named Stepansky. The two families had intermarried several times over and were the true Jewish roots of the town. David-Yosel Moser, Esther's father and the patriarch of the Moser family, was one of the *chazzans* (cantors) of Stavishche and, as such, held a high position in the Jewish community. David-Yosel became famous throughout Russia for training his brother-in-law, who became one of the world's first blind cantors, Leaper the Blinder (the Blind One).

As a blind cantor, Leaper was unable to read directly from the Torah, as proscribed by Jewish law, and was forbidden from reciting the words of the scroll by heart. However, Leaper was so talented, and had such an incredible mind, that David-Yosel was able to teach him the entire *Haftorah* (readings from the Prophets, corresponding to the Torah section read in the synagogue on the Sabbath) by memory. It was through his association with Leaper that David-Yosel became known as an esteemed teacher.

When David-Yosel's wife, Pessie, was pregnant with Esther, the cantor made a *shidduch* (arranged marriage) with one of the Stepanskys, whose wife was also expecting a baby at the same time. If these children were born of the opposite sex, which they were, the prospective marriage would be finalized shortly after their births.

This agreement did not sit well with young Esther, who grew up to dislike the Stepansky boy. However, since a written contract of their engagement existed, it could not be broken. In 1903, Esther was pressured to go through with the wedding, but afterward refused to live or sleep with her new husband. Following the nuptials, she had the chutzpah to tell her esteemed father, "You wanted me to marry him, now you go and live with him!" Not surprisingly, Esther's new (and probably distraught) husband asked the rabbi for a get.

David-Yosel was well aware that his daughter was in love with Yunkel Cutler. In fact, everyone in town knew that Esther was smitten with Yunkel from the moment she laid eyes on him at her uncle Yoske Stepansky's blacksmith shop. The old cantor soon realized that there was no keeping the young couple apart. The sweethearts then faced only one more potential obstacle. Since the bride-to-be had been married before, it would now be up to the groom's mother to *khapn a keek* (grab a look) at her son's prospective wife to approve of the match.

Although Esther Moser came from a family with a higher social standing than the Cutlers, Fay Cutler, who was once the subject of gossip after her own divorce, nonetheless traveled the traditional road from Skibin to give—or deny—her blessing. After meeting the chazzan's beautiful young daughter, and seeing the sparkle in her middle son Yunkel's eyes, Fay's decision was made easy. "I don't blame you!" she said to her relieved son, "You SHOULD marry her!"

In 1904, Yunkel Cutler became Esther Moser's second husband. Yunkel was so in love with Esther that he left behind his profitable business that he shared with his older brother, Shalum, in Belaya Tserkov so that he and Esther could live closer to her family in Stavishche.

In Stavishche they raised two boys, Daniel and Paul, and two girls named Sarah and Sheva.* Family members endearingly called the girls "the *shvesters*" (the sisters); the beauties looked almost like twins.

Esther and Yunkel lived on the far side of town, in one of the houses that was built near the river. For decades, the Jews of Stavishche called the river "Lazy Tikatch" because it winded in so many directions. In Russian, it was called "Gniloi Tikich" and in Ukrainian, "Hnylyi Tikych." The Polish nobles in town called it "Tykicz Gnily." From their home, the young family could see the factory across the wide body of water where bricks were made, so the *landslayt* referred to it as "The Brick River." Further on, there was a part of the same river that was called "Near the Post Office."

Rebecca

Rebecca, the second daughter born to Fay and Carl, was a statuesque girl with gorgeous, thick black wavy hair that she wore braided and pinned on top of her head. Her eyes were a sparkling blue under dark brows; she was an exotic beauty. In 1909, the nineteen-year-old was involved in a love affair with a handsome young shoemaker named Isaac Caprove, who was older than her by just nine days.

Isaac was the grandson of Rabbi Meir Caprove, originally from Talnoe, who became one of the few prominent and influential spiritual leaders to serve Stavishche during the mid-to-late 1800s. Isaac's father, Beryl, had died when Isaac was just seven years old, leaving behind a distraught wife, Sarah Leah,† and five children. Isaac's mother, who was terribly shaken by her thirty-year-old husband's death, had no means to support her two sons, Isaac and Moishe, and

---

*   Sheva was also known as Bessie, the same name as her aunt.

†   Sarah Leah was the daughter of Motes Vinokurov, a resident of Tarashcha.

three daughters, Shifka, Piya,* and Rosa, and therefore allowed her father-in-law to step in. The elderly rabbi, who was already raising five other grandchildren who had been tragically orphaned years earlier, placed the young children to live with families across Stavishche. Isaac was sent to a foster home, where he became an apprentice to a shoemaker.[†]

The Caprove siblings would soon face another heartbreaking tragedy: the youngest and most beautiful sister, Rosa, became ill with a fever and she lost her life at age eighteen. Rosa's devastated siblings gathered together to bury the teenager at the Stavishche cemetery. Her brothers, reciting the words of the *Kaddish* taught to them years earlier by their grandfather, led the small graveside service.

Isaac had no way of foreseeing that his unfortunate childhood would later lessen his desirability as a groom. Wedding plans were arranged for the happy young couple, and, as was routinely done in those days, official engagement papers, called *Tenaim*, were signed. Isaac and Rebecca were soon to be married.

But if Rebecca's oldest brother, Shalum Cutler, were to have had his way, which he almost did, this wedding would never have taken place. Shalum, a wealthy blacksmith in Belaya Tserkov who made his fortune by mass-producing horseshoes and iron wagon wheels for the tsar's army, had a long history for causing tension among his family members.[‡] He believed that his social status earned him the right to interfere with the love affair of his younger sister. His unwelcome meddling in Rebecca's life began when he sent her a letter in which he delivered the following ultimatum:

> *My Dear Sister,*
>
> *I was recently informed of your impending wedding plans. I disapprove of your engagement, and, as your oldest brother, forbid it. Marrying Isaac Caprove would be a disgrace to our family. He has such a lowly vocation—a mere shoemaker—and even worse, he's an orphan!*

---

* Channa called her aunt Shifka by the name Shiva or Sheva, possibly derived from Bathsheba. Her family in Europe called her Shifka. Piya was Channa's pronunciation for Pollya.

† Although most orphans who were apprenticed to learn these poor artisan trades would never be educated, the rabbi oversaw his grandsons' education and provided the necessary funds for Isaac and his brother to attend *chedar*, a Jewish school where they learned to read and write.

‡ One might be forgiven for thinking that since Shalum's fortune came from suppling the tsar's army with equipment, that he would be a great supporter of Nicholas II. However, a nephew believed he was both an idealist and Communist and he later volunteered to become a commander of a detachment during the Revolution and fought against the tsar.

What kind of a life can an orphan offer you? If you marry him, I shall
have nothing more to do with you.
    Shalum

Rebecca was accustomed to her brother's interference and took no notice of his letter. She was a headstrong young woman who was very much in love with Isaac and determined to marry him despite her brother's objections. She felt that Shalum, who lived nearly thirty miles away and hardly ever saw his family, had no right to interfere in her life. Annoyed, she tossed the letter aside, carelessly leaving it on a table.

Soon after, Rebecca's dashing young suitor, Isaac Caprove, appeared at the door. When there was no response to his knock, Isaac let himself in. He couldn't help but notice the letter that was lying open on a table beside the family's steaming samovar. As it was a rare occurrence in those days to receive a letter, he became curious and casually picked it up. Naturally, Isaac was devastated to learn that Rebecca's brother did not deem him worthy of her hand in marriage.

After reading Shalum's letter, Isaac's pride was so crushed that he quietly left town, vanishing from Rebecca's life for a couple of years. She desperately wanted to contact him but had no way of finding him. Two years passed before Rebecca finally spotted Isaac at the other end of the busy town market. Rebecca pushed her way through the crowd of bargainers and tried to reason with him. "Isaac, we love each other," she pleaded, "we could be together and live happily."

Her declaration of unwavering love would not change Isaac's stubborn mind. When Rebecca saw him leaving the market that day accompanied by her mother's relatives, it finally occurred to her where he had been living for the past two years. Rebecca felt so betrayed that she declared to everyone around her that she didn't want to be engaged to Isaac anymore; she now knew where to send him a letter telling him so.

During the two years following his disappearance, Isaac had been living with Fay's prominent relatives, who also employed him. After returning from that fateful meeting with Rebecca at the marketplace, Isaac discovered from Fay's relatives the scandalous secret that had plagued Rebecca's mother's youth.

Shortly after, Isaac received Rebecca's letter officially breaking off their engagement. He immediately realized what a fool he had been; it was as if a brick had suddenly fallen from the sky and knocked some sense into him. More than anything, he longed to marry Rebecca, but after two years of constant heartbreak, she no longer wanted him back.

And so the saga continued: When she wanted him, he didn't want her. When he wanted her, she didn't want him. This back-and-forth continued until they both reached the age of twenty-one. In Russia, men at that age were automatically drafted into the tsar's army. Before Isaac went into the army, he came to her with one last plea. "Marry me now, or it's all over."

Rebecca may have been stubborn, but she was no fool. Rebecca Cutler married her childhood sweetheart, Isaac Caprove, just three months later, on August 10, 1911.

CHAPTER TWO

A TOTAL ECLIPSE

Stavishche: 1911–1917

Soon after his marriage to Rebecca, Isaac was drafted into the Russian army under Tsar Nicholas II. As a member of a select group of young men whose physical fitness rendered them more capable than others to sustain rougher climates, he became a shooter with the 39th Siberian Rifle Regiment. He was sent to Khabarovsk, Siberia, located on the eastern end of the Russian Empire, just nineteen miles from the Chinese border. One could see the shores of China by standing on the Khabarovsk side of the Amur River.

Isaac, along with many other young soldiers from nearby villages, gathered at the station in Belaya Tserkov before traveling forty days and nights by train to get to his unit in Khabarovsk. As his train departed, the new recruit caught a fleeting glimpse of his new bride through the window but had no idea that she was already expecting their first child.

Although Isaac was stationed in Siberia—famous for its exiled prisoners and frigid temperatures—it was the only warm winter that he ever spent in Russia. He slept in a bunk by an ongoing fire in an officer's wooden cabin, where he was ordered to remain near the heat of the flames to help shape the leather he used in making the commanders' boots. On his breaks, the young soldier swaddled his feet with flannel *portyanki* before donning his own boots. Isaac enjoyed time away from his assigned shoemaking duties with long walks in the crisp, Siberian air. It was a dry and pristine climate with the most spectacular snowfall.

Back in Skibin, on August 11, 1912, exactly one year and one day after her parents' wedding, Channa Caprove, a chubby ten-pounder with large, almond-shaped eyes and a heap of dark hair, entered the world. Shortly after the birth, Rebecca, who supported herself as a seamstress, moved out of her family's over-crowded homestead in Skibin with her cherub-cheeked baby and into a one-room place six miles away in Stavishche.

The highlight of her social life as a young mother and wife of a soldier was the weekly gathering of her friends at her home every Sabbath evening. Just before sundown, they met by the fields neighboring their local pond and dug up and filled their pails with yellowish clay. The group then looked forward to their main event: they painted Rebecca's floors after smoothing them over with clay! This seemingly mundane activity gave young people in small *shtetlach* across Russia an excuse to socialize.

With Isaac away, Rebecca and her group of friends were unaware of the mounting anti-Semitism growing around them. In nearby Kiev, a Jewish super-intendent of a brick kiln was falsely accused of murdering a boy in a Jewish ritual blood libel case that drew international attention. Despite the promotion of anti-Jewish sentiments led by the Black Hundreds throughout the trial, Menahem Mendel Beilis was acquitted by a jury in October 1913.

Rebecca also did not know of a minor assassination that took place in another small corner of a long-forgotten empire—one that would soon thrust Russia and its soldiers into a global conflict. The June 28, 1914, murder of Archduke Franz Ferdinand, heir to the Austro-Hungarian throne, by a Bosnian Serb student in Sarajevo set in motion a series of fast-moving events that soon escalated into a full-scale war.

Isaac, preparing for his return home to Stavishche after a three-year stint as a soldier in the largest army in the world, was called back to his post. Russia, which was bound by a treaty with Serbia, announced the mobilization of its vast army in her defense. Isaac soon found himself getting ready for combat in what would later be dubbed "the War to End All Wars."

World War I—Impending Doom

On the eve of World War I, two-year-old Channa had still never laid eyes on her father. The precocious toddler envied her pretty but skinny four-year-old neighbor, Rose Lechtzer, whose father, Elia, received a medical exemption from serving as a soldier in the tsar's army and remained home with his family during the war.

Just twenty days after Germany declared war on Russia, Channa and her mother stood in the same crowd as Rose and Elia when a natural phenomenon catapulted over the skies of Stavishche. Channa watched as Rose sat on her father's shoulders while "looking through a piece of smoked glass at the sun." Somehow Elia, a bright Jewish wheat and grain dealer, knew that there was a complete eclipse of the sun. "Everyone was sure it forebode an evil event," Rose would later write.[*]

It was August 21, 1914, a somewhat cloudy morning, when astronomers from around the world gathered in Russia to stargaze and unlock the secrets of the universe. Curious onlookers flocked to the center of Channa's village just a few hundred miles north of the Crimean expedition, where the path of the total eclipse of the sun would fall. By midday the clouds seemed to disappear. The superstitious people of Stavishche interpreted the scientifically spectacular event as a sign of impending doom. However, the evil event that the Jews spoke of would not show its ugly face in the pleasant townlet for another three years.

Isaac Caprove finally returned home to Stavishche in 1915 as a war hero. He endured two gunshot wounds to the legs and spent several months lying on his back in a sparse Russian hospital room. While anxiously making his way back to his bride, the newly discharged soldier showed off his war wounds to his childhood buddies, which included a scar where a bullet entered and passed through the soft tissue in his upper thigh. After finally arriving on Rebecca's doorstep, the biggest news that he would learn, both to his shock and joy, was that he had fathered a little girl.

Soon after his arrival home, the young shoemaker rented one of the many tiny houses that were attached to the Stavishcha Inn and settled his family in the back rooms. At the front of the building was a large display window, where people could look in and watch Isaac in his new boot factory, as he made high leather boots by hand, using the finest nails to attach the soles.

---

[*] Source: Both quotes from this paragraph are from the written family history of Rose Lechtzer/ Lichtzer (Lessure) Mayers.

Nine months later, in July 1916,* Channa's younger sister, Sarah Leah, who was named after Isaac's mother, entered the world. Isaac, who had missed Channa's entire infancy, was overwhelmed with happiness at being present for the birth of his second daughter and was in absolute awe of this little creature, whom they nicknamed Sunny. While up until this point, Rebecca had been the sole recipient of Isaac's adoration, this attention was now superseded by their second child. Sunny forever remained Isaac's favorite.

Living in a town without running water, the modest Caprove home benefitted from a prime location close to a well. Their *vaser deliverer* (water deliverer), Chaim-Mayer, performed a daily balancing act with two pails attached to a wooden rod, which hung over his shoulders. He pumped fresh well water into the pails and then filled up the large barrels on top of his wagon before delivering them to his customers. If he missed a few days of work, his customers had to bathe in the bathing pond.

Inside the Caprove family's house, a large fireplace and chimney, which was heated with wood, straw, or charcoal, resembled a small baker's oven. It served a dual purpose: to cook and to heat both sides of the wall. The floors, made of hardened clay, were cold, so they would huddle by the fireplace for warmth. Above the oven was a crawlspace that was accessible to Channa and Sunny by climbing a small ladder. The girls passed many evenings there together, where they cuddled to keep warm in their cozy hiding place.

One of the family's biggest pleasures came during the warmer months, when they took long walks to the outskirts of town. After all their chores were completed, friends and relatives would follow a path to Count Branicki's estate. All residents of Stavishche were given free access to the grounds of the count's estate and enjoyed sitting on the benches that were shaded by very old pine and poplar trees leading up to Branicki Palace. In the flat valley where the grand manor house stood in the shape of a horseshoe, it was as if they had accidentally stumbled upon paradise. Botanical gardens with exquisite plants, roses, and lilac bushes were set among wooded rolling hills.

---

* Sunny's birth entry was recorded on July 22, 1916, in the metric book for Stavishche. However, it is not known if that was the actual date of birth or the date it was finally recorded. Sunny celebrated her birthday in June.

On the slopes of a few hills that were connected to the gardens below, a beautiful, landscaped square had been set up by Count Branicki's father more than half a century earlier. While standing at the highest point of the Stavishche Park, the Caprove family could look down and see a stunning view of a huge pond linked to the Gniloi Tikich River; from another slope they could see the charming village, filled with white cottages trimmed with green lawns.

Not far from the cottages, up a hill near a wide, old-fashioned Ukrainian road, there stood an old brick windmill weathered by time and missing many of its sails. Artists often sketched the blackened windmill, which also caught the attention and imagination of Polish writer Tadeusz Micinski, who set his novel *Wita* in Stavishche.

Channa's *bubbe* Fay Cutler loved to join her daughter's family on their walks whenever she was visiting from nearby Skibin. Young Channa always made a point of picking small bouquets of lilacs that grew in the count's gardens because they were her grandmother's favorite flowers. The grouping of the purple lilacs in bloom that formed a hedge in the botanical gardens was a constant attribute of springtime in Stavishche. Fay's eyes lit up at the sight of the vast gardens that were in full bloom. It was almost as if she was reminded of another life as she inhaled the intoxicating fragrances of those lilacs.

❖

As Isaac's business blossomed, Rebecca hired a maid, a peasant woman named Sophia. For two and a half years, they lived a comfortable life. Since Channa was the daughter of a tsar's soldier, she was one of a handful of Jewish children who would soon be eligible to attend a Russian *gymnasium* (school).

To prepare their four-year-old daughter for school, Channa's parents arranged for an old rabbi to tutor her at home. The children in Stavishche playfully called him "Mosh-calla-zoo-doelus," a nickname that the old and impatient rabbi failed to appreciate. The first day that he came over to tutor her, Channa infuriated him by running and hiding under a table. "You can't find me, Mosh-calla-zoo-doelus!" the little girl screamed out to him. She clearly wanted the rabbi to come and search for her; it was all a game. Her embarrassed mother angrily yelled, "Channa, come out this instant!"

The rabbi was educated in the *yeshiva;* he was considered a *melamed* (teacher of young children). The scene was reminiscent of that described in the old Yiddish lullaby "Oyfn Pripetshik":*

> *Oyfn pripetshik brent a fayerl, Un in shtub iz heys;*
> *Un der rebbe lernt kleyne kinderlech dem alefbeyz;*
> *Un der rebbe lernt kleyne kinderlech dem alefbeyz.*
> *Zet zhe, kinderlech, gedenkt zhe tayere, vos ir lernt do;*
> *Zogt zhe noch a mol un take noch a mol: Komets alef o.*

(On the hearth a fire burns, and the room has heat.
And the rabbi teaches all the little ones all their ABCs;
And the rabbi teaches all the little ones all their ABCs.
See now, little ones, listen children, don't forget it please.
Say it once for me and say it once again, all your ABCs.)

The children who had already mastered their *alefbeyz* under the tutelage of the old melamed went on to continue their studies at either the Jewish *chedar* or the Stavishche School, which the peasants simply referred to as "the Teaching Place."

Although times were still relatively peaceful in town, early signs of religious discord were becoming more frequent at the Stavishche School, where three of Channa's older cousins, Sarah, Sheva, and Daniel Cutler, were students. Jewish enrollment was severely limited, but the Cutler children were allowed to attend because their father, Yunkel, had once been a master iron worker for the tsar's army. Two other Jewish girls in town, Dvora Golditch and Rochela Faynzilberg, also attended classes with them.

After peasant boys threw pebbles at Dvora and Rochela as they walked together to school, Dvora's father, Shika de Potch, insisted on driving them to and from the schoolroom each day in his fancy horse and carriage. In another act of anti-Semitism, the same boys chased Sarah and Sheva and pulled harshly on their hair.

The greatest act of violence was directed at their brother Daniel. With Daniel present, the teacher openly displayed anti-Semitism in the classroom. One day,

---

* "Oyfn Pripetshik" (On the Hearth) is a well-known Yiddish song written by Mark Warshawsky (1848–1907).

the school master singled Daniel out when he announced to the class, "Do you know why Daniel was not in school yesterday? Yesterday was a Jewish holiday; Daniel is a Jew."

The peasant children stared and made faces at him that entire morning in the classroom. After school ended, the children were allowed, and even encouraged, to beat Daniel up. With their teacher's approval, they tore his clothes and kicked him.

The black cloud that the Jews of Stavishche feared would appear after the moon's spectacular alignment between the earth and the sun now hovered directly over them.

CHAPTER THREE

A PASSOVER TRAGEDY

April 14, 1917

There were two entrances to their house in Stavishche. The front had a gate, but during the harsh Russian winters it was always snowed in, so the Caprove family was forced to enter through the back door.

It was the last day of Passover—April 14, 1917. Channa was four and a half. She balanced on a window seat and watched through the window as her father, Isaac, and three maternal uncles—Avrum, Yunkel, and Shalum—opened the front entrance that was used only during milder weather. The men carried in a large wooden box.

Her mother and aunts covered all the mirrors and pictures in the house. Channa had no idea what was going on. Now there were so many people—almost one hundred—who came to visit the family in their cramped living quarters.

They were the Jews of Stavishche, who arrived armed with homemade delicacies, such as *kugels*, *rugelach*, and *challahs*. While Channa didn't recognize everyone, they all knew who she was.

"Channa," an old woman said as she approached her, "you don't remember me, but I knew you when you were this big." As she held up her wrinkled hands as high as Channa's knee, the girl could hear another elderly lady cornering her older cousin, "Oh, Daniel, I knew you when you were this big. . . ."

Isaac appeared from a back room, calling out anxiously for another man to make a *minyan*, a quorum with ten men. He grabbed Uncle Avrum, who, at twenty-one, was the youngest and most handsome of her mother Rebecca's brothers. They shut the door behind them, but through the paper-thin walls the child could hear the men chanting the Kaddish, the Mourner's Prayer.

Among the crowd in her house that day were the two Gentile peasants who worked for her father in his shoe factory that was located in the front of the dwelling. Mykola,* a lanky fellow, lived with his parents and three burly brothers on a vegetable farm on the outskirts of Stavishche. This friendly Christian family was proud that Mykola was chosen to be an apprentice of a shoemaker. To most Jews, an apprenticeship to a shoemaker was considered an inferior position, although Isaac himself had started out in this way after he was orphaned. To the Gentile peasants, however, many whose skills didn't extend much further than farming, it was commendable to have a family member learning a trade.

Standing next to Mykola was the despised peasant, Vasyl. The Jewish merchants in Stavishche refused to employ him because he was a known trouble-maker and a thief. Isaac took him under his wing and taught him the shoemaking trade, and, in return, Vasyl was loyal to him.

Vasyl always said that Isaac was the only Jew in Stavishche to ever show him kindness. While many of the Jews visiting the house that day came over to greet Mykola, Vasyl was met with disapproving stares, which he ignored. To him, paying his respects and expressing his sympathy to Isaac and Rebecca before heading home was more important.

Also among the crowd of visitors was Isaac's only brother, Channa's handsome uncle Moishe Caprove. Sporting a new thin mustache, he brought with him his plain wife, Bubkah, who was short with black curly hair. Family members whispered that she was frugal, except when spending on her obsession—jewelry. She arrived that afternoon wearing several of her favorite pieces: long necklaces and pins on her dress, as well as a couple of sparkling rings. Running around the Caprove home were the couple's two young children: a daughter, Sima, the mirror image of her mother, and a young son, Beryl.

Moishe was two years older than Isaac. Everyone in the family adored him, including his sister-in-law Rebecca. Channa watched her mother that day holding on to her baby sister while weeping on Moishe's shoulder.

---

*   Mykola is a Ukrainian masculine name for Nicholas.

Although she didn't know what was wrong—Channa was just a little girl, after all—she could sense that something terrible had happened. She heard someone talk about death, a word that, up until that day, was foreign to her. Confused, she was determined to investigate. Later that evening, after all the visitors had left, she sneaked out of the bed she shared with her baby sister, Sunny, and into the room where the long pine box rested on a table. She quietly stood on a chair so that she could reach over and see what was inside.

To her horror, she was shocked to discover that inside of this mysterious box lay her grandmother Fay Cutler. She reached over and touched the long strands of her graying red hair. When she felt her forehead, it was cold and clammy. Channa tried pulling at her arm, desperate to wake her up, but she would not move or stir; Channa felt the scream rise in her throat.

Rebecca and Isaac heard Channa's cries and ran into the room where they found their daughter standing over her dead grandmother. "What happened, Mama?" she shrieked, large tears rolling down her face. "Why isn't she moving?"

Rebecca gently picked her up and moved away from her own mother's coffin. Her arms embraced the girl as tears streamed from her own eyes. Rebecca rocked her little girl in her arms and said, "Someday, Channa, there will come a time when the living will envy the dead."

CHAPTER FOUR

DAYS OF INNOCENCE

Stavishche: Just Before the Revolution

U p until the turn of the 20th century, mostly peaceful times prevailed between Christians and Jews in Stavishche. Nestled in a green valley on the road from Kiev to Uman, the small Russian village remained unscathed during the religious discord that plagued so many of its neighboring towns in 1905.* The Gentiles who broke their backs tilling the soil and the Jewish merchants and artisans who struggled to earn a living on a daily basis tried to respect each other's hardships.

Stavishche, a land isolated by rivers and ponds and surrounded on one side by an overcrowded pine tree forest, had a long, rich history of Jewish culture and life. By 1763, the Jewish population in town was already well established, with sixty-one Jewish households appearing in a census. One hundred and fifty years later, just prior to the Revolution of 1917, half of the 8,500 residents of Stavishche were Jewish. Most of the Jews were concentrated in the center of town, forming a ghetto. The majority of their houses had clay floors and straw roofs; they were built on crooked streets, with no greenery surrounding them.

On a chilly but sunny spring afternoon in 1917, villagers came out from every corner of town. Rabbi Pitsie Avram and Cantor David-Yosel Moser met

---

* In 1903-1906, anti-Jewish riots left an estimated one to three thousand Jews dead across Russia. In 1905, these riots flared up in villages surrounding Stavishche.

at Golub's bookstore, sitting and discussing the latest newspaper stories on the porch.

"Another false accusation of Jewish blood libel,"* the rabbi read. "It's been over three years since the acquittal of Beilis, yet their hatred for us grows. They'll never let us live in peace."

"That is my prayer—that my grandchildren should only know peace," David-Yosel answered.

"Ah, speaking of grandchildren . . . ," the rabbi said, while lifting his bearded face up from behind the newspaper. "I see two of them now. It looks as if Isaac has put Daniel and Sol to work."

"Indeed, it does."

The cantor watched as his two grandsons pushed an old wooden handcart piled high with shoes and boots earmarked for deliveries.

It was a familiar sight: Isaac sent his young daughter Channa, along with Rebecca's nephew, Daniel Cutler, to make deliveries throughout the shtetl. Sol Moser, Daniel's older cousin and the son of Itzie Moser,† the bakery owner, joined them. The three children were excited. They wandered freely through the one-horse town on Alexandria Street, the main road, which was paved in cobblestone.

As usual, they began their journey at Isaac's old-fashioned boot factory and were expected to make stops around the village, eventually finishing at the town's gates, near Count Branicki's vast estate. Surrounding the Polish landowner's manor were many stately homes inhabited by those who worked for him. There were very few deliveries on the outskirts of town, where impoverished Christian peasants lived on farms.

The trio looked forward to their interesting encounters with many colorful personalities of their village. As was almost always the case, they first spotted Leaper the Blinder, who lived behind Alexandria Street on the *intergesl* (side street or alley), not far from the boot factory near the Stavishcha Inn. It didn't matter what the weather was like, Leaper the Blinder made the trip every day to visit his aunt Haika at the family bakery on the other side of town. Today,

---

* This term refers to a false accusation, centuries old, that Jews murdered Christians, in particular young children, to drain and use their blood for the making of Passover *matzahs* and other ritual purposes.

† Daniel's mother, Esther Moser Cutler, and Sol's father, Itzie Moser, were siblings. The boys shared the same grandfather, Cantor David-Yosel Moser.

the ground was very muddy, but somehow, even though he couldn't see a thing, Leaper managed to avoid the mud and kept his boots clean!

"How do you do it?" Sol asked.

"My cane guides me . . . ," Leaper answered.

The local celebrity, who was wearing his signature opera hat and a cape, sensed that Sol was not alone. "Call out to me, children, so I know who's here!"

"Hello, Leaper!" Daniel said.

"You're Yunkel's son," Leaper said to Daniel.

"Hello, sir!" young Channa said.

"You're Isaac the shoemaker's daughter!" he answered.

The children giggled and were thoroughly amused. The blind and brilliant chazzan instantly recognized their voices. It was a game to everyone in Stavishche: Leaper was always right.

"Did you children hear the performance of the famous tenor Pinchas Siegal at the large *shul* on Synagogue Street last week?" Leaper asked. "He is beginning to call himself Pierre Pinchik."*

"Papa said that the crowds rushed to hear his concert, but Pinchas stood there in his tall chazzan hat and refused to sing a single note until there was absolute silence," Sol answered.

"Yes, since he made his debut a few years ago at the Kiev Synagogue, he has become quite the temperamental performer," Leaper answered. "And he now wears a hat even taller than mine!

"Good day, children," the cantor said, tipping his top hat toward the youngsters, "I'm off to greet my favorite *tante*, Haika de Zhitomir."

As the blind cantor continued on his way, Daniel questioned Sol. "Why did Leaper say that your mother is from Zhitomir?" he asked. "Hasn't the Stepansky family always lived here in Stavishche?"

"No, she and her eight brothers and sisters, including my two uncles, Lepe the egg merchant and Yoske the blacksmith, fled from their hometown years ago. There was a pogrom there that killed many people, including children," Sol answered.

What Sol didn't mention to his young cousin was that the Zhitomir pogrom was an exceptionally brutal one: Jewish babies were murdered by being thrown into the air and caught on the tips of the bandits' swords. The Stepansky family

---

* Siegal or Segal officially took on the stage name Pinchik in the 1920s.

resettled in Stavishche, where Haika's husband, Itzie Moser, grew up. Along with the Moser family, they became, in many of the villagers' opinions, the true Jewish roots of the town.

Daniel wandered off the main thoroughfare and then flagged over his two cousins. He pointed out the house of Chiah Sura Spivack, well-known in town for practicing her hot "cupping"* techniques on family members to soothe their pain. The children of Stavishche were fascinated by cupping, known as *bankes* in Yiddish, an ancient Jewish folk remedy similar to acupressure that was popular in Russia in the early 1900s. Although they did not have a shoe delivery for her, the kids peeked through the unsuspecting Chiah Sura's window, each getting a glimpse of how she magically created a vacuum by air (heated by fire) in glass cups that she placed flush against the skin of her current patient.

"Did you know that Chiah Sura is Avrum Postrelko's aunt?" Daniel asked Channa, who shook her head. "A few years ago, he escaped exile near Yakutsk and fled to the Holy Land. He now calls himself Avraham Harzfeld and is starting to become a big deal in Eretz Yisrael."

"No, I didn't know," Channa answered, unsure where Eretz Yisrael was. The young girl's attention was, however, quickly diverted by the appearance of Pitsie Sheynes, the husband of Shika de Potch's sister Pearl, as he walked down the path that they just strayed from. He was a handsome tailor whom some considered, from head to toe, to be one of the best-dressed men in town. His modern topcoat was only partially buttoned, exposing a fancy suit underneath; he even wore his dress shoes while walking through the muddy thoroughfare.

"I know of two other Pitsies," Daniel said, and laughed while following Channa back to the cobblestone road. "There is a man called Pitsic Postrel, the overseer of the forest and the keeper of the bathhouse. And the other is . . ."

"Pitsie Avram!" Sol and Channa shouted out together, laughing in harmony. Everyone in town knew Stavishche's most famous and beloved "Pitseleh" (an unusual but endearing name, meaning "little one"). He was the esteemed and learned rabbi of the village. The children did not realize that they had just passed the rabbi and the cantor sitting on Golub's porch.

"And Pitsie Avram now has famous cousins!" Daniel added, as the children continued on their way. "I heard that the Zionist from Zhashkov, Eliyahu Dayan, along with his brother Shmuel, who has been living in the *kibbutz* Deganyah,

---

* There is a well-known and humorous Yiddish proverb: *"Es vet hlefn vi-a toyten bankes"* ("It would help like cupping a corpse").

near the Sea of Galilee, came to visit him recently."* Shmuel Dayan was the
father of Moshe Dayan, who would years later become a politician, military
hero, and leader in Israel.

The children jumped off the main pathway, allowing a horse and buggy to
pass them; they knew that it was owned by Shika de Potch (the nickname for
Yehoshua Golditch the Postmaster). It was headed, with a sick passenger in tow,
to Count Branicki's Free Hospital for the Poor, which was a long walk from the
Jewish quarter of town. Shika never charged a sick person for using one of
the twenty-four stallions or eight buggies that were sitting in his barn.

The children headed toward the brick part of the river, where Daniel lived.
His mother, Esther, was expecting a leather boot that Isaac had repaired for her
daughter Sarah. The children left the boot by Esther's door and ran out back to
play by the river.

Esther smiled as she watched through her back window, remembering the
children's last delivery just a few months earlier; it was back during the winter,
on January 19. The cousins pulled sleds out of a shed and ran eagerly to the frozen
Gniloi Tikich River to take a break from their duties. They skidded playfully on
the ice and pulled the homemade sleds, made by Yunkel's skilled hands.

They made their way to the ice while a famous ceremony was held out on the
frozen river. The town's peasantry gathered there once a year to commemorate
the baptism of the infant Jesus in the River Jordan. It was the celebration of
Epiphany, known as *Kreshchenie*, the twelfth day of Christmas for Russian
Orthodox believers. Christian peasants walked out on the frozen river with
their priest.

Jewish mothers, Esther included, whose houses were built along the river,
tried each year to distract their children from watching the procession. Even
Rebecca instructed Channa not to venture out onto the ice. It wasn't just fear for
their children's safety out on the ice that drove the women to discourage their
children from viewing the ceremony. They were afraid that their children might
become influenced as a result of their exposure to anything Christian. However, the
women's efforts were in vain. Despite the objections of their parents, Channa and her
cousins, along with many of the Jewish children of Stavishche, watched and were
absolutely mesmerized by the beautiful ritual of Epiphany.

---

* Eliyahu and Shmuel Dayan's father, Reb Avraham Dayan, was the son of Reb Pinhas, the *shohet*
and *dayan* "judge" of Zhashkov. They were most likely half brothers who descended from a folk *rebbe*,
Rabbi Aryeh Leib of Uman (1724–1811), known as the "Shpole Zeide."

During the ceremony, the youngsters looked on as peasants cut a cross out of the ice and prayed as the priest sanctified the water. Some dipped themselves into the cross-shaped ice hole,* others just bent down to fill their bottles with this water that was considered to be holy. Christian peasants kept the bottled water all year long, believing that it would help heal any sicknesses and would chase evil spirits away.

The young trio's second-to-last scheduled stop was the fair in Stavishche. Known as the *yarid*, it was, every day except Tuesday, just an empty plaza with wooden gates near the highway, not far from Channa's home. Isaac had instructed the children to make two deliveries to merchants at the fair. One merchant was friendly with Daniel's father, Yunkel. The other delivery was for Avrum, Channa and Daniel's youngest uncle. Each manned a booth at the fair where Avrum sold wheat and Yunkel sold handmade wagons. During the remainder of the week, they worked at markets in neighboring towns, much like their father, Carl Cutler, had done years earlier.

The fair lasted an entire day. Everyone in Stavishche was either buying or selling in an attempt to make a living. On the day of the fair, there was never an empty space at the market because Christians and Jews sold their wares alongside each other. Stavishche's rich soil made the cultivation and sale of corn, watermelons, grapes, peaches, and apricots popular at the market. Fresh carp, the tastiest fish in the province, was caught from the surrounding ponds and sold at the fair. Farm goods like potatoes and raw bags of wheat were brought in by horse and wagon.

Those who didn't have horses used pushcarts. Those who didn't have wheat brought live chickens. The children wandered near the chickens that were tied by their legs; Channa wasn't surprised to see the peasants hanging them upside down. Farmers also brought along their pigs and other livestock.

The fair was noisy and lively. Yosl Golub, the handsome son of Soloman the bookstore owner, whom Channa had a crush on, wrote about the market many decades after leaving Stavishche. He perfectly captured the essence of the hustle and bustle that the children experienced that day at the yarid: "When the fair came, everyone was busy with commerce, buying and selling, with lively noisy merriment. . . . The various sounds of the fair, the shouting and bargaining of buyers and sellers, the cries of drunkards and the music of the beggars playing

---

* Although Yasha Kainer didn't identify the celebration of Epiphany by name, he did describe the ceremony in a story by Emily Bayard.

their banduras, the crying of babies, the neighing of horses, the barking of dogs and the lowing of cattle—all blended into a noisy symphony—the fair in Stavishche."[*]

The bustling open marketplace in Stavishche was often the scene of many love matches, as well as countless numbers of lovers' quarrels. For Channa's mother, Rebecca, it was a glimpse of her long-lost love Isaac at the fair back in 1911 that marked a turning point in reuniting the young couple.

The Stavishche marketplace also played an important role in the life of the great Jewish writer Sholem Aleichem. In 1883, he married Olga "Bibi" Loyev, whose family, the Loyevs and the Mazurs, were prominent Jews with familial ties to Stavishche. Sholem often visited his wife's father, Elimelich Loyev, at the Stavishche yarid; his first meeting with his father-in-law (at another nearby marketplace) is vividly described in a chapter in the writer's autobiographical masterpiece, *From the Fair*.[†]

Channa and Daniel spotted their youngest uncle, Avrum Cutler, standing by a nearby table, selling wheat. He gave each child a warm hug.

"I have good news," he announced. "But you must promise to keep it a secret. I'm about to sign engagement papers; you will soon be dancing at my wedding!"

The children were so excited by Avrum's news that they forgot all about their final stop at the home of the *poritz*, a nobleman and customer of Isaac's who lived near the town's gates, not far from Count Branicki. Instead, they accidentally abandoned the wooden handcart that held his boots. They made their way back home in the dark, exhausted but elated by their uncle's happy announcement.

---

[*] From a story written by Channa's childhood acquaintance Yosl Golub, in the *Stavishche Yizkor Book*.

[†] Aleichem does not specifically name Stavishche in his autobiography, but many Stavishchers knew that he visited their local yarid on many occasions. His wife was born in nearby Shubovka.

CHAPTER FIVE

AVRUM CUTLER'S BRIEF BETROTHALS

1917–1918

A vrum Cutler's secret would soon be out.

The youngest of Channa's three maternal uncles, Avrum was blessed with the most handsome looks in a large family of siblings who were all considered attractive. This fact went undisputed mostly because he was tall like his father and had blue eyes that were always smiling.

The story the family told is that Avrum served as a Cossack with special privileges in the army of Tsar Nicholas II. His height, blondish hair, fair complexion, and ability to speak Russian fluently never gave the Cossacks any cause to suspect he was Jewish. His nieces Channa, Sarah, and Sheva, could not help but laugh at such a thought. After all, they questioned, didn't Avrum bathe with the other soldiers? And what about when he needed to relieve himself? Somehow, though, Avrum explained, the other Cossacks never caught on to his ruse.

When Avrum returned home in 1917 after briefly serving in the army,* he took pleasure in socializing with young Jewish men and women from neighboring towns. Avrum was charming and popular among the ladies and could have married almost anyone he desired. When he met a lovely girl from Stavishche, he

---

* Shortly after his mother Fay's funeral, Avrum became his sister Rebecca's houseguest in Stavishche, visiting from his home in nearby Skibin.

became quickly infatuated and fell instantly in love with her. As a token of his commitment, he gave her a pair of expensive earrings that symbolized their love for each other. About a month before the wedding, he accepted an invitation to spend a long weekend with the family of his new fiancée.

His soon-to-be in-laws supported the engagement and welcomed Avrum with open arms; he was likewise impressed with his fiancée's family. All went well with the visit until it became apparent to Avrum that his girlfriend may have been lovely and charming, but she was far from capable. He watched miserably as his fiancée's mother did all the cooking, sewing, and cleaning in the family's household. The breaking point came when Avrum realized that his bride-to-be was not able to dress herself; her mother even had to wash her daughter's hair for her.

Avrum began to wonder what kind of life he would have with such an incompetent woman. His infatuation quickly dissolved, and he wasted no time in breaking off the engagement. When Avrum confided in Rebecca, his older sister and closest confidante, she was extremely upset and disappointed by the news. In those days, breaking an engagement was sinful. Superstitious Jews like Rebecca believed that the shame resulting from the broken contract would be accompanied by a curse that would bring both bad luck and unhappiness to the couple who had parted ways. What made matters worse was that the sensational news of the breakup spread quickly throughout the entire town and its surrounding villages. The Jewish community already knew of the impending nuptials because the bride's family had hired in advance what was left of Mendel-Ber's feuding orchestra to play at the wedding.

Rebecca's fear of bad luck striking her favorite brother was soon realized. When Avrum's seasonal job at the sugar factory in Zhashkov ended,* he managed to once again trade briefly in wheat, like his father, but a poor crop limited his success. As his new business began to fail, he could not repay the start-up money that he had borrowed from family members, friends, and the local townsfolk. As an ethical person who suddenly found himself deeply in debt, Avrum didn't know how to handle his failure. It was whispered around town that his lovely ex-fiancée, who was distraught and embarrassed over their broken engagement,

---

* Zhashkov was 10.2 miles south-southwest of Stavishche with a Jewish population of 2,445 in 1900. The sugar factory in Zhashkov had commercial ties to Stavishche through Count Branicki, who cultivated the confectionary industry on his vast properties in Kiev Province.

followed an even more troubled path. Apparently, her heart was so broken that she made an unsuccessful suicide attempt.

1918

Just eighteen miles northeast of Stavishche, on the affluent side of Tarashcha, a successful matchmaker paced the floors of an estate owned by a Jewish man named Myer Ova Denka. It just so happened that Myer Ova Denka, a shoe-maker by trade, once made a pair of leather boots by hand for someone of great prestige—Tsar Nicholas II. Tsar Nicholas was extremely impressed that the boots made for him by Ova Denka were a perfect fit. The last tsar to rule all the Russias couldn't understand how a shoemaker from the town of Tarashcha would know what size would fit his royal feet.

To demonstrate his appreciation, Nicholas II sent a servant to travel from the palace all the way to Tarashcha to personally deliver Ova Denka a special gift. Inside the package was a golden statue of a two-headed eagle, the Romanov seal of approval.

As the entire town looked on, Myer Ova Denka proudly displayed the impe-rial gift in the window of his shoe factory. The shoemaker was granted permission by the tsar to use the royal insignia on a sign that hung outside his shoe shop. Despite the royal servant's monumental efforts on behalf of the tsar to discover just how Ova Denka knew the exact size of the emperor's feet, the stubborn shoemaker refused to shed any light on the mystery.

News of the tsar's lavish gift spread quickly among local aristocrats. These wealthy nobles, who lived on the outskirts of Tarashcha and included some minor Polish nobles connected to Count Branicki, patronized the shoemaker. There became a terrific demand for his boots, and Ova Denka soon became a wealthy man.

Now Ova Denka was in search of a husband for his daughter and was willing and able to pay a generous dowry. His daughter, Slova,* who was both out-spoken and opinionated, insisted that if her father was to pay such a large dowry, her bridegroom should at least be handsome.

The matchmaker assessed the rich man's daughter with frustration: she was unwavering in her demands for a tall, good-looking husband, yet she was already

---

* Her name was also spelled Sluva. On the US census, she was listed as Sylvia. Avrum was Abraham.

twenty-six, and was short and fairly overweight. How could the matchmaker possibly find the "perfect man" for this woman? But Ova Denka was a prominent and influential man, and she was determined to be the one to find a match for his daughter.

Refusing to give up, the matchmaker racked her brains until an interesting thought occurred to her. She recalled hearing the townspeople at the yarid in Stavishche talking about Avrum Cutler's broken engagement. Years before, she had actually met Avrum and remembered that he was tall, blond, and handsome. More recently, she'd heard rumors that he was heavily in debt.

The determined matchmaker made her way over to see Avrum and proposed a solution to his financial troubles. "I've got the perfect girl for you," she announced as she looked Avrum directly in the eyes. "Not only is she very rich and from a good family, but she is also intelligent, well educated and has an attractive face." Avrum was naturally enthusiastic after such a glowing description of the woman, and plans were made to finalize the engagement, even before the couple had a chance to meet.

The matchmaker, of course, had failed to mention that Slova was a bit *zaftig.** The couple, however, met for the first time and immediately agreed to the engagement. When Isaac and Rebecca were introduced to their future sister-in-law, they were shocked to discover that Avrum had only met her the day before. Learning that her brother was marrying a complete stranger, Rebecca was at a loss for words. Isaac could do nothing more than embrace his wife, who was heartbroken at the thought of her youngest brother never experiencing the magic of old-fashioned romance and love, as she and Isaac had. But the marriage was an arrangement that suited both parties: Avrum had a debt to pay, and Slova's father had the money to clear all his debts. The couple willingly entered into the union with open eyes, even though they barely knew each other.

Avrum's life after the wedding soon became what he described to Rebecca as a very difficult time. He complained that his wife never stopped eating. When he saw Slova drinking hot tea, it drove him crazy to watch her fill half her cup with sugar. His wife, in all fairness, also had cause for complaint. Because Avrum came from a poorer family than she did, she had little respect at first for her husband and was frustrated with his inability to make a good living. Avrum, in turn, was annoyed at her condescending attitude toward him.

---

*   Many men, often equating a woman's large, voluptuous size with beauty, find zaftig women (those who are heavyset) very attractive. Channa heard her aunts say (in Yiddish) of a woman: "*Zi iz azoy sheyn, az zi ken nisht pasik durkh di tir aun*" ("She is so beautiful that she can't fit through the door").

After Slova gave birth to their first child in 1919, a girl named Fay after Avrum's mother, life became even more unbearable for the bickering couple.* Avrum went to visit his sister and confidante Rebecca in Stavishche and revealed that both he and his wife were considering a divorce.

Superstitious in nature, Rebecca was as opposed to the idea of divorce as she was to Avrum's previous broken engagement and told Avrum in no uncertain terms that if a man divorced a woman after having a child with her, it would be as if he were making that child an orphan. As her daughter Channa looked on, she pleaded with Avrum to do the right thing and stay with his wife and infant daughter, fearing God's wrath if he abandoned his family. Avrum came to his senses, as did Slova, and listened to his sister; they remained together. Although their early married years were far from peaceful, he and Slova managed to work things out. After all, each spouse got exactly what they asked for: Avrum landed a rich wife who was intelligent and could no doubt run a household, and Slova landed a husband who was extremely handsome.

In the end, the matchmaker proved to be right. The couple, who married as complete strangers, eventually fell in love and had two more children. Slova's resourcefulness combined with Avrum's Gentile good looks would prove pivotal in their survival. The once-feuding couple soon discovered, as did all of Russia's Jews, that their biggest war was yet to come.

---

* These observations were witnessed by Channa as a child. Her mother, Rebecca, Avrum's sister, also told her of the couple's marital problems during the early years of their marriage in Europe.

CHAPTER SIX

COUNT WLADYSLAW BRANICKI AND THE NOBLE FAMILY OF STAVISHCHE

It was on a market day, sometime during the early days of the Revolution, when violence invaded the peaceful townlet. Five-year-old Channa heard a commotion coming from outside of her father's shoe shop. She watched through a window as peasants, carrying large flags, jubilantly marched through the streets singing patriotic songs. They were drunk, looting, and very boisterous. It was like watching a play. Even as a child, Channa couldn't understand how they could act that way—and why? She learned soon enough.

As the mobs passed, more and more peasants were spurred on to join them. Channa looked on as the maid, Sophia, who lived with the family, dropped what she was doing and ran out to join the crowd.

The young girl was curious and wandered after her, following the mob as they marched to the end of the town where the count's heirs, his staff, and other minor aristocrats lived. The unruly peasants were bent on looting the rich. They attacked the *graf*'s* estate, as well as those of the other surrounding nobles, and robbed them of their valuables. The peasants went wild ransacking the grand palace. Channa looked on as dozens of peasants ran past her, cradling priceless pieces of china, silver, statues, bedding, and draperies. Men lifted up and carried away elegant pieces of furniture. They pillaged paintings from the art galleries that

---

* *Graf* is a Germanic/Yiddish term meaning "noble" or "count."

connected the two side wings to the main house of the grand estate.* Bronzes, portraits, eastern-style carpets, marble figurines and statues, and exquisite pieces of furniture were among the many treasures looted by the peasantry.

They stripped the estate of its treasures before setting fire to parts of the Branicki family's magnificent horseshoe-shaped palace. Clouds of black smoke hovered in the sky and could be seen from every corner of town. Channa became afraid—she was trapped in the crowd as people ran in all directions after the fire began.[†]

From a distance, she spotted her seven-year-old neighbor Rose Lechtzer. A peasant farmer passed by Rose, dragging a very large mirror through the muddy streets of the shtetl. He had stolen it from the castle that was inherited by Count Branicki's third daughter, the last heiress of Stavishche, Countess Julia Wladyslawowna Potocka.[‡] When he found that it was too large to fit through the doorway of his small house, he stuck it instead in his barn, where his nervous cow caught a glimpse of her own image for the first time. Stories circulated for days around town that for his trouble, this peasant farmer ended up "with a shattered mirror and a bleeding cow!"[§]

Channa was relieved when her father found her in the mob and carried her home to safety. She soon learned that her parents and the Jews in Stavishche did not share in the jubilation of the enraged peasants. Over the years, the poor Christian masses had become increasingly resentful of the Branicki family's growing fortune, while the Jews, who, like Isaac, tended to be more prosperous than their Gentile neighbors, accepted their wealth as a matter of fact.

Rebecca and Isaac were particularly distraught. They had grown to trust, and even respect, many of the nobles, who often patronized Isaac's business, and were deeply saddened by this latest turn of events. Despite their sympathy for the Count's family, the couple felt impotent in the face of such brutal violence. It

---

* During a tour of the estate in 1881, writer A. Chlopicki described in detail many of the valuables and objets d'art found inside of the palace, which included two paintings by Reubens hanging in the tea room. It is not known which valuables were saved and sent to another of the count's estates at the beginning of the war, or which exact items were looted during this revolt.

† Luckily, the Branicki and Potocki families were not in Stavishche during the fire.

‡ Julia, the wife of Count Henryk (Henry) Potocki, inherited the estate in Stavishche from her father, Count Wladyslaw Branicki, after his death in 1914. She most likely owned it until the Treaty of Riga in 1921. The last Polish king gifted the estate to her great-great-grandfather in 1774.

§ From the written family history of and an interview with Rose Lechtzer/Lichtzer (Lessure) Mayers.

would not be long, they predicted, before this uncontrollable peasant mob would turn their misguided rage in another direction: the Jews of the town would no doubt be the next victims of looting and deadly acts of violence.

Channa watched her mother's reaction when their peasant maid Sophia returned to the house. Sophia brought back a sack filled with beautiful items that she had stolen from the countess's estate during the raids. When she shamelessly began to show off her new possessions that she robbed from Branicki Palace, Rebecca screamed at the top of her lungs for Sophia to leave her home.

They never saw the maid again.

In the aftermath of the revolt, Rebecca and Isaac took a walk to inspect the grounds of the once grand estate. Channa and Sunny, who had just learned how to walk, followed them to the site. Tears quickly filled all their eyes. Fire compromised the palatial dwelling.[*] The young family solemnly gathered by a small section of the foundation of the building, obscured by massive heaps of rubble and ashes. Smoking embers flickered throughout the air. The fire set by the hands of the insurgent peasant mob had spread mercilessly to the count's vast botanical gardens, leaving little trace of greenery or life in its path.

The main building, imposing in size but not uniform in height, had been looted and charred by fire. Gone was the beauty of its lavish landscaped park and vast botanical gardens that Count Alexander Branicki, the current Count Wladyslaw's father, had commissioned back in 1857.[†] The hothouse that stood on the right wing of the palace where tropical plants were stored during the winter months was destroyed. Gone were the exotic plants and colorful flowers that the Jewish children in Stavishche enjoyed picking and arranging as bouquets for their mothers' Sabbath tables.

The spectacular gardens were gone. Just months earlier, in the spring, Channa had gathered, for the last time, a lovely bunch of lilacs from the count's estate. At the Jewish cemetery with her grieving mother by her side, she leaned down and

---

[*] Witnesses described different degrees of damage to the building and estate by the fire. It is generally agreed that between the damage caused by both the looting and the fire, the estate as it was once known was essentially considered to be destroyed.

[†] The gardens were set up and managed by the great botanic scholar Antoni Andrzejowski until his death in 1868. Andrzejowski also wrote the count's memoir.

spread their opulent trusses across her grandmother's fresh grave. The sensitive little girl hoped that their heavy scent, a favorite of her bubbe's, would reach Fay in heaven.

Channa searched for the exotic birds—mostly peacocks with colorful feathers—that had promenaded around the gardens.* She could not find any sign of them. Isaac walked over to the partially blackened low brick wall that encompassed the grounds of the Holy Trinity, the Catholic Church. The church had always been easily accessible to the townspeople with a gate that opened from the walkway on the main thoroughfare. The small courtyard opposite that gate, which earlier in the week was filled with pine trees, had burned.

Two of the properties surrounding the other side of the manor to survive the attack were the dwellings of the steward and one of the three doctors in town. Count Branicki's Free Hospital for the Poor, which was located nearby on a small hill by a structure that housed a peculiar-looking water pump, also survived the rampage.

The family somberly left the still smoldering grounds and returned to their humble quarters near the Stavishcha Inn. Behind them stood the ruins of a palace that once captured the imagination of the count's subjects with fascinating tales and stories of great splendor.

Stavishche's Last Count: Wladyslaw Branicki

Wladyslaw was the great-grandson of Stavishche's first count, Franciszek Ksawery Branicki, and his beautiful young wife, Aleksandra Engelhardt, who was rumored to be the secret daughter of Catherine the Great of Russia.[†] After the death of his father, Alexander, in 1877, Count Wladyslaw Branicki inherited the vast estate and its riches.[‡] The nobleman, who was often described as shy and unassuming,[§] was concerned about the welfare of widows and orphans,

---

[*] Count Alexander Branicki and his brother, Konstanty, were well-known patrons of zoology with a special interest in ornithology, and brought exotic birds to live on the estate.

[†] See Appendix A.

[‡] Wladyslaw's mother, Anna Holynska, the daughter of Elizabeth, Countess Tolstoy, also retained a residence at the estate until her death in 1907.

[§] From the family history written by Count W. Branicki's great-grandson, Count Ladislas Tarnowski.

and frequently supported them anonymously through intermediaries. Branicki devoted his life to various charities.

Count Wladyslaw Branicki was a man of merit who cared deeply about people, including the Jews of his village whom he offered, along with the local Christian population, free medical care. Many Jews in Stavishche believed he had considerable influence in the court of the tsar, where he was supportive of the Jewish community.[*]

In the winter of 1887, a Hebrew language newspaper, *Hazefirah,* openly praised Count Branicki's generosity to the town's poor. When a great number of residents were starving, he contributed one hundred silver rubles for food and gifted free wood to heat their homes. He also donated an additional one thousand silver rubles for those who suffered losses during fires in Stavishche. The same newspaper specifically thanked Count Branicki and publicly proclaimed: "May he be rewarded in full."[†]

To the Polish people in his employ, who formed an interesting community around him, as well as to the locals, Count Branicki was a very popular lord and the subject of many tales. A young Polish poet, Jaroslaw Iwaszkiewicz, who visited the estate, wrote that like Casimir the Great, Count Branicki often visited those on his properties dressed in a simple outfit and traveling in an ordinary-looking wagon. He enjoyed taking part in the daily lives of the peasants and often acted as godfather in children's christenings.

All of his properties were well-manicured with flower gardens and plush greenery. The perfumed aroma of the count's lilac bushes mingled with the scent of pine trees that surrounded the castle, and many locals were drawn to the estate to inhale the fresh air.

On one of Wladyslaw's many trips abroad, he purchased a drilling machine that he sent back to Stavishche. A well was dug near his palace that provided the townsfolk with both a drink of ice-cold water and a beautiful gathering place near the gardens to share stories of the mysterious nobleman.[‡]

The fabricated tales that circulated had many of the Jewish children in town believing that he was a famous Russian general from the royal family. In reality,

---

[*]   Shimon Kushnir. *The Village Builder: A Biography of Abraham Harzfeld.* Translated by Abraham Regelson and Gertrude Hirschler. New York: Herzl Press, 1967, page 34.

[†]   Hachovesh. *Hazefirah.* Translated by Yale J. Reisner. Warsaw, Russian Poland, February 9, 1887, page 2.

[‡]   Kushnir, *The Village Builder,* page 34.

Count Branicki was a Polish magnate whose ancestors retained ownership of the land, despite Russia's annexation of Ukraine in 1793.

On the opposite side of town, down the hill, past the pond on the way to the nearby shtetl of Zhashkov, was Count Branicki's dense pine forest. Under the century-old pine trees that margined Stavishche's border, youngsters played hide-and-seek while inhaling woodsy smells and feeling the wet earth beneath their toes. Young Jewish children, including Channa and her sister, Sunny, her neighbor Rose, and her cousins, watched and listened as Christian peasant boys sang Ukrainian folk songs while herding goats and performing their daily chores.

The Count's Arabian Stallion

The local townsfolk, socializing at the well, often told tales of the Branicki family's love of Arabian horses, which were, at that time, rare in Europe. Stavishche, though, was famous for its horses. Arabians adorned the estate of the count, who set up stables for his twenty thoroughbreds and three dozen saddle and harness horses. One of the biggest pleasures of those who lived on the Branicki estate was the morning horseback rides on the most beautiful of stallions.

The father of A. Ben-Hayim of Stavishche, who was known to spin tales about Count Wladyslaw Branicki, recalled the noble's much-talked-about purchase of an Arabian horse while traveling abroad. Rebecca told a similar tale of the count's purchase from Cairo; Isaac thought it was Damascus.[*] Branicki decided to have his new prized possession sent back to his estate in Stavishche. Apparently, Wladyslaw spared no expense in sending his horse and its trainer by ship in first-class accommodations.

Although pampered, Count Branicki's new Arabian horse had difficulty adjusting to its new environment in Stavishche. Against the trainer's advice, Count Branicki decided to saddle his prized Arabian and parade it around town. As word spread that the count would be making an appearance on horseback, the people of Stavishche, who usually waited for the wind to carry away the dirt and the dust, took out their brooms and swept the streets in anticipation of his arrival. Nobles, Jews, and peasants then gathered together and watched and waved with admiration as the kind Polish magnate rode his prized new

[*] Stories similar to A. Ben-Hayim's account in the *Stavishche (Stavisht) Yizkor Book* circulated around town; Channa's parents told a similar tale.

horse around Stavishche. Men, women, and children ran out into the street and watched with the crowd as Count Branicki proudly paraded his favorite stallion.

The count traveled to the outskirts of town, but when he returned to the gates of Stavishche, the horse had had enough. Before the eyes of the entire village, the noble's priceless Arabian, with Count Branicki proudly saddled on top of him, collapsed and died.

Arabian horses were not the count's only passion—he was the proud owner of the first automobile in the town. During one of his last visits to his estate just before his death, Count Branicki had his chauffeur drive him around town in his fancy new car, probably imported from America.

"Look at that—no horses, nothing!*" exclaimed little Benny Golditch, the son of Shika de Potch, who, in 1913, captured the excitement of the people as they gathered for their first glimpse of an automobile. The townsfolk rushed to the streets to witness the miracle. A Jewish girl from Stavishche was so enamored with Count Branicki's automobile that she caused a scandal when she ran away with the graf's driver just before the onset of the First World War.

Count Wladyslaw Branicki, one of the last members of the Polish border gentry, died in April 1914. At the time of his passing, the nobleman owned more than seven thousand acres of land in Tarashcha District, where Stavishche is located. He also held title to both the brewery and the seventy-four-year-old vineyard in the town. Many of his grandchildren later told their children that the nobleman loved Stavishche and its environs so much, that the events that followed his death three years later in 1917 would have been a great affliction for him.†

---

* From a family interview by Dr. Murry Rich.

† Count Paul Potocki, Wladyslaw's great-grandson, stated a similar sentiment in a letter to the author.

PART II

THE POGROMS
1917–1920

CHAPTER SEVEN

STAVISHCHE UNDER SIEGE

1917–1918

I t started with the violent destruction of noble estates across Russia by peasant mobs.

Rebecca and Isaac feared that the pattern of violence sweeping the country would soon be redirected toward the Jews. They saw with their own eyes the vicious attack against Count Branicki's palace and the torching of his botanical gardens in Stavishche.

Russia and Ukraine had a long tradition of anti-Semitism, and Jews were a popular scapegoat for the oppressed peasants. Following the tsar's murder, when nationalists fought the Bolshevik armies in 1918–1921, they ensured the support of the uneducated Ukrainian peasant population by associating the Jews as Bolsheviks, stirring up anti-Semitism. Pogroms against Jews, whose beliefs, dress, language, holidays, and traditions set them apart from the rest of the country, were now an incentive for the nationalist troops to fight against the Reds.

The Jews of Stavishche were not spared from anti-Semitic outbreaks and pogroms. On October 17, 1917, Stavishche's spiritual leader, Yitzhak Avraham Gaisinsky (Haissinsky in Yiddish),* affectionately known to all as Rabbi Pitsie Avram, received troubling news. The local Jewish Communal Council was

---

* After the deaths of his father, Rabbi Israel Gaisinsky, and of Isaac Caprove's grandfather, Rabbi Meir Caprove, the Jews of Stavishche looked to Rabbi Yitzhak Avraham Gaisinsky for leadership.

preparing to send an urgent telegram to the Jewish National Secretariat in regard to not only a pogrom in Stavishche, but also of twelve others in nearby villages that were committed simultaneously earlier that day by peasants.[*] The pogrom in Stavishche appears to be one of the earliest on record there during this time period, but it was only the beginning of many.

Less than a year later, in August 1918, Khlavna Kohen (Kagan), a Jewish former member of the Stavishche Town Authority, presented a document to the rabbi detailing another raid by the Bolshevik leader, Gribenko. Gribenko led a few thousand peasants in a pogrom against the Jews, whom they accused of bringing in the Germans. Before taking over Stavishche, Gribenko and his followers began a killing spree in nearby villages, leaving a trail of over one hundred Jewish corpses.

All too aware of the volatile situation in Stavishche, as well as in its neighboring villages, Rabbi Pitsie Avram decided it was time to take action. After witnessing continuous carnage in his beloved town, Pitsie Avram sat by his desk near a kerosene lamp with a pen in hand. He composed, with great forethought, the following letter of alarm[†] to the chief rabbi of Kiev, Rabbi Shelomoh Aharonson.[‡] In 1911–1913, Rabbi Aharonson had played an active role in successfully defending Menahem Mendel Beilis, a Jewish brick factory supervisor who was tried and acquitted in the notorious blood libel trial in Kiev that made headlines worldwide. The Stavishche rabbi pleaded for help.

LETTER OF ALARM TO THE RABBI OF KIEV
WRITTEN BY YITZHAK AVRAHAM GAISINSKY, RABBI OF STAVISHCHE

Stavishche, 5 Elul, 5678 (August 13, 1918)

To His Honor, the Honored and Learned Rabbi of the Congregation of Kiev and Environs, Rabbi Shelomoh Aharonson, the Priest of God On High Peace!

---

[*]   According to the Committee of Jewish Delegations, this widespread violence in the region included a bloody riot that exploded at a fair eighty-five miles away in Pogrebishtche.

[†]   The letter appeared in Hebrew in the *Stavishche Yizkor Book*. It was translated from Hebrew to English by Dr. Ida Selevan Schwarcz. English translation courtesy of Dr. Robert Barnes. The *Stavishche Yizkor Book* credits YIVO Institute for Jewish Research, New York, for their documents. (See Notes.)

[‡]   Rabbi Shelomoh Aharonson, the intended recipient of Rabbi Pitsie Avram's letter of alarm, served as the chief rabbi of Kiev from 1906 to 1921. Aharonson later became a rabbi in Tel Aviv.

We, the representatives of the Jews in Stavishche, pour forth our plea to you, our rabbi, to stand by us in this hour of mortal danger, which is over us, for of the ten measures of suffering which have been afflicted on the Jews of (the) Ukraine in this time of emergency, nine measures have come upon us.

Our isolated town, fifty viorst [a Russian measure of distance equal to about 3,500 feet, a kilometer, or .662 mile] from the railroad, is in the center of the land where the partisan uprising is happening. About six weeks ago our town was filled with the sound of army boots of the partisans, with Gribenko at their head. They declared a draft of all men aged eighteen to forty. Afterwards they lay a fine upon our town of 15,000 rubles. They were given all the money and they nullified the draft order. They confiscated much merchandise for which they sometimes paid a small sum. There is almost no shop which has not suffered from this confiscation.

In the early period the partisans seemed to be satisfied with taking money and merchandise and did not cause violence and the spilling of blood, because there was a certain amount of discipline imposed by their leaders, to whom we could turn for protection. However, now the situation has completely changed. Two weeks ago, a group of Germans came to town and the partisans left. On the second day a battle began between the two camps. It started outside of Stavishche but little by little the partisans were forced to retreat into the town and the narrow streets became killing fields. For seven hours without cease there was thunder of rifles and grenades and a rain of fire on the town. Of the Jews there were four dead and many wounded because the bullets of death penetrated the walls into the houses. But our most terrible sufferings began after the battle.

The leaders and some of the partisans retreated and left our area and found refuge on the other side of the Dnieper. However, a large portion of them, peasants from the area, returned to their homes, hid their arms, and posed as peasants going about their work. The Germans could not find them, because their families would not give them up. The Germans stayed in town five days and as soon as they left, the partisans removed their disguises, took up their arms, and became rulers. Since they had no leaders, they were simply a band of robbers and murderers. They would gather into bands of ten or more men, lay ambushes on the roads and kill all the Jews passing by, after taking everything they had. Every day one or two dead Jews are brought into town. No one dares to leave for fear of these bandits.

The sources of income have stopped, and the lives of the residents hang by a thread. The bandits are not satisfied with ambush only, but invade the town, band by band, armed with swords, rifles, and grenades; they attack houses and rob them, enter the stores and take merchandise, then require tribute from the town.

For example, on Sunday, this week, a band of eleven bandits came into town, armed with grenades, and demanded a tribute of 25,000 rubles. After much begging by the rabbi, in tears, they lowered the sum to 15,000 rubles. They gave us one hour to collect the money. Now there is a rumor that they are planning to set fire to the whole town, after they have plundered it. Our small community is in the midst of tens of villages filled with murderers and robbers, armed to the teeth. We are like a lamb ringed by seventy wolves. We are poor and without weapons to defend ourselves. Have mercy, Rabbi, on our unfortunate community, and send us assistance in our time of trouble. Let the authorities know that they must send us a defense force immediately, for death awaits us and our wives and children, horrible death by sword and fire.

We have been informed that a German unit is approaching but will be here only a few days, and afterwards the bandits will again wreak havoc upon us. We ask and plead in the name of one thousand Jewish families for help. Please send us a permanent defense force so that the Germans will not just come in and out for they do nothing to prevent the violence and the robbery.

So says the member of the Judicial Authority [signature]

So says Yitzhak Avraham Gaisinsky, Rabbi of Stavishche [signature]

P.S. Since the letter has been delayed until today, the tenth of Elul [August 18], more dead bodies have been gathered that were found on the roads. Yesterday they found nine dead Jews, five men and four women, near the village Zshidivsko Grebli. In another place there were dead Gentiles. Even though the Germans are in town and protect it against attack, the roads are still dangerous.

Received: August 23, 1918

There are no known surviving documents confirming whether Rabbi Pitsie Avram's plea for help was ever answered. Four days after the rabbi drafted the letter, a battle transpired between the peasants and the Germans, who eventually drove Gribenko out of Stavishche. While retreating, the peasants killed six Jews in town. The pogrom attacks targeting the Jews of Stavishche continued on a steady basis between the years 1918 and 1921.

CHAPTER EIGHT

GRIGORIEV'S BANDITS

June 5–16, 1919

On Thursday morning, June 5, 1919, the second day of Shavuot, the day of Pentecost, gunfire erupted on the road leading to the nearby town of Tarashcha. The bandit leaders Zhelezniak, Yatsenko, and Voytsekovsky, underlings from *Ataman* Nikifor Grigoriev's unit, burst into Stavishche on horseback with a five-thousand-man unit looking to wreak havoc upon its Jewish population, which numbered roughly four and a half thousand people. Eyewitnesses stated that this group declared themselves to be "White-Guards."[*]

Yunkel and Esther Cutler's oldest son, nine-year-old Daniel Cutler, was in town with an elderly Jewish friend when the two heard the commotion of four drunken peasants in the street. The boisterous gang became separated from the thousands of other bandits who were making their way toward the synagogue. Daniel and the older gentleman quickly took shelter under a stairwell, but peasants encircled another elderly Jewish man, who hadn't managed to take cover. They laughed, amused by his terrified expression as they aimed a gun at his head.

"Dance, Jew, dance!" the peasants drunkenly demanded him.

The old man, with a gun cocked at his head, obeyed.

"Dance faster, Jew, faster!" another peasant yelled out.

---

[*] The "White Guards" opposed the Reds (Bolsheviks) after the October 1917 Revolution.

The old man began to dance even faster.

"You're not dancing fast enough, old Jew!"

The old man tried his hardest to keep up, but instead collapsed. One of the drunkards brought over a hot iron that he had stolen from a nearby blacksmith shop. He motioned for the others to force open the hand of the petrified man. "This is for you, Jew!" the peasant laughed. As the compression of the hot iron caused his palm to sizzle, the man let out a curdling yell.

Daniel's friend, who had been hiding with him under the stairwell, risked their safety when he lifted his head to observe. The peasant wielding the weapon spotted him and fired a fatal gunshot between his eyes.

The sight of an old Jewish woman running out into the street soon diverted the peasants' attention away from the stairwell, where Daniel, frozen with fear, remained alone in hiding. The intoxicated peasants surrounded the woman, who had left her house to see the cause of the commotion. They encircled her, ripping at her clothes. As she screamed for help, each peasant took a turn raping her. During the assault, the old Jewish man, whom they had just burned and tortured, rallied to come to her aid, lifting his battered body off the ground while desperately trying to reach her. In response, one of the murderers fired a final shot at him.

Petrified by the sight of his friend's bloody, lifeless body sprawled out next to him on the ground and fearful for his own life, Daniel waited for the cover of darkness before running home to safety.

The boy first fled to the nearby shoe factory of Isaac Caprove, where he frantically pounded on his stunned aunt and uncle's door. He recounted the horror that he witnessed. "Bandits are here!" Daniel screamed to Rebecca and Isaac, referring to the large group of *sikrikim* or *sikriks.*[*]

Daniel ran home and warned everyone that the town was under siege. The boy had witnessed the first two casualties of what was just the beginning of a long and treacherous pogrom. Isaac and Rebecca wrongly assumed it was an isolated incident.

The next afternoon, when Isaac went to synagogue, he was stunned to discover that the town was still under attack. Arriving at the temple, he was grabbed at gunpoint and taken hostage with those who had gathered the day before to celebrate Shavuot. Throughout the day, the three top henchmen of Grigoriev, with

---

[*] *Sikrikim* or *sikriks* is a Hebrew term derived from the Latin *sicarii*, or "those armed with curved daggers." Rosenthal (MH) uses all three words to describe this particular group of bandits.

Zhelezniak clearly in charge, herded dozens of Jews who entered the building until there was standing room only. Zhelezniak's men waved their guns and surrounded the hostages inside of the synagogue. Over and over again the bandits shouted in Russian, "Jews are Communists!"

The Jewish men in the room knew that there were no Communists among them. After a meeting with a group of peasants from the nearby village of Pshienka, Zhelezniak announced to his hostages that it was decided that instead of killing everyone, they would allow the Jews from Stavishche to buy their freedom by paying a ransom.[*]

Isaac watched as his rabbi, Pitsie Avram, was ordered to collect a contribution of 400,000 rubles from the Jews of the town, along with eight hundred measures of cloth and six hundred sets of underwear. The rabbi, clutching his uneven white beard in amazement, studied the familiar faces of some of his captors and could not believe his eyes. He, along with other witnesses, recognized these bandits as some of the local priests, landowners, students, teachers, and peasants.[†] The rabbi knew the deacon of one of the nearby villages who stood up and announced that he would take it upon himself the "good deed" of revenge on the Jews.[‡]

The brilliant rabbi was forced at gunpoint to knock door to door and request from his followers: "Give me your rubles and your underwear." With the assistance of several well-respected men from Stavishche, however, the rabbi was successful in collecting a considerable sum.

At the end of the day, Pitsie Avram and his assistants returned to the shul where Isaac and the other hostages witnessed their esteemed rabbi handing over 357,000 rubles to Zhelezniak. When Pitsie Avram remarked to Zhelezniak that the money was taken from poor people, the ataman "showed mercy and handed back seven-thousand."[§]

The rabbi, however, was unable to meet all of the captors' demands. While he was successful in collecting most of the ransom, finding cloth and underwear in such large quantities, especially since undergarments were not yet mass-produced in Russia, was an impossible task. Zhelezniak's men, who were drunk

---

[*]   From the archival manuscript *Megilat Ha-tevah* (see Bibliography).

[†]   Elias Heifetz, *The Slaughter of the Jews in the Ukraine in 1919*. New York: Thomas Seltzer, 1921. (See Notes.)

[‡]   From the archival manuscript, *Megilat Ha-tevah*.

[§]   Heifetz, *Slaughter of the Jews in the Ukraine in 1919*, page 287.

and out of control, meted revenge on a handful of Jews. In addition to the two victims whose brutal deaths were witnessed by Daniel Cutler, several others were slaughtered in town.

The rabbi and his men reported to those being held captive in the shul that Isaac's thirty-year-old neighbor, Phillip "Yitzhak" Kohen, had been killed. Phillip's brother-in-law Israel Senderowitz, standing with Isaac, heard the news first-hand: Phillip, a new father, was shot by a drunken bandit as he lay sleeping in his bed.*

The men, including Isaac, who had been imprisoned inside the synagogue, were eventually released. Israel Senderowitz and Isaac were among the last hostages to leave. Zhelezniak admitted that he was unable to restrain his men. The bandit leader gave Senderowitz money to distribute among those Jewish families in Stavishche who had lost their loved ones, with several thousand rubles to be given to Israel's newly widowed sister, Chaika, and her baby daughter, Bella.

Two Days Later: Shabbat, June 7, 1919

The gang returned to town once more. They tortured and raped many women and injured more than eighty Jews, including young children, slashing at them with their swords. They ransacked Jewish houses and loaded 180 wagons with all kinds of goods, such as food, clothing, large pieces of furniture, draperies, goose-down pillows, bed linens, dishes, silverware, Shabbat candlesticks, and jewelry. They also helped themselves to two and a half dozen heads of cattle, horses, and wagons.

The townspeople quietly spoke about the atrocities inflicted upon their friends and neighbors. Three old women told of the unthinkable torture of a thirteen-year-old fatherless girl whose family was named Wilfond after having witnessed it from a nearby room in their house. The teenager was dragged into a wooden structure and then raped and beaten. During the attack, the old women overheard the girl's assailants threatening to kill her if she screamed. After the bandits fled, the women ran to help her, but they found her suffering from serious injuries and were shocked to see that her beautiful brown hair had turned white. She died a short time later in their presence.†

---

* Source: Israel Senderowitz's story in the *Stavishche Yizkor Book*.

† Source: The Wilfond girl's attack was reported in *Megilat Ha-tevah* (see Notes).

For Isaac, there was more bad news. When he heard rumors that two of his acquaintances, Hirsh Zagatovtchik, another shoemaker in town, and Motel Tsirolnick, had been murdered, Isaac sought out Rabbi Pitsie Avram for more information. The rabbi confirmed what others had reported to him. Bandits burst into Hirsh Zagatovtchik's home, relentlessly chasing him and trapping him in his courtyard. He turned over all the money that he had hidden to his pursuers, and then escaped while they were counting it. On Bathhouse Street, the murderers caught up with him. They slashed a bayonet through Hirsh's head, but he was strong as an ox and did not die quickly. Three more assassins beat him to death using the butts of their rifles.*

"What happened to Motel?" Isaac asked Pitsie Avram.

The rabbi told him that a Christian neighbor of Motel's reported to a group of local bandits that Tsirolnick made a negative comment about the Ataman Zhelezniak. To make a personal example of Motel, Zhelezniak responded to the insult by hunting him down. The hetman then killed Motel by shooting him in the mouth.†

Isaac, devastated, returned home to his wife and daughters, who were still in shock after hearing about the Wilfond girl's murder.

During the week Zhelezniak's men occupied the town, they forced their way into Zaslawsky's printer's shop. The establishment on the hill was owned by the wealthiest man in town, whose son, David, was married to Rabbi Pitsie Avram's youngest daughter, Havah. After breaking into the shop, bandits printed large anti-Semitic posters filled with poisonous lies about the Jews.

When the gang finally departed for Tarashcha, the Jews had no way of anticipating that the Red Army would inadvertently drive these killers back to Stavishche. Their most lethal raid caught everyone by surprise on the evening of June 15–16, 1919, when locals brutally assisted Zhelezniak's mob in the attacks.

The two factions terrorizing the Jews of Stavishche clearly defined themselves by the weapons they chose to brutalize their victims with. Zhelezniak's *pogrom-chiks* armed themselves with guns, rifles, and bayonets. Local peasant thugs who joined in the bloodbath attacked with farming tools, such as axes and pitchforks. Together they began by storming the street near the Stavishcha Inn, where Isaac,

---

*   Confirmation source: *Megilat Ha-tevah* (see Notes).

†   Confirmation source: *Megilat Ha-tevah* (see Notes).

Rebecca, and their young daughters resided. They wildly smashed windows, axed down doors, and brutally murdered those not in hiding.

Isaac and Rebecca's House: The Next Morning, June 16, 1919

From every corner the neighborhood was coming out of hiding, hugging and crying or screaming next to the victims of the pogrom. Rebecca and Isaac, who crawled out of the root cellar as soon as the violence stopped, ran quickly to their house. They opened the back door, which was still closed and intact, and rushed to their daughters' bed.

Their legs froze in place, preparing for the worst. Rebecca felt an awful pit in her stomach, afraid of what horrible scene they might find. Instead, they found the girls safe in their bed; they slept through the night!

The violent mob passed over their house!

Rebecca looked at her husband. His cheeks had gone white. Hands shaking, he picked up Sunny, who stretched and smiled. Rebecca broke down and sobbed uncontrollably into Channa's long, brown hair. Confused, the girls looked around with wide eyes. The children, unintentionally left alone in their bed as their worried parents feared for their lives, were oblivious to what had happened.

"Nothing—nothing touched," Isaac said, wondering. "Why did they spare us?"

"Isaac!" a howl came from outside the front door, followed by loud banging. "Isaac! Isaac Caprove! Your peasant Vasyl has murdered my wife!"

Isaac, visibly shaken and still damp from the root cellar where he had just spent a harrowing night in hiding while separated from his daughters, waited for the pounding to stop. He took a few minutes to compose himself before carrying Sunny with him to open the door.

Outside on the street, in front of his shoe factory, a couple dozen Jewish men and women congregated, distraught and still terrified.

Rebecca followed, her oldest daughter huddled against her leg. Channa heard the group of men talking, too many of them at once. Their voices were low and urgent.

"Itsie Shadken was shot in the leg! They took him to Count Branicki's hospital but he died on the way. He bled to death!"

"That handsome student? He should never have come home for the summer!"

"I heard that Mordechai Gutharts was murdered. Isn't he the young man who headed the Committee for the Poor?"

"They killed Chaim Mayer's stepson, Asher!"

"Who did this horror?"

"Zhelezniak and his thugs came back!"

"Vasyl and his local gang joined Zhelezniak's men. He led the raid down our street!"

"Yes, it was Vasyl!" another man told Isaac. "I was hiding under the stairwell of the inn. I heard him—it was your apprentice"—he sneered at Isaac—"leading those drunken Ukrainians, egging them on, then yelling at them to leave your house alone. He stopped the murderers from hacking down your door. He wouldn't allow anyone to enter your house!" The man gestured to Isaac's front door, which was still intact, and his factory window, the only unbroken one on the block.

Channa listened in shock. She knew Vasyl well: he worked for her father. She often played with his little girl. Isaac had met him a couple of years before at the town yarid (market). Vasyl had been caught stealing peaches and apricots from the stand of a Jewish peddler. An angry crowd surrounded the peasant when Isaac noticed the young daughter who was with him: she was about Channa's age. Starving, the girl was devouring a peach that her father had stolen. Isaac felt sorry for her, so he stepped in and paid the merchant for Vasyl's stolen fruit and demanded that the growing crowd of onlookers disperse. Believing that every man should have the chance to earn an honest living to feed his family, Ivan offered the peasant a job in his one-room shoe factory resulting in Vasyl learning the shoemaking trade and remaining a loyal employee.

Vasyl always said that Isaac was the only Jew in Stavishche to ever show him kindness. He promised Isaac that one day he would return the kindness that he had shown him. That's why Channa and Sunny weren't murdered in their beds.

"Isaac Caprove, you took in a murderer," an older man spat. "My wife is dead because of Vasyl, that troublemaker . . . thief . . . murderer! He kept those thugs from harming you!"

Isaac's eyes flashed. "Would you blame me for that peasant's murderous ways? Do you really resent me for still having my wife and children alive? My girls were sleeping in that house!"

"If only we had known," Rebecca wept, dropping to her knees. "We would have had everyone hiding in our home." The men who had been arguing all turned toward her; the sight of the beautiful, pregnant twenty-seven-year-old brunette on the ground shaking and crying helped to break the mounting tension around her.

"Rebecca," Isaac reached out to her, in a comforting tone. Channa saw the love and despair in her father's face.

Channa recognized the newly widowed merchant as he raised his voice. "What will we do? Nearly thirty of us are dead; so many are hurt. Our women were beaten and raped in their own homes. Our houses are in shambles. We're not safe!"

"We can't turn on each other," Isaac said.

"You won't be so safe next time!" the elderly man responded. "I'm taking what's left of my family to Belaya Tserkov."

"Volodarka!" another said. "The rabbi is heading there."

The murmurs grew. Channa felt her mother tighten her grip against her. "Belaya Tserkov," Rebecca said. Her sister Molly and brother Shalum lived there; she felt they'd be safer in the larger city.

First Escape from Stavishche

"Belaya Tserkov," Rebecca kept insisting to Isaac, as she grabbed what she could in a panic. She gathered her jewelry and whatever clothing and food that she could carry. She knew that her husband was torn. Isaac was contemplating fleeing to Volodarka, a village only fifteen miles away, in nearby Skvira district, whereas Belaya Tserkov was twenty-nine miles north. But she was insistent.

Isaac closed the door to the house gently behind him, and, with a sigh, the family began walking swiftly to Belaya Tserkov, ears alert for the sounds of returning thugs. Nearly eight hundred Jews filled the cobblestone and dusty dirt Stavishche streets, carrying their belongings, their eyes weary and grief-stricken. They were leaving the only home many had known. Children with runny noses held their parents' hands.

"Channa, you will carry the bread," Rebecca instructed. The little girl obeyed, and followed her mother, father, and sister on foot, holding the long loaf.

Sunny, a toddler, complained constantly that she was tired. It would be a whole day and night's walk on foot. Isaac had to carry her, but it was no easy task: she was a hefty little thing. As the long line of people reached the crossroads at the edge of town, Channa saw a smaller group with Rabbi Pitsie Avram walking in a slightly different direction, northwest toward Volodarka. The newlyweds Rachel and Elias, who hid during the night with Rebecca and Isaac in the root cellar, held hands as they followed the rabbi's procession.

Next to Pitsie Avram, Channa eyed his grandson Laizer, a thin, handsome boy her age. Laizer didn't smile, but he waved to her. Channa noticed that he, too, was carrying a large loaf of bread.

After what felt like a week of walking, Isaac led his hungry family off the main thoroughfare to a dirt wagon-rutted road and across a field to a small peasant's hut. "We can't make it on foot. We need food. I know this man," he said. "Rebecca, give me your locket and your ring." Isaac returned with a local peasant who agreed to transport the family north on his old horse and wagon, which were kept behind a barn.

Isaac silently held out three dirty potatoes. Rebecca used her skirt to wipe the dirt off the potatoes and handed one to each girl. "Eat everything, even the skin," she said. "It would be sinful to waste it."

Lying in the wagon under a musty burlap cover, Channa took a bite of the gritty, metallic-tasting spud. Her teeth and tongue rebelled, but she followed her mother's instructions. She was so hungry that the potato was gone almost immediately. As the horse clopped on and on, Channa and Sunny fell asleep.

Pitsie Avram's small flock veered off the main road and crossed the wooden bridge built over the Ros River leading to Volodarka. Unbeknownst to the rabbi's group, the bandits, after looting many of the homes that were abandoned by Jews in Stavishche, also headed in that direction, much to the horror of those who just fled from them. After Zhelezniak's men arrived on their heels, they demanded that all the Jews from Stavishche be handed over to their hetman.

The attention of the thugs soon shifted.

"The Reds are coming—burn the bridge!" one of their leaders yelled.

Bandits lit torches and set fire to the old, wooden bridge, keeping out the (Regional) Red Army that were pursuing them on horses from Tarashcha. In doing so, they trapped the Jews of Stavishche in Volodarka with no way to return home.

Once again Rabbi Pitsie Avram went over to privately negotiate with Zhelezniak, who showed great respect for the gutsy, revered rabbi.

"Bring out boards for a makeshift bridge!" Zhelezniak ordered the locals, who obeyed by layering sheets of wood over the shallow part of the river, allowing the Jews to return to Stavishche.

Pitsie Avram waited by the edge of the Ros River until all his people crossed over safely. The rabbi was such a brave, charismatic, and effective negotiator that he even managed to convince Zhelezniak to give the small group of frazzled Jews bread to eat during their long journey home.

Among those returning with this group was the rabbi's seven-year-old grandson, Channa's neighborhood friend Laizer Spector, the child of Pitsie Avram's daughter Libby.* A few days afterward, the Jews who returned to Stavishche from Volodarka selected a day to fast as a remembrance for their neighbors slain by Zhelezniak's gang.†

Isaac, Rebecca, and their young daughters narrowly escaped with their lives by fleeing with the larger group farther north to Belaya Tserkov (Russian for "White Church"). The following day, as the exhausted refugees entered the city full of white domes and cathedrals, they could not help but be reminded of the negative attitude that they felt the Church had toward them as Jews. Isaac's heart sunk, fearing that he'd supported the wrong choice and led his family deeper into danger. Under her breath, however, Rebecca was quietly relieved: they had finally arrived safely in Shvartse Tume.‡

---

* Laizer and Channa, both soon approaching their seventh birthdays, were born just two days apart.

† Source: Laizer Spector, "The Adventures of My Life."

‡ Jewish folklore quietly refers to Belaya Tserkov as *Shvartse Tume,* which was a Yiddish play on its name (Russian: "White Church") meaning "Black Abomination" or "Black Impurity." Perhaps it was the only way Jews felt that they could quietly respond to the anti-Semitism that they felt the Church exhibited toward them during this time period, by using their wits—hence the name change. The same town was also referred to in Hebrew as S'deh Lavan, meaning "White Field." Please note: While the family felt the sting of anti-Semitism, there were also brave Christians from their village who risked their lives to save them. (See chapters 9 and 12.)

CHAPTER NINE

FROM VILLAGE TO VILLAGE

1919–1920

Belaya Tserkov was the largest city on the way to Kiev, making it a natural destination for the several hundred Jews who were desperate to flee from Stavishche. In general, the larger cities were more peaceful, because they tended to be less of a target. When a rumor circulated that another wave of bandits was approaching, even more Stavishche Jews picked up their children without thinking twice, and began running.

Belaya Tserkov was a day and night's journey from Stavishche, even by horse and wagon.* Rebecca had both a brother and a sister living in Belaya Tserkov. She had taken Channa and Sunny there only once before to visit her oldest brother, Shalum Cutler, and his wife, Baila. The couple's vast holdings included a great deal of acreage covered with beautiful flowers and roses. Their main dwelling stood on a hill with a view overlooking the picturesque city full of white domes and churches.

Even more impressive was the fact that all seven of their children, including the daughters, attended a gymnasium, a privilege that was rarely afforded to

---

* Belaya Tserkov had the nearest train station on the road to Kiev, and whenever the tsar's mother, Marie Feodorovna, visited the city, everyone in town would stop what they were doing to watch her grand entrance. From the moment that the attractive widowed empress stepped off the train, red carpets were spread and rolled out before her feet until she reached her accommodation for the night.

Jewish children. An exception was made for Shalum on account of his work as a blacksmith for Tsar Nicholas's army. Despite Shalum's apparent monetary success, it wasn't his help that Rebecca sought out in Belaya Tserkov. She was much closer to her sister Molly, whose doorstep the family landed on.

Two Years Earlier: Stavishche, 1917

Just a few months after losing their mother, Fay, Molly, a gorgeous, blue-eyed brunette with a slender figure, surprised her older sister Rebecca with a visit. "I've just spent the summer with Shalum and Baila," she told Rebecca, as five-year-old Channa listened in. "I had no idea there were so many eligible men in Belaya Tserkov!"

"You've come miles out of your way to see me; did you meet a man?" Rebecca asked Molly.

"Not exactly one."

"Two?"

"No, not two."

"Three?" Rebecca asked surprisingly.

Molly shook her head.

"Four?"

"I've received four marriage proposals! I need your advice: I don't know what to do," Molly said. "I want to marry for love, just like you and Isaac did."

"Then why did you agree to a matchmaker?"

"I refused to see the matchmaker. Baila took it upon herself; she spread the word that her younger sister-in-law was in Belaya Tserkov looking for a husband. Suddenly, Shalum and Baila had lots of unexpected visitors."

"Which man did you chose?" Rebecca asked.

"I haven't decided yet; that's why I've come to Stavishche to speak with you. Baila pointed out that I am already twenty-three, I have no dowry, and in Skibin, there are no marriage prospects for me. She urged me to choose one and marry him."

"Do you favor one over the others?"

"There is one man, an established tailor with a large house, who is a bit older than me. He is a widower named Itzie with two young boys. Shalum and Baila invited him to a large dinner party, and after the meal, he led the dancing there. He asked me to dance. He is the best dancer I have ever partnered with—sparks flew! Later that evening he told me that I am the first woman to capture his heart since his wife, Gittel, died."

"What about the others?"

"They are all much younger than him, closer to my age. I really don't know any of them very well. What do you think I should I do?"

Molly saw that her older sister was at a loss for words, a problem she rarely struggled with.

"I've made up my mind," Molly declared out of frustration. "The next man who comes to my door, I shall marry!"

That is truly what happened. The next suitor to knock at her door, after travelling all the way from Belaya Tserkov to Skibin, was Itzie Stumacher, the widower sixteen years her senior. He had suffered the painful losses of his twenty-nine-year-old wife[*] and their youngest daughter, Libby.

On December 23, 1917, twenty-three-year-old Molly Cutler wed thirty-nine-year-old Itzie Stumacher in Stavishche.[†] At first, his eleven- and six-year-old sons, Ruby and Moe, made their young stepmother's life a living nightmare. But eventually, they managed to overcome their grief at the thought of another woman replacing their dear mother and saw Molly for the kind woman she was. It wasn't long before they began to call her their mother.

Itzie, whose father and grandfather were well-respected men in Belaya Tserkov, was considered to be an established man, and certainly, in comparison to Molly's family, was financially secure. The beautiful twin house that he owned in Belaya Tserkov had a rental apartment attached to it with four large rooms.[‡]

In June 1919, when the Caprove family finally arrived at Itzie's stately dwelling after fleeing the pogrom in Stavishche, Channa could not believe that her new uncle was so rich. The large wooden and brick dwelling had two front doors and

---

[*]   Gittel died of an infection following an appendicitis attack. She was the daughter of Baila and Leib Dimenstein of Belaya Tserkov.

[†]   Itzie was also known as Izzy, Isidore or Isadore.

[‡]   Itzie's address in Belaya Tserkov is thought to be 32 Gravana Ulitsa.

two chimneys; one for the main house, and the other for the rental apartment. She looked up at the dark, picket fence that stood taller than she did; it was at least five feet in height. The points on top of the slats were triangular and painted white, giving the encompassed property a stately feel. The fence encased not only the house, but also a large porch that extended around the entire perimeter of the building. There was a large stoop in front of each front door where the family sat and enjoyed the sunny breeze. Every few feet, beautifully crafted windows, all rectangular, were open, allowing those inside the house to enjoy the fresh summer air.

Tarashcha, 1919

While the situation seemed to be calming down in Stavishche, the same could not be said for Tarashcha, located 18.5 miles northeast of Stavishche. Tsar Nicholas's famous boot maker, Myer Ova Denka, the father-in-law of Rebecca's brother, Avrum Cutler, was standing alone on the cobblestone street just outside of his shoe factory when a pogrom took him by surprise. A small group of Cossacks surrounded him and began taunting him mercilessly until one took it a step too far. Myer's daughter, Slova, Avrum's feisty wife, looked through a window and saw a pistol being placed in her father's mouth.

The full-figured Slova bravely ran out into the street and cocked her own pistol to the head of the bandit whose gun was pointed at her father. "If you hurt my father, I will pull the trigger!" she screamed madly in Russian.*

The peasants, laughing nervously, could not believe their eyes: a Jewish woman defiantly holding a gun to the head of their comrade. The peasant slowly removed his gun from inside of Myer's mouth and laughed, "I'll let you both live because of the bravery of the young Jewess!"

The Cossacks let it be known that they released father and daughter because they were amused by Avrum's gutsy wife. However, anyone who knew Slova believed that she meant business. Secretly, they were probably scared that she would not have hesitated to blow the head off of anyone who dared to hurt her beloved father.

---

* Source: Charles Cutler, in an interview with the author.

Back in Stavishche: June–July 1919

Rebecca wanted nothing more than to be back in her own home when she gave birth to her third child. A Jewish committee of aid set up in Belaya Tserkov to assist the refugees from Stavishche had assured the family that it was safe to return. Like most of the Jews from Stavishche, they believed what they were told and were relieved to be on their way.

Shortly after their return home, rumors spread that bandits were approaching the town. It happened on a quiet, peaceful summer night. Windows were open everywhere, yet there was no movement in the air. At ten o'clock the tranquility was abruptly broken by the sound of screaming in the streets, alerting residents of impending danger. Rebecca, Isaac, and their girls found themselves throwing on their clothes and running for their lives with many others toward a public house, the bet hamidrash.

Once inside, Channa immediately spotted her eleven-year-old neighbor Rochela Feinzilberg, the daughter of the apothecary owner, huddled in a corner with her parents and sisters. The frightened girls locked eyes. In the midst of the commotion, each child prayed in silence to survive the night. The noise and screaming outside were horrifying, and many were crying hysterically.

The girls watched as mothers were trying to calm their little ones. Men paced the room while discussing what to do. They did not know whether or not to run again. Everyone knew that they could die at any moment; Rochela couldn't imagine her life ending that evening. She thought to herself that just outside the door, there was such beauty in nature nearby. It began as such a lovely, calm evening; to even think that people could be so cruel toward others and to show such hatred was unimaginable.[*]

When the sun rose the next morning and all was quiet, it was clear that the impending threat had passed. The girls gave a heavy sigh of relief, and everyone was thankful for their good fortune. God finally heard their prayers—it was truly a miracle.

The stress that Channa's family endured after returning to Stavishche surely contributed to Rebecca going into labor a few weeks earlier than expected. During both of her previous pregnancies, she had delivered large babies after long and difficult labors, and this time was no different. Rebecca's anxious

---

[*]   Source: From an oral story by Channa, and also a composition written by Rochela Feinzilberg.

husband and two young daughters listened from another room in their home as she screamed out in pain.

Naturally, Channa's father was hoping for his first son, who would become a bar mitzvah and would one day be able to recite *Kaddish* for his parents. Sunny, Isaac's favorite, was cuddled in his lap when the midwife finally appeared cradling a tiny newborn covered in a white blanket.

"Isaac, you have another beautiful daughter," she told him.

For a moment, Channa thought that she detected a look of disappointment on her papa's face; now he had three daughters and no sons. However, as he held the delicate infant in his arms for the first time and saw his daughter's tiny head and large eyes peeping out of the blanket, it was apparent to all that he fell instantly in love.

"What will we name her?" Channa asked her father.

"Your mama has already named her Fay," the midwife told them.

Another pregnant woman on the block gave birth on the same day to a healthy son. A joint celebration was planned for the birth of Stavishche's two newest and tiniest residents, and the Jewish women in town busied themselves baking and cooking for the event.

It resembled a scene that one might find in a Sholem Aleichem story: when a couple got married, the entire village showed up for the wedding. When someone laughed, the whole town laughed. When a baby was born, the whole community—men, women, and children—celebrated. Despite recent tragedies, everyone from the shtetl, between 4,000 and 4,500 Jews, was invited to join the celebration and eat cake and homemade strudel.

On July 31, 1919, seven-year-old Channa joined the other children as they went from door to door collecting cakes for the celebrations.* As the group of Jewish children passed the town's church, they all crossed themselves and then pointed their fingers at their derrieres. It was a defiant gesture made by young children who, at that time, felt persecuted by the Church.†

The children were simply reacting to the fear of the times, not knowing who to trust or what horrible circumstance they might witness next. Their reaction

---

* One of the celebrations included a *brit milah* (circumcision), since the other child born that day was a boy.

† Upon reflection, years later, Channa felt that the children should not have made disrespectful gestures when passing the Church. Not all Christians in Stavishche persecuted Jews. Many of the Christian peasants were good people, who had helped her family, even when it was unsafe for them to do so.

was understandable in light of the fact that the bandits that led the pogroms were Christian peasants. Jewish children grew up fearing the Church.[*] Published testimony suggests that even some of the priests were among the bandits in Stavishche.[†]

Despite the tension and hostility between many of the Christians and Jews at that time, life continued as normal—and the Jewish children of Stavishche were caught up in the excitement of the festivities. But it seemed that their excitement was short-lived. No sooner had the festivities begun when a messenger arrived, screaming, "Run—be careful, they're attacking!" Gunshots were audible from a distance. Many of those who had gathered for the *brit milah* fled to their cellars or any other safe hiding place. Isaac grabbed Channa and Sunny in each hand, and their mother cradled her newborn baby, as the family headed for the woods to hide. Earlier in the day, just hours before the celebration, it had rained, and the woods were swampy and full of water; they soon found themselves all covered in mud. They slept in the marshes that night.

Inside Stavishche, another murderous band of several thousand bandits, headed by Ataman Zeleny, began breaking into homes and looting Jewish shops. The son of a poor peasant, Danylo Trepylo had been given the nickname Zeleny, Russian for "green," by his band of followers after hiding in green valleys near his village by the Dnieper River. Green soon became the color symbolic of the peasant uprisings. Zeleny was a central figure in the attacks against Kiev and a fierce enemy of the Reds, a band that he once supported. The hetman was "the prototypical representative of the rebel movement from the Ukrainian villages of this period."[‡]

---

[*] Dr. Abraham Gannes, the late Jewish educator and author, summed up the possible reasons why some Jews in Ukraine may have at that time feared the Church: "In Jewish history, generally, the Church was the millennial symbol of Christianity's anti-Semitic teachings, calling Jews Christ killers, attempting to convert them, overtly and covertly inciting their adherents to terror and pogroms, and holding them responsible for the economic and social chaos, anarchy and communism. Fear of the Church was a constant in Jewish life."

[†] There were also many kind priests in Ukraine, like the one in nearby Winograd, who risked his life while sheltering Jews in his cellar during a pogrom. He even fought for and helped win the release of a sixteen-year-old Jewish boy from that city being held by a group of bandits. Then there was the Peshinke priest, Leyavitsh, who allowed a Jewish boy from Stavishche to hide from Zhelezniak's gang in his home.

[‡] Source: Elias Tcherikower. *Di Ukrainer Pogromen in Yor 1919.* Translated by Janie Respitz. New York: YIVO Institute for Jewish Research, 1965.

After the Bolsheviks tried to capture Zeleny in 1919, he clashed with Stavishche. Several thousand of his followers stormed the town, many armed with axes. The Jews hid in their cellars, attics, and in secret rooms in their houses.

In the woods, Channa's family could hear the stomping of Zeleny's men's horses as they rode by. If the Jews didn't make it back in time to their houses, they hid in the woods or in a garden. Some sought shelter in the homes of friendly Christians who saved them.

Tired, wet, and hungry, Isaac led his family on foot to the home of a *poritz*, a Polish Catholic noble who was his friend and a customer at the shoe factory. The nobleman lived in a fine home located near the ruins of what once was Count Branicki's magical estate, destroyed by the revolting peasants nearly two years earlier. As a poritz, he had suffered the loss of his wealth and valuables but was able to continue living on the count's vast property, far from the Jewish quarter of town. Since he wasn't a Jew, the nobleman's home was safe. It was during the early hours of the morning when the poritz covered the exhausted family with warm blankets while his wife, the *preetza*, showed kindness by serving them a hot breakfast.

When it was safe for the family to return home, the noble took them by horse and wagon back to their living quarters in the center of town. His peasant wagon driver had abandoned him during the early days of the Revolution, so the noble positioned himself on the hay-cushioned driver's box seat and grabbed the leather reins and whip. Isaac sat up front beside the nobleman and placed Channa on his lap. She sat in awe, mesmerized by the constant tick of the horse's pointy ears and the bobbing up and down of its flowing, stringy mane.

The child was awakened from her pleasant but momentary trance by a startled cry coming from her mother, who was sitting behind her. Channa looked down and was terrified to see two corpses lying in pools of blood on the cobblestone street before her. Rebecca turned protectively to Sunny, but she was not sitting near enough to her oldest daughter to cover her eyes, and Isaac did not react fast enough to do so. The men from one of the victim's family had already gathered and were hammering a pine box to be used for his burial. A wagon stood waiting to take his body to one of the two Jewish cemeteries in town; those close to him waited to follow on foot behind the casket of their loved one.

News of Zeleny's attack quickly spread around town. The people of Stavishche soon learned what Rebecca and Isaac had witnessed while hiding in the woods the night before: the bravery of their rabbi, Pitsie Avram.

CHAPTER TEN

ATAMAN ZELENY MEETS RABBI PITSIE AVRAM

Kol Yisrael Arevim Ze ba Ze
All Jews are responsible one for the other.

Stavishche, July 1919

Rabbi Pitsie Avram had his own special interpretation of this famous Talmudic statement. When several thousand murderous bandits took the shtetl of Stavishche by storm on July 31, 1919, Pitsie Avram felt compelled to save the Jews of the town. While everyone in town feared for their lives, the sixty-two-year-old rabbi, much to the dismay of his wife, Sara, who begged him not to draw attention to himself, ran out openly into the street and was arrested by the infamous Zeleny's bandits.

"Take me to your ataman!" he demanded.

A dark-haired, lightly bearded man in his thirties stepped forward. "I am Ataman Zeleny," answered Danylo Ilkovych Terpylo, the hetman from the village of Tripoliye. "I believe you were asking for me."

The white-bearded rabbi, standing before him with a gun pointed at his head, spoke in Russian, the ataman's native language, hoping to use diplomacy as a way of protecting his people from any further violence. His heroic negotiation with Zeleny was within earshot of Rebecca, who, while hiding in the nearby muddy woods with Isaac and their three daughters, translated the fiery exchange for her husband.

"I am Yitzhak Avraham Gaisinsky, the rabbi of Stavishche," he told the bandit, a former carpenter in the Kiev train yards. "Since you and your soldiers are our guests, we wish to provide you with boots, sugar, salt, and money, on the condition that you protect the town."*

"You show great courage," the hetman responded. "This is something I have not seen before in a Jewish leader."

By a great stroke of luck, Ataman Zeleny liked, and even admired, the brave rabbi, and agreed to send two of his soldiers to accompany Pitsie Avram on a house-to-house collection. Six hundred thousand rubles were collected from the town's population, and a group of nearly thirty men, who had been arrested and taken hostage during the initial tumult, were released unharmed. Only two or three murders were committed during the raid, minimal in comparison to the devastating trail of bodies that Zeleny's soldiers had left behind in other villages. Zeleny, out of great respect for the rabbi's fierce and unyielding determination to shield his people from danger, prevented his henchmen from committing any further lootings, robberies, and murders on that summer day. The Red Army, on the trail of the bandits, soon appeared and chased the thousands of hooligans out of town.

When he boldly demanded a meeting with the infamous bandit, the rabbi exhibited an innate understanding of human nature. In this instance, it was almost as if he had been given access to one of Zeleny's earlier speeches, which expressed the murderous ataman's views on the Jewish "question." Less than seven months earlier, Zeleny, a gifted orator, delivered a speech in the town of Borispol, located twenty miles east southeast of Kiev, which was later reported on by eyewitnesses.

> I am neither a Jew-lover, nor a Jew hater. It is not because of hatred that we do not take Jews into our ranks. We are fighting for freedom and land; with freedom every resident of the Ukraine will benefit, but the land belongs only to the Ukrainians. The Jews certainly cannot take offense at this. The Jew does not need land.

---

* This was also a recollection by the rabbi's granddaughter Havah (Eva) Haissinsky Goldman (see Notes).

The Jew does not want to toil, just as the Jew does not want to fight a war. . . . A Jew needs freedom, and he will get it. Let him do as much business as his heart desires, as long as it is of honest and respectable character. In return for the freedom we will bring to the Jews, they should help us out with money.[*]

Who was this fearless rabbi who risked his life for the Jews of his shtetl?

Without question, Pitsie Avram was Stavishche's greatest Jewish homegrown scholar as well as its strongest personality. While there were other fine rabbis in the town, such as Yaakov Yosef, Eliyahu Sohet, and the Zionist leader HaLevi from Lida, it was Pitsie Avram's remarkable courage that stood out, ensuring his legendary status. Even a half-century after his death in 1942, Stavishche landsmen shared fond memories of the colorful rabbi.

While his proper name was Rabbi Yitzhak Avraham Gaisinsky (Haissinsky in Yiddish), he was known to everyone in Stavishche simply as "Rabbi Pitsie Avram."

All that is really known about Pitsie Avram's childhood is that he was born in Stavishche to Rabbi Israel Haissinsky and his wife, Libby, on June 5, 1857, and that he came from a long line of rabbis. He was ordained by Rabbi Michel of Belaya Tserkov. In 1883, Pitsie Avram succeeded his late father as the Jewish spiritual leader of Stavishche. His grandfather Isaac and his great-grandfather Nissan had both served as rabbis of the community, and his mentor and uncle, Rabbi Raphael Haissinsky, was an outstanding scholar and teacher.[†]

Pitsie Avram's oldest child and only son, Nissan, was a rabbi and an "honored merchant in the town of Talnoye, Kiev District."[‡] The esteemed rabbi upheld family tradition by marrying off the three oldest of his five daughters to the sons of other well-established rabbinical families in (what is now) Ukraine.[§] His oldest daughter, Fruma, married Rabbi Zelig Tanicki of Boguslav, and a second daughter, Golda, became the wife of Rabbi Dov Ber Czarne of Monasterzyce. A

---

[*]   Source: Tcherikower, *Di Ukrainer Pogromen in Yor 1919*.

[†]   Source: Gottlieb, S.N. *Ohole-Schem, Biografien und Adressen d. Rabbiners*. Translated by Yale J. Reisner. Pinsk: MM Glouberman Printer, 1912.

[‡]   Source: Gottlieb, *Ohole-Schem, Biografien und Adressen d. Rabbiners*. Family members state that Nissan also had familial ties to Tarashcha. His last residence in Ukraine was in Talnoe in 1927.

[§]   The only child of Rabbi Pitsie Avram and his wife, Sara, who is not mentioned within the text is his fourth-born daughter, Rose, who remained in Europe.

third daughter, Liba (Libby), married Rabbi Aryeh Judah Spector of Zhivotov.[*] Rabbi Spector, the esteemed teacher of the teen songbird Pinchas Segal (Pierre Pinchik), was murdered while heroically trying to warn Jewish families of an imminent pogrom.

Pitsie Avram insisted that his young and brilliant grandson Moise Haissinsky, son of Nissan, leave his parents' home in Tarashcha to be raised by him as a rabbi in Stavishche. Moise, who inherited the rabbi's keen intellect, eventually left Stavishche for other parts of Europe, leaving behind all the rabbinical aspirations his grandfather had for him. In France, he became a well-respected scientist, assisting Marie Curie in her famous laboratory. Today, Pitsie Avram's grandson is considered to be one of the founders of radiochemistry.[†]

The esteemed rabbi's granddaughter (and Moise's sister) Eva Haissinsky Goldman recalled that for four decades, the residents of Stavishche would turn to her *zeyde* (grandfather) for advice in all important life-altering discussions: engagements, weddings, divorces, business arrangements and disagreements, and the settling of other disputes. In addition to being wise, he was a skilled diplomat. It would not be an unusual sight for his many young grandchildren, including Moise and Eva, to witness both sides of disputing parties arguing and yelling before him. According to Eva, the old rabbi would then hold out his kerchief, letting it be known that he had made his decision.[‡]

All facets of life in the town revolved around Pitsie Avram and his influence. Although he was known as the rabbi of the common people and prayed with them at both the bet hamidrash and the Sokolovka kloyz, he was respected by almost everyone in Stavishche.[§] His display of courage in protecting all the Jews in town during times of distress, regardless of their religious level and affiliation, awarded him heroic status.

His youngest daughter, Havah, who earned a chemistry degree and worked in Stavishche as a pharmacist, worshipped her father. She would later write of him proudly:

---

[*]   Source: Gottlieb, *Ohole-Schem, Biografien und Adressen d. Rabbiners.*

[†]   *Rossiyskaya Evreiskaya Entsiclopediya*, entry 1354.

[‡]   Source: Eva Haissinsky Goldman describes her grandfather's influence in a story in the *Stavishche Yizkor Book.*

[§]   In addition to Rabbi Pitsie Avram's followers in the bet hamidrash and the Sokolovka kloyz, many Stavishchers were followers of the rabbis from the Zionist, Hassidic, Talnoe, or Makarov kloyz.

Besides being a pious scholar, he was also very wise. He was the religious leader of the town, the adviser, the peace maker, the representative of all the Jews before God and before the world. He helped the
Jews of Stavishche at all times, especially in time of war. At the time
of the pogroms he rescued them from the murderers' hands. With his
great wisdom he saved the Jews from the greatest dangers.*

After exiting Stavishche, Zeleny and thousands of his men rode by horseback
and soon reached the town of Sokolovka Justingrad. As they passed through a
nearby shtetl, Jewish eyewitnesses described seeing as many as five thousand to
ten thousand of his followers. Unfortunately for the Jewish population of Sokolovka Justingrad, Zeleny did not take such a liking to their rabbi.

---

*   Source: Havah Zaslawsky's story in the *Stavishche Yizkor Book*.

CHAPTER ELEVEN

THE MURDER OF
BESSIE CUTLER'S HUSBAND

Sokolovka Justingrad/Konela, 1919

In 1919, 2,500 Jews lived in Sokolovka Justingrad, twenty-five miles south of Stavishche, and a few hundred occupied the surrounding dorfs. Bessie Cutler, Rebecca's youngest sister, lived with her husband, Karl, and their infant daughter in nearby Konela, a tiny village found by following the old channel two or three miles north.[*]

Tensions flared within the Jewish community of Sokolovka Justingrad when, just prior to Passover 1919, Alexander Kraidin, a young matzah maker, was jailed on suspicion of committing a Jewish blood libel murder.[†] Although the young teen was released a week later after his "victim" showed up in town alive and well, tensions did not subside.

Four months later, on August 2, 1919, a pleasant summer day, thousands of Ataman Zeleny's men stormed into the town on horseback. They had just left

---

[*] Source: Joseph M. Gillman, in collaboration with Etta C. Gillman. *The B'Nai Khaim in America: A Study of Cultural Change in a Jewish Group*. Philadelphia: Dorrance & Company, 1969.

[†] A blood libel murder, also known as a ritual murder, is a false allegation that Jews used the blood of slain Christian children for ritual purposes, particularly when preparing matzah for Passover.

Stavishche, where Rabbi Pitsie Avram had successfully negotiated face-to-face with the henchman Zeleny, thus saving the town's Jews.

Rabbi Pinchas Rabinowitz, Sokolovka Justingrad's spiritual leader and folk hero, promised that "as long as I live, no blood will be spilled in my town."* When the lives of his people were miraculously spared during two prior attacks,† Jews and Christians from the shtetl and its environs began to believe the rabbi's promise. Many also thought that he'd placed a curse on the bandits. The murderers were determined to end the life of the revered rabbi, believing, as did the local peasantry, that as long as there was "light in his eyes,"‡ Rabbi Rabinowitz possessed the power, using prayer, to defeat the pogrom bandits.

A few mounted horsemen made their way to the house of the beloved Reb Pinchas'l, as he was affectionately known to Sokolovka's Jewish community. A bandit entered the rabbi's large courtyard, brandishing a gun. In the dining room, the pious and humble rabbi and several of his Hassidim friends were finishing their third meal of the Sabbath.§ The bandit asked which man was the rabbi: Reb Pinchas'l stood up and was shot after identifying himself.¶

The murderers' motives were clear. Now that they had killed the seventy-six-year-old Torah-chanting rabbi, they were free to shed the blood of Sokolovka's Jews. They then massacred the young men of the town—approximately 150 were shot by a hidden machine gun.**

Fortunately, Bessie, her husband, and their infant daughter were at home in Konela during the summer bloodbath.

---

* While the rabbi's famous words are well-documented in several written sources, Channa herself heard of the rabbi's fearless words as a child while living in Stavishche and never forgot the story of his tragic fate.

† During one pogrom, local Christians rescued their Jewish neighbors from a bridge in Sokolovka.

‡ Source: *Megilat Ha-tevah*.

§ Leo and Diana Miller also discuss the rabbi's murder in *Sokolievka/Justingrad: A Century of Struggle and Suffering in a Ukrainian Shtetl*. page 54.

¶ The rabbi may have been survived by a son-in-law, the Hassidic Rebbi Reb Yehoshua Heskl Rabinowitz of Monistritch. It is unknown whether he was present when the rabbi was murdered. The rabbi's twenty-two-year-old grandson, Gedalya Mandel son of Yehoshua, was murdered during one of the bloodbaths that followed.

** Unconfirmed, heartbreaking stories circulated that as the men were shot, the Jews of the village cried out the *Sh'ma* (a prayer, also known as Shema)

The notorious bandit Kebe was born and raised in the nearby village of Popivka and later served in Sokolovka Justingrad's militia.[*] When a group of Jews in Sokolovka accused him of first stealing hides from them, and then selling them, he was convicted and punished for his crimes. Kebe subsequently joined the partisans and swore vengeance on all the Jews of Sokolovka.[†]

On his second killing spree, which took place right after Zeleny's summer massacre, Kebe led a band of hooligans who set fire to parts of Sokolovka. He then hunted down a group of Jews who had fled the flames to nearby Konela, and murdered thirty-six of his prey, leaving their bloodied bodies sprawled out on a field by the windmills at the entrance of the tiny village. The scene of mass murder near the spinning sails of Konela's flour mills was an unforgettable sight for the 120 Jewish families and their many friendly Christian neighbors who lived in this tiny dorf.

Among the witnesses was Channa's youngest and favorite aunt, Bessie Cutler, who had grown up with Channa's mother in the much smaller countryside dorf of Skibin. Their upbringing turned out to be a blessing—as with very few Jewish families in Skibin, it forced all seven of the Cutler children to pick up the language of his or her neighbors. When most Jews spoke Russian, their Yiddish accents gave them away. Peasants usually had no problem distinguishing between a Christian and a Jew. But Bessie spoke Russian fluently without an accent. In fact, when Jews from larger towns heard her speak Yiddish, they could easily detect that she had grown up in a dorf and made fun of her thick Yiddish accent. During a time when being Jewish could mean losing your life, it was a blessing that Bessie spoke Russian so well.

Not only was Bessie fluent in Russian, but with a tall, statuesque figure, blue eyes, and long golden hair, many mistook her for a Gentile. In Konela, she deliberately wore peasant-style clothing that she sewed herself in order to mingle freely and blend in among the local peasantry. When the peasant farmers boycotted selling Jews any fruit, vegetables, and chickens, they sold them to Bessie. When they would not speak freely in front of a Jew, they gladly conversed with her. When Jewish women feared for their lives as they walked down the street, the local male populace smiled pleasantly at her.

---

[*]   Popivka was a village two miles southwest of Sokolovka Justingrad.

[†]   Kebe's second raid probably took place in late 1919. Source: *Megilat Ha-tevah*.

Bessie had gotten married in 1917 to a red-headed young man named Karl who adored her. Karl was born and raised in Konela, where the teenaged couple now made their home. They became parents to a beautiful baby girl and were happy with their lives until fate cruelly intervened.

At the very end of 1919, General Anton Denikin's army, retreating from a loss in Belaya Tserkov, sent word out in Sokolovka Justingrad that they wanted to hold a meeting in a field near the river with all the Jewish men from the town. It was hinted that they wanted to talk about peace. Denikin, the commander and chief of the White forces (Russians) in the civil war against the Bolsheviks, had little control over his followers, who often committed violent pogroms against the Jews. Bessie had the advantage of being able to converse with the local peasantry. From what she had gleaned from their conversation, she was naturally suspicious about the true intentions of Denikin's soldiers. She begged her husband not to attend and implored him to hide in their root cellar in Konela while this meeting was set to take place.

Assured that her young husband was safely in hiding, Bessie, with her infant daughter, made the long walk into Sokolovka to shop for eggs and milk at the marketplace. She was startled by a series of explosions that sounded like cannon fire: blasts continued one after another as the ground shook beneath her. They appeared to have originated from the direction near the river where the meeting was rumored to have taken place. In between the shots, she could make out the faint but heart wrenching echoes of a familiar prayer, *"Sh'ma Yisrael Adonai Eloheinu Adonai Ehad."* "Hear, O Israel: the Lord is our God, the Lord is One."*

Cradling her young child in her arms, Bessie rushed home. When she opened the cellar door, she was certain that she would find her husband. But Karl had broken his promise to her and had gone to the meeting. Before leaving, Karl had confided in a female neighbor that he felt it was an act of cowardice to hide when all the other men in the village were attending the gathering. On what must have been pure adrenaline, Bessie ran until she reached the outskirts of the field near the river.

She could not believe the gruesome sight that greeted her. Two hundred bloodied bodies were lying before her, mangled together in the snow. The unarmed men had gathered there in hopes of making peace, but instead were

---

* While this prayer serves as a centerpiece of the morning and evening Jewish prayer services, it has also been traditional to recite the Sh'ma as one's last words.

ruthlessly ambushed by Denikin's hooligans. In shock, Bessie desperately searched for her husband; she found his lifeless body dangling from a wagon. Dazed, she stood there, helpless. Bessie looked around the frozen killing field and realized that, with the exception of a few men who were tending to the bodies, she and her baby were the only ones alive. Others who had heard the gunfire and had reached the sight of the massacre just before her were murdered in the streets, shot by the bandits on horseback as they were exiting Sokolovka.

In an absolute state of shock, Bessie held on to her child for dear life and started walking. As she passed the frozen river, her boots brushed against the corpses of dozens of men who had been ambushed earlier in the day. The men had been stripped naked of their coats, clothing, shoes, and underwear by Denikin's soldiers, who then tied the hands of their victims and bound them together. The naked men were then thrown out on the frozen river and left to freeze to death. Unable to process her thoughts, Bessie mindlessly headed toward her sister Hiya's house, which was several miles away. She walked through the snow in the bitter cold and had no idea how long it took her to reach her sister's house.

The first night following the massacre, Bessie woke up screaming and shaking from a vivid nightmare. "Karl came to me in my dream," she cried to Hiya. "He told me that he wants the baby with him." Hiya sat by her traumatized sister's bedside until Bessie, who lovingly cradled her precious infant daughter in her arms, fell back to sleep.

A few days later, Bessie's dream turned out to be prophetic: her seemingly healthy little girl died mysteriously.* Within just days, Bessie had witnessed a massacre and lost both a husband and a child. Now widowed and childless, she remained under the loving and nurturing care of her older sister, who was a great comfort to her.

Channa's youngest and sweetest aunt, an innocent victim of General Denikin's fury, was just eighteen years old when her life came crumbling down around her.

The pogrom that took the life of Bessie Cutler's young husband also spelled the end of the century-old shtetl.†

---

* Other family members told slightly different versions of the story; this is Channa's.

† A small handful of Jews and their descendants remained in the town until they were shot during the Holocaust.

CHAPTER TWELVE

GENERAL DENIKIN'S MILITIA

Scenes from the week long raids:
Stavishche, November–December 1919

On Simchat Torah 5680 (1919), the Jews of Stavishche danced in celebration, feeling revived.* Arks in the synagogues were opened, and men carried and kissed the precious Torah scrolls. In Pitsie Avram's shul, Isaac and Rebecca looked on proudly as Channa and Sunny joined the procession of children who paraded around the building carrying little blue-and-white flags with an apple and a lighted candle on top.† It was just a brief moment of happiness before the next wave of anti-Semitic violence entered the already pogrom-ravaged village.

It was as if the bandits believed that the Jews were hiding an infinite supply of riches. Many different bands of hoodlums in Ukraine continued targeting Jews by pillaging their homes in town after town. By the end of November 1919, the Jews of Stavishche had already endured the raids of Dabravalsky, Kravtshenko,

---

* Many of the 4,500 Jews who lived in Stavishche had returned to their homes.

† The children carried flags on Simchat Torah to symbolize the tribal flags under which the Israelites marched in the desert. Blue-and-white flags were first adopted by the Zionist Movement back in 1897; it was later used as the official flag of Israel in 1948. The colors blue and white represent the colors of the Jewish prayer shawl. The apple with a candle on top was meant to evoke images of Torah as light. This procession was recalled by both Channa in an interview and her childhood friend Yosl Golub in the *Stavishche Yizkor Book* (see Notes). It is unclear if there was a separation of the boys and girls.

Gribenko, the Bazenevtes, Zhelezniak, Petliura, Karnivsky, Mazali, Zeleny, and various other wandering and intermittent peasant gangs. While local thugs continued their plundering, the Denikins, under the leadership of the Russian general Anton Denikin, who led the White forces, also raided Stavishche.

Channa's uncle, Yunkel Cutler, experienced firsthand the brutality of the Denikins. After violating his home during the last week of November, the thugs threw Yunkel violently against the wall to shoot him. Despite their young age, his four children, Sarah, Sheva, Daniel, and Paul, understood all too well what was happening to their father. Watching the barrel of a loaded gun pointed at his father's face, ten-year-old Daniel started screaming, "You can't shoot my father; he hasn't done anything to you!"

The Denikin soldier warned Daniel to move aside or he'd hit him with the butt of his gun. Daniel, who was a fearless child, screamed back in Russian, "You can hit me or shoot me, but you can't shoot my father!"

Daniel's mother, Esther, hurriedly threw some money in a refuse pail; it was just a few hundred rubles, but enough to momentarily distract the peasants. Yunkel, a powerful blacksmith, took advantage of the distraction and managed to pull the barrel of the gun away from his face while screaming for the others inside the house to run. Fifteen Jews, including Yunkel and his family, ran out of the back door toward the river; all but a sick woman and Daniel fled from the house. After seeing the fear in her eyes, the young boy, who did not know the woman well, felt compelled to remain behind to help her. In their rush to flee the home, the others did not realize that she was too weak to run on her own accord.

Daniel, who was mature well beyond his years, began screaming and crying, trying to further distract the bandits. One of the Denikins actually felt sorry for him and tried to console the young, fair-haired boy. The bandit took some cookies out of his pocket that he had stolen from a Jewish woman who had baked them earlier in the day. "Here, have this, youngster, and don't cry."

The sympathetic Denikin showed Daniel the door. The bandits could have shot and killed everyone in that house, and nobody would have known. They could have easily buried the bodies beneath the ice of the frozen Gniloi Tikich River out back.

❖

Fools rush in where angels fear to tread.
—Alexander Pope

After fleeing their home, Daniel and Sarah became separated from the rest of their family, but ran into their cousin, Sol Moser, while wandering by the river. Without their parents' knowledge, the three children ran around town during the height of trouble. They disregarded the imminent danger around them. On account of their blondish hair, flawless Russian, and peasant clothing, the youngsters were able to move around freely during the Denikin raids without attracting the unwanted attention of the murderous "soldiers."

The trio, while out near the Gniloi Tikich River, heard bloodcurdling screams coming from inside of their uncle Yoske Stepansky's blacksmith shop. They ran over to the establishment and took turns peering through the window. Unnoticed by the bandits who had broken into the shop, the children witnessed the torture and murder of one of their cousins, Elek Stepansky.

A formidable man and a powerful blacksmith, Elek found himself outnumbered and cornered by this group of Denikin's thugs. Forced at gunpoint to heat up and grab a blacksmith's iron with his bare hands, the children looked on in silent horror and cringed as Elek's palms sizzled from the burns. The bandits did not spare the life of the young husband and father of three. Later that same evening in Stavishche, Elek's younger brother Mendel suffered a similar fate while their grandmother was axed to death.

Elek Stepansky's young widow, Sheindel, felt the sharp sting of the pogroms as, one by one, the bandits claimed the lives of so many of her loved ones. Her father, Stavishche's popular sixty-year-old wagon driver, Nachum Velvel Bershadsky, was slain by Petliura's band; her uncle Yonah Bershadsky, a driver whose open wagon route covered the distance between Tarashcha and Stavishche, also lost his life in a pogrom attack. Two of her brothers, both soldiers in the tsar's army, disappeared in the Crimea, and her young brother-in-law perished shortly after fleeing Stavishche to Belaya Tserkov during the raids.

As if the young widow hadn't already suffered enough, the most painful horror would soon befall her. Hours after her husband's vicious murder, Sheindel and her three small children sought refuge with a group of other Jews in the basement of a home belonging to a Gentile friend. When bandits burst into the house where they were hiding, her beautiful baby boy began to cry. In a desperate effort to keep him quiet, someone overpowered the young mother and forced a pillow over his tiny mouth, asphyxiating him. Devastated that she was unable to protect her child, Sheindel cried as she cradled the limp baby in her arms.[*]

As the middle of the night approached during the raids, more gunfire could be heard in Stavishche. Ten Jewish homes, some with families still inside of them, were set on fire. Esther and Yunkel Cutler and their four children, who escaped an attack by Denikin's soldiers earlier in the day by fleeing through a back door of their home, reunited once again after walking aimlessly for hours through the thick smoke along the river's edge. Esther was holding her son Daniel's hand when a bandit on horseback began hitting the crowd with a whip to break them up. When the bandit struck Daniel in the head with his whip, the boy automatically let go of his mother's hand, causing them to become briefly separated yet another time in the crowd during the mass evacuation.

After finding each other amid the turmoil, the Cutler family traveled all night by foot with many other refugees toward Belaya Tserkov. Along the way, the group came across a barn with inviting stacks of hay inside. Hungry, weak, and depleted of energy, they were so exhausted that they lay down on the hay and instantly fell asleep. Esther, who was thrilled to be reunited with Daniel again, fell asleep in the barn with her arms wrapped protectively around her son. However, Daniel could not ignore his growling stomach and left his mother's side in search of food.

As he walked over to a gate, Daniel noticed a peasant farmer who was sharpening knives to cut the grass. Dogs started barking at Daniel, and the peasant looked up at him and said, "What is it, kid; what do you want?"

"I'm hungry."

The farmer took in Daniel's disheveled appearance and offered the boy a piece of bread with relish and some cider.

"Who are you with?" the farmer asked.

"My family," Daniel told him.

---

[*] Soon afterward, her father-in-law, Yoske Stepansky, whose own brother, Lepe, the egg merchant, was shot and killed by bandits while he stood on his front doorstep, arranged for Sheindel and her two remaining children, Ite and Zelig, to flee the country. They finally settled safely in Argentina in 1926.

The kindness of the farmer reminded the boy that not all Ukrainian peasants were anti-Semites. The farmer took out a loaf of black bread and a couple dozen eggs that he had cooked for the field workers, and handed them over to Daniel. Unable to believe his good luck, the boy dragged the food back toward the barn when he heard his mother frantically calling out for him.

"*Meyn kind, meyn kind!*"* she yelled.

"Don't worry, Mama. Look—I've got something to eat!"

Upon hearing mention of food, three heads emerged from a pile of hay, and another three heads appeared from another pile of hay . . .

"Don't worry," Esther said. "Whatever we've got, we'll share."

They shared their good fortune with everyone in the barn that night.

Chaos continued in all corners of Stavishche. At the other end of the town stood Sol Moser's house, owned by his parents, Itzie and Haika. The dwelling was a large two-story building with wooden floors and a tin roof. By contrast, the poorer Jewish homes in Stavishche had clay floors and straw roofs. From each of the two beautiful balconies, one could see ducks and geese scurrying around in the yard.

The Mosers' house was attached to their business. They owned a bakery with two ovens: one above the ground and one below. All the bandit groups raiding Stavishche stopped first at the bakery for bread to feed their men. The cellar that housed the underground bakery was dug into the earth. For the three days the Denikins raided Stavishche, between 150 and 200 Jews found refuge in this cellar. A big trunk on top of a trap door camouflaged the stairway leading down to the basement. While Jews from that side of town knew about the hiding place, strangers had no clue of its existence. A working stove used for baking bread made sure that there was no shortage of food downstairs.

As the Denikins began retreating from Stavishche, the Red Army soon took their place. The first scout that the Red Army sent into Stavishche had heard that inside of the Moser household was a Jewish bakery. In the middle of the night, at around one or two o'clock in the morning, Itzie Moser heard from the basement loud banging at his front door. Many Jews were still hiding in his basement, and

---

* Yiddish for "My child, my child!"

he turned to two of his sons, Sol and Schmuelik, in despair. If he answered the door and it turned out to be the Denikins, they would surely kill him. True, it was a strong door, but the bandits would only need to break a window to force their way in.

Within minutes, Itzie heard a man call out in Yiddish amid the noise, "I'm a Jew, and a friend of all Jews!" ("Jews and comrades!" is a more literal translation.) Relieved at the sound of Yiddish, Itzie came out of hiding and went upstairs.

Three or four men were standing at his door with guns. The one who had knocked was only five feet tall, and his gun was bigger than he was. He said to Itzie, "Have no fear, we are not going to bother you; we're from the Red Army."

By this time, many Jews had enlisted in the Red Army. The soldiers only wanted to know when the Denikins had last raided the town. As time passed, and it was clear that the Denikins had truly left, Itzie put on the kerosene lamps, which shined down into the basement and illuminated the entire house. After three terrifying days, he announced to everyone that it was now safe to come out of hiding. For a very short time, anyway, the good guys were the Bolsheviks!*

As a result of being so closely confined indoors during the weeklong raids, a mysterious illness paralyzed Stavishche, causing devastation so great that the death toll nearly surpassed the number of murder victims. A fever that many believed registered as high as 107.6 degrees Fahrenheit† spread quickly, claiming victims from almost every Jewish family in town.‡

Convinced that it would be safer to return to Belaya Tserkov, Isaac and Rebecca prepared to leave once again, as did many of the Jews from their village. Although they didn't realize it at the time, this would be the last time they would lay eyes on their hometown. On a cold December evening, as Denikin's soldiers neared the end of their reign of terror over the town, the family fled under the

---

* There were some Jews who joined the Bolsheviks, and others who would never do so. In this particular instance, the Moser family was just relieved to see Jewish soldiers at their door.

† This figure was converted into Fahrenheit: the results were dependent on the accuracy of the measuring devices available in Europe in 1919.

‡ During the week that Denikin's army raided the town, a few of Channa's neighbors were brought to the hospital, where they died from a high fever.

cover of darkness to Mykola's chicken farm on the outskirts of Stavishche. Isaac trusted that his young Gentile apprentice would shield his family from danger.

Mykola's parents showed their guests a crawl space built above a baker's oven, where the Jewish family could hide without being seen by any visitors. The old farmhouse, which was damp from the lack of coverings over its clay flooring, had a shelf that Mykola's father built above that oven where the Caprove family huddled together to keep warm. Isaac's family hid in that crawl space for several days, during both daylight and starlight, as they never knew who could be trusted. Bandits were known for betraying their own neighbors for money.

When things seemed quieter the following morning, Rebecca ventured out into the town to listen for news of the attacks. Like her sisters, she spoke fluent Russian and could easily circulate around Stavishche without fear of being detected as Jewish. When she finally returned to the farm that afternoon, her husband and daughters could see in her eyes that something was terribly wrong; she had been crying and was unable to look Isaac directly in the eyes.

"What is it?" Isaac asked.

Rebecca could barely get the words out.

"It's Moishe—he's gone."

When Isaac heard that his only brother was dead, the shock was so great that he was rendered speechless. Channa and Sunny began crying hysterically; the girls adored their uncle Moishe, and they could not believe that they would never see him again. Their uncle was just thirty-two years old when he died. One of their last images of him, as a vibrant soldier in the tsar's 31st Aleksopol Infantry Regiment, remained vivid in their minds. Moishe was an expert marksman and a decorated soldier who had been stationed just a few years earlier in Skierniewice, Poland. He had survived the war only to lose his life in a way that would never make sense to his family.

Isaac insisted that his wife take him to the Stavishche Hospital, Count Branicki's Free Hospital for the Poor, where she had heard that Moishe had died. The cause of his death was unclear; the couple did not know if Moishe had suffered from the deadly illness that had spread across town or if he was a victim of violence. At the hospital, they met a nurse who knew Moishe and had tried to care for him herself.

"He had no money, so they took him on as a charity case," she told the grieving couple. "A great number of those injured during the raids were brought here last night. Our beds were already filled with patients suffering from a fever. Their families were paying off doctors so that their loved ones would receive preferential treatment. Moishe passed away before a doctor could even examine him."

Isaac was inconsolable. If only he had known, he would have paid any price for his brother to have received prompt medical treatment.

When her parents finally returned to the farm, eight-year-old Channa was relieved beyond words. She had been left in charge of four-year-old Sunny and her baby sister Fay, who had been crying all afternoon. She was grateful to finally hand the fussy infant over to her mother. After the family members were reunited again in the crawl space, Rebecca tried nursing the baby, but her breast milk supply had almost dried up.

That evening, a burly peasant, armed with two rifles, stopped by the farmhouse unannounced, leaving his horse with friends who waited for him outside. The family overheard the peasant questioning Mykola's oldest brother. The peasant had noticed fresh wagon prints and consequently suspected that there were Jews hiding somewhere on the property. When he came inside to look around, Isaac, Rebecca, and their daughters held their breath, careful not to make the slightest sound. All of a sudden, Channa's baby sister Fay, who couldn't suckle enough of her Mama's breast milk in order to satisfy her hunger, let out a loud cry.

It was one of those moments in life that could have changed everything. It would have been so much easier for Mykola's Christian family to give up the Jewish family in order to save themselves; instead, they chose to protect their friends. The Caproves listened as Mykola, his father, and three older brothers encircled the armed hoodlum and pushed him roughly against the wall. The brothers were big fellows, and the peasant had good reason to be scared. Before the bandit had a chance to react, Mikola grabbed both guns from him.

"If you say anything, we'll kill you right here!" Mykola threatened, knowing that there were others waiting outside.

"If we ever see or hear from you again, my sons will hunt you down like an animal and make you wish that you never stepped foot in my house!" the father promised.

The bandit was relieved to get out of the house alive. There was likely no doubt in his mind that Mykola and his brothers would not have hesitated to kill him on the spot.

Like most of the Jews from Stavishche, Isaac, Rebecca, and their three daughters left town and headed toward Belaya Tserkov again.

❖

When a few remaining soldiers, under the leadership of the gray-bearded General Denikin, gathered a small group of Jews at gunpoint in the bet hamidrash, they forced everyone to strip off their clothing and confiscated all their belongings. The bandits then threatened to set the house of worship on fire. The elderly wife of the town's travel agent became so afraid during the hostage crisis that she suffered a fatal heart attack and collapsed.

When Rabbi Pitsie Avram later arrived, he distracted the bandits by conversing with them in their native Russian. While the bandits were still immersed in conversation, the rabbi instructed the naked Jews in Yiddish to slip out of the back door, which they did, carrying out the old lady's body with them. When the Denikins discovered his ruse, they threatened to cut off the rabbi's right hand, but he begged and pleaded so wholeheartedly that they took pity on him and decided to hang him instead. They made the rabbi step up on a bench and were ready to hang him from the hook of a hanging lamp when their leader walked in. He stopped the execution and took the heroic rabbi home.

The last of Denikin's hooligans left in the town feasted on food and liquor that they had ordered be brought to the bet hamidrash. As they sat around eating and drinking merrily, they toasted and shouted that all Christians should live a long life, and all Jews should die.[*]

---

[*]   Khlavna Kohen, a former member of the Stavishche Town Authority, reported the physical threat against the rabbi and the singing of the drunken bandits in a circa 1920–1921 document entitled "Pogrom Happenings in Stavishche." See Notes.

CHAPTER THIRTEEN

REFUGE IN BELAYA TSERKOV

1919–1920

W hen his mother's sister Sonia found nine-year-old Sol on her doorstep, lice were crawling all over his body. The night before wandering into Belaya Tserkov, he had slept on horse manure to keep warm, and he stank. Lice creeping up the legs of his black pants made them appear white. When nobody wanted to look at him, Sonia gave him a bath; she then burned his clothing and sewed her young nephew a new pair of pants out of a burlap bag.

Sol Moser was an orphan. Over the course of a few weeks, his father, Itzie Moser, the owner and proprietor of the Jewish bakery in Stavishche, had fallen sick and died from an appendicitis attack. His mother, Haika Stepansky-Moser, suffered from a large, untreated goiter and choked to death. The oldest of his eleven siblings died in a pogrom.

Sol was forced to walk the twenty-eight miles to Belaya Tserkov with no shoes. Gone were the days when the young boy joined Channa and Daniel on happy excursions around town making shoe deliveries for Isaac. Ironically, he now found himself desperately in need of boots, but never made it to the other side of town to Isaac's shoe factory to ask for his help.

He survived on his own for a few months in Stavishche, stealing bread and fruit at the Tuesday market with a group of homeless kids. The children, who were from both Jewish and Christian backgrounds, bonded over the one thing that they all shared in common—hunger. Together, they devised a plan to steal and then pass the stolen food down a line, arranging to meet up afterward to divide the fruits of their labor. The plan was clever enough to protect a child who was caught in the act of stealing. Since the stolen items would be passed from one person to another, the thief would never be caught holding the shoplifted merchandise.

While fleeing Stavishche in the direction of Belaya Tserkov during one of the many bandit raids, Sol, who began his journey with another aunt and his older sister Goldie, became separated from them. He wandered that winter evening into a stable and slept curled up to the stalls; he was warmed by the heat radiating from the horses and their manure.

The resilient boy "staved off the worst hunger by catching the sunflower seeds that fell from the horses' feedbags."[*] Sol smartly picked up the excess seeds and pocketed them. When he collected enough, he cracked the shells open with his teeth and swallowed the seeds in one large mouthful; they were delicious and even healthy. Sol was a strong boy with good survival instincts; after arriving in Belaya Tserkov, he landed on the doorstep of yet another maternal aunt. No longer forced to manage on his own without adult supervision, he would now have hope for a better future.

Food was scarce in Belaya Tserkov. Although the larger cities were generally safer, and the Jews who had flocked there from Stavishche could sleep more peacefully at night, there wasn't much to eat. Everyone was malnourished. After Channa's family returned to her aunt Molly's apartment in Belaya Tserkov, she met up with Sol Moser, who took her with him to his cousin Davy Berkowitz's house. Davy was three months younger than Sol, and he had a sister who was about Channa's age, seven years old. They were four kids home alone, moving furniture around at Davy's house when they stumbled upon a piece of moldy bread. It was as hard as a rock, but when the children tried to wash the mold off, the water softened the bread, making it less repulsive to eat.

The four playmates were about to sit down and divide up the moldy bread when Davy's older brother Louie walked in the door. Louie Berkowitz was a young man of maybe eighteen years of age, and his father, who had left for America before the war, used to work for Sol's father in the bakery in Stavishche. Channa recalled giggling at the image of Louie standing at the door, holding a

---

[*] Source: From a letter written to the author by Sol's granddaughter Elise Moser.

gun with a bayonet in one hand, and three loaves of black bread in another. At five feet tall, the gun was almost as large as Louie. The starving children, who ate to their hearts' content that day, would never forget Louie Berkowitz.

❖

Bubkah Caprove's Hidden Jewels

Isaac found them on his doorstep in Belaya Tserkov half-starved. Bubkah Caprove, his brother Moishe's widow, was standing there, frail and thin, with her two waiflike children. All three were ready to collapse from dehydration and starvation. They had arrived at Molly's doorstep with nowhere to go after escaping Stavishche. Bubkah had remembered that Rebecca's sister Molly lived in Belaya Tserkov, and it did not take long for her to locate her husband's family. She also knew the great pain that Isaac had suffered after losing his older brother. But no matter how tough things were, Isaac would never turn Moishe's widow and children away to live on the streets.

When Isaac invited Bubkah and her children to join them in his brother-in-law's spare apartment, there were already eleven people occupying four rooms. In order to provide sustenance for his extended family, Isaac rented a small office in town where he was making a meager living by repairing boots.

One afternoon, when Isaac and Rebecca left Bubkah in charge of watching all the children, her pretty, curly-haired daughter, Sima, who was the same age as Channa, almost eight, brought out her mother's secret box of jewels to play with. The young cousins innocently emptied the small chest of its magnificent trinkets: rings, necklaces, bracelets, chains, watches, and gold earrings. Channa's eyes popped when she saw her aunt's silver and gold pieces. The girls were trying on the many gems when Bubkah caught them wearing her prized possessions.

"What do you girls think you are doing?" she screamed at the children in Yiddish, as she repossessed her treasures, one by one. "Give me those!"

Bubkah sat herself down at the kitchen table and made certain that not only was every piece accounted for, but that they were arranged in the box to her satisfaction. In those days, regular currency was worth something one day and nothing the next, so jewelry, gold, and silver pieces were used to trade for food and shelter.

When Isaac and Rebecca arrived home, they were stunned to find Bubkah sitting at their table examining the baubles that were spread out before her.

"Where did you get all of those jewels?" Rebecca asked her in amazement. Times were so desperate it was hard to imagine that anyone in Belaya Tserkov had a jewelry collection left of that magnitude.

"I've been saving them," was all she answered.

Rebecca and Isaac became very upset with Bubkah. After all, she and her children had shown up on their doorstep starving. They argued in front of the children that she could have sold or traded her jewels to help feed herself and her family.

Isaac was truly devastated that his only brother, Moishe, had been taken to the hospital as a charity case; he died before ever seeing a doctor. After seeing the jewels, he questioned whether his sister-in-law could have at least tried to do more. *Could she have sold her jewels to help pay off a doctor?* he wondered. Isaac would never know if doing so would have made a difference, but his heart was clearly broken.

No amount of screaming that day would give him any answers that made sense. Times were terrible, even for Bubkah, and there was no explaining why she did or didn't act in a certain way that others expected of her. Perhaps she was scared, and rhyme and reason simply went out the door. It did not, however, bode well for family relations. The family was in survival mode and could not understand her actions. In front of young Channa, Isaac told Bubkah, who was clutching her valuable trinket box, to leave the apartment that day. Sadly, it was the last time that Isaac or Rebecca ever saw or heard from Bubkah Caprove or her children.*

By 1919, Belaya Tserkov was home to thousands of Jews.[†] As a larger city, it was generally considered to be a safe haven from the chaos that plagued the smaller

---

*   It is important to note that this event was witnessed and interpreted by Channa, who was just a young girl at the time. Bubkah and her children remained in Ukraine, but her son died as a soldier during World War II.

†   The Jewish population of Belaya Tserkov in 1900 was nineteen thousand. According to an entry in the *Megilat Ha-tevah,* the Jewish population in that city in 1919 was thought to be as high as forty thousand, but this number could be inflated and is unconfirmed.

shtetls. However, just three months before the Jews of Stavishche fled from the Denikin raids to seek their final refuge in Belaya Tserkov, a violent pogrom by the same gang devastated the city.

On the first of Elul 1919 (Wednesday, August 27, 1919), also known as Rosh Chodesh Elul, hooligans entered the city famous for its white domes and churches. By Saturday, the followers of General Anton Denikin[*] invaded the town, setting Jewish buildings and homes on fire. The battalion killed, robbed, tortured, and raped the Jewish people of Belaya Tserkov. Three hundred and fifty Jews lost their lives; this number did not include the many men, women, and children who died in the fields or on their way to the fields to hide. The Jews of the city declared a day of mourning in remembrance of the victims.[†]

By year's end, despite the violence in the city, the Caprove, Cutler, and Stumacher families managed to enjoy some happy days in Belaya Tserkov. Through harsh conditions, the spirit of family unity often prevailed over the difficult times. During the cold winter months at the end of 1919, the women took great pleasure in baking bread in preparation for the Sabbath. Next door, in Molly's kitchen, they would somehow always find enough flour to bake the weekly challah. The daughters watched as Molly, Esther, and Rebecca prepared the Friday night meals.

Molly and Itzie Stumacher had become parents to a baby daughter whom they also named Fay, after her grandmother. Channa, Sunny, and their two older cousins Sarah and Sheva now had two active babies named Fay to look after as the women were busy baking.

When flour was scarce and there was not enough to bake bread for the Sabbath, Itzie's oldest son, Ruby, who was about thirteen years old at the time, went to work at the train station in Belaya Tserkov. During freezing winter nights, he sold matches and cigarettes to the soldiers who were passing through. Ruby was a resourceful boy who teamed up with an old Jewish man in Belaya Tserkov who studied how to fabricate these matches: a carpenter's tool with a blade, called a plane, would be used to shave a large handful of matchsticks from a piece of

---

[*]   General Anton Denikin, under the name Antoine Deinikine, entered the Port of New York on December 7, 1945. He listed himself on the passenger manifest as both a "writer" and a "stateless person." Denikin remained in the United States until his death in 1947.

[†]   A smaller pogrom also occurred in Belaya Tserkov at the beginning of August 1919.

wood taken from the forest.* These sticks were then dipped into a compound of sulfur, phosphor, and other chemicals to make the matches. Ruby would then either use the money that he made by selling these matches to buy the women flour, or he would trade the matches and cigarettes with the soldiers for their loaves of bread.

Ruby was also sent out on the Sabbath with Yunkel and Esther's son Daniel in search of wood to keep a fire burning all evening. Before the boys began their walk to the forest, which was a couple of miles away, their mothers filled the pockets of their coats with challah bread. Hours later, they would return with sacks full of branches.

Molly's house didn't have much in the way of furniture, but the women were all accomplished seamstresses, and there were plenty of handmade quilts to keep everyone warm. During chilly evenings, the women spread out all the quilts across the room on the clay floors, and they would all lay together under them; as the heat of the fire warmed them during the brisk nights in Belaya Tserkov, the family happily sang variations of many songs in Yiddish, Ukrainian, and Russian.

Out of all the extended family, Ruby was the most musical, and his voice was both melodious and innocent. His little brother, Moe, also loved to sing while Ruby played his mandolin. Their father, Itzie, was a dancing instructor, a talent for which he was famous in Belaya Tserkov. People in the city thought of him as the dancing tailor! On nights like these, Itzie instructed the adults, who took turns dancing around the room. The children snuggled and sang merrily as Molly plucked the three strings of her balalaika, an instrument that she had learned to play as a child in Skibin. It was highly entertaining to watch Itzie's dances, and others in Belaya Tserkov craved his company as well. During more peaceful times, Molly and Itzie were often invited for suppers at different houses around town, and he would lead the dancing there.

The Fires in Stavishche

In the spring of 1920, 1,500 to 2,000 Jews were burned alive in the synagogue in the nearby city of Tetiev by the followers of Ataman A. Kurovsky, a former

---

* Ruby Stumacher described making matches as did Yasha Kainer. Yasha gave great detail about the process in a separate story by Emily Bayard.

officer under Symon Petliura. The Caprove family heard rumors from the safety of their apartment in Belaya Tserkov that these hooligans were headed toward Stavishche. By then, the majority of Jews who still remained in the town were the sick, disabled, and elderly. The spiritual leaders and their families also remained behind in support of their people who were unable to flee. A group of vicious local peasants entered Stavishche on the heels of Kurovsky's men, who had left the shtetl as quickly as they entered it. On a beautiful spring day, these bandits set a few buildings on fire in the Jewish quarter of town.

Havah Zaslawsky, the devoted daughter of Rabbi Pitsie Avram, ran down the street in panic during the fires in search of her father, fearing that he had been killed. When she saw the flames rise near the synagogue (probably the Sokolovka kloyz, one of six in town), Havah instinctively knew that her father had rushed to open the ark for the last time. The rabbi, with his flowing white beard and large sunken eyes, suddenly emerged from the burning synagogue cradling his sacred Torah, its breastplate, and a pair of matching antique silver Torah crowns. The tiny bells that hung in layers from the priceless *keters* (crowns) jingled as he ran for his life.[*]

Escaping the flames of the fires that spread quickly behind them, Pitsie Avram and his youngest daughter fled down the street together, meeting up with other family members along the way. At the Jewish Bikur Holim (Home for the Aged Hospital), six elderly female and two male residents were slaughtered. In the home of Shlomo Zalman Frankel, thugs tied him to a pig and set both on fire.[†]

As the rabbi's group fled, they were unaware as murderers searched house to house for Jews and tore the screaming, bedridden, and elderly from their beds. Within minutes they herded twenty-six Jews to another synagogue and slit their throats. Barking dogs began eating away at the dead.[‡]

At yet another Stavishche house of worship, Cantor David-Yosel Moser was inside chanting words from his precious Torah when bandits stormed in and confiscated his sacred scroll. Tossing the fragile parchment across the floor, the

---

[*] This story was shared with the author by the rabbi's youngest grandson, Max, who heard it from his mother. The rabbi and his family returned again to the town after the fires to assist those in need.

[†] The brutal murder of Shlomo Zalman Frankel was reported by Khlavna Kohen, a former member of the Stavishche Town Authority, in his report entitled "Pogrom Happenings in Stavishche" (see Notes).

[‡] A local group of hooligans from Stavishche were arrested some time later for the murders committed during this time period, and documents were found on them proving their participation in the massacres. The Bolsheviks, who were then in power, eventually released them.

thugs then raped a Jewish woman on top of its pages. When that was not sufficient enough in their drunken minds to desecrate the holy scrolls, they brought in a horse to defile it.

Cantor David-Yosel stood helpless as the assassins torched his *Sefer Torah* (Torah scroll). Finally, the old chazzan's heart gave out. He dropped to the floor, dying beside the thing that he loved most in the world. The old cantor, who in happier times loved entertaining the children of Stavishche by cutting out beautiful parchment chains of paper birds, died beside his burning Torah. This destruction, however, could not kill the spirit of either, for the spirit of the chazzan David-Yosel and his parchment scroll are both indestructible; they are eternal, beyond time.*

---

* The cantor perished trying to save his sacred Torah. The Torah that the beloved Rabbi Pitsie Avram cradled as he exited the blazing town was carried by him across many countries in Europe, including a trek that covered southern Ukraine, Romania, and many other lands until he reached England. He eventually carried the precious Stavishche Torah items with him when he sailed to America in 1928.

PART III

EXODUS TO THE GOLDENE MEDINA
1920–1925

CHAPTER FOURTEEN

THERE WAS A PLACE NEARBY, WHERE THEY MADE THE LITTLE COFFINS

Belaya Tserkov, 1920

Times were difficult in Belaya Tserkov; even if Isaac had the money to buy food for his growing family, very little was available. Hunger was so rampant in Ukraine that people were literally dying around them each day. Starvation, possibly the greatest hardship that they had ever encountered, left an even greater void in their hearts than their stomachs.

A Jewish boy who lived near the Caprove family in Stavishche later recalled that while in the city of Nikolayev, near the Dnieper, he heard a rumor that young children were being kidnapped and murdered for their human flesh, which was then being passed off and sold as animal meat. It was unknown whether there was any truth to these cannibalistic tales, but Stavishchers who fled to that city were terrified by these stories and kept a close eye on their children.

In Belaya Tserkov, a malnourished Rebecca had been ill for some time with a high fever, and for a while, Isaac feared his wife would not recover. Rebecca had fallen victim to the typhus epidemic, which spread quickly in Ukraine. She could hardly nurse, her breast milk supply dried up, and one miserable day, the couple's baby daughter Fay died of malnutrition while Rebecca lay whimpering in bed.

Rebecca, bedridden and delirious, watched helplessly as seven men entered the apartment and removed her beautiful dead baby from the bed. In front of her two horrified daughters, they wrapped Fay up in a white sheet and carried her tiny body off to her little grave. There was a place nearby where they made the little coffins.

Channa and Sunny cried day and night for their baby sister. Channa, who, as the older sister, had the advantage of age and more words at her disposal, turned to her father for answers: "How could this happen?" It wasn't that as a child she had no experience of death—people were dropping like flies every day, and the memory of her grandmother's passing was still vivid in her mind—but when her innocent little baby sister shared the same cruel fate, she was in a state of disbelief.

With their mother so ill, it was up to Isaac to comfort the girls. He held his daughters in his arms, telling them soothingly, "There will come a time when everybody will get together in the sky, and all of the people who have passed away will be there. Fay will come back to us then, and we will all see her again."

Channa and Sunny clung to that story with desperation; each girl wished with all their heart and soul for it to be true.

Their grieving mother, her body ravished from typhus, could not even summon the strength to lift her head up off the bed where her youngest child drew her last breath. Channa watched as her heartbroken father sat by her mother's side with Sunny clinging to him. He may have been able to comfort his daughters, but he didn't know how to console Rebecca.

Outside on their stoop, Channa sat alone, watching beggars roam the street, pleading with passersby for a piece of bread. How could Fay be gone? The pain seemed unbearable for an eight-year-old to endure. The only way that she could find comfort was to think of happier days.

She closed her eyes and summoned up wonderful memories in Stavishche, when children ran barefoot through Count Branicki's magical gardens. The perfumed fragrances of rosebushes and the sheer beauty of purple lilacs in bloom were not far from her mind. The scent of those tall pine trees that lined the forest where she once ran joyfully through the woods with other boys and girls was such a delight!

How Channa would have loved to catch another glimpse of those little peacocks fluttering their feathers while tiptoeing around the nobleman's exotic park. She yearned to stand again at sunset in the rolling valleys of her homeland as peasant boys, singing folk songs, passed her by.

How she missed those fleeting days before the Revolution, when life was simple yet charming, before innocent lives were inexplicably snuffed out. Channa longed for the time when the galoshes-maker was more prosperous, and in greater demand, than the tombstone-maker. How she longed for the days when the main cause of death was old age.

When Isaac found his oldest daughter sitting on the stoop and interrupted her from her wistful daydreaming, the painful reality of Fay's death hit the child once more. Although Rebecca eventually recuperated from typhus, she never fully recovered from her baby's death. None of them did.

CHAPTER FIFTEEN

THE UNLIKELY ARRIVAL OF BARNEY STUMACHER, AN AMERICAN HERO

Yom Kippur 1920

There are some stories in life that are more compelling than fiction. They are the tales of seemingly ordinary men who, against all odds, accomplish extraordinary feats. It is with great wonderment that the triumph of one such man, Barney Stumacher, the first cousin of Molly Cutler's husband, Itzie Stumacher, is now recounted.

In mid-August 1920, twenty-eight-year-old veteran of World War I Barney Stumacher left his home in New York City and set out on an almost impossible mission to rescue his parents and three of his five sisters, who were living in the city of Belaya Tserkov, which was then in Ukraine.

The gutsy young cloaks salesman[*] had made this cross-Atlantic journey once before, in the opposite direction. Almost a decade earlier, at the beginning of 1911, the dark reddish-haired teenage adventurer bid farewell to his family in Belaya Tserkov and sailed alone from Liverpool to New York. With only twenty-five

---

[*] According to the United States Federal Census, Barney was working as a cloaks salesman in New York City at the beginning of 1920.

dollars in his pocket, Barney boarded the SS *Franconia* under his Jewish name, Benzion Stomachin and prepared himself to begin a new life in America.*

The handsome bachelor's remarkable sojourn unfolded almost ten years later, in the summer of 1920, when Barney and his sisters Freada and Pauline finally received word from their father, Nechame Stumacher,† who smuggled a note out to them from Belaya Tserkov. The letter was delivered to the Henry Street home where Barney was living with his sister and brother-in-law, Freada and David Picheny, and their four children. Due to the war, the siblings had not heard any news of their family in Europe since 1914. Until the arrival of this long-awaited letter, they had no idea whether their loved ones in Russia had survived.

Barney read the undated letter aloud to his two sisters and brother-in-law:‡

> *Dear Son!*
>
> *Thank God, we are well now. God keep us in the future from the terrible murderers. What shall I write you, dear son? It is five years that we haven't heard from you. Now, as God has sent us an American, and we have an opportunity to write you a letter, as he promised to deliver the letter to you, I write you to have pity on us and to come and save us from these murderers, as we cannot be here. We have had many pogroms here; they robbed us in such a way, that we were left without any clothes on our backs. We haven't enough money to carry us through each day, and my son-in-law Nissel, when he had the store, used to help us. Now, everything was taken from him too and the store was burned. They, themselves are starving, he has two children and hasn't enough bread for them. The misfortunes through which we have lived are beyond my ability to write. Many people were killed, and our daughter, Basse,§ had married, but her husband was murdered. Now she is left with a child, and has no means with which to keep it. They are starving. We beg you, dear son, have pity on us; talk this over with David, Freide, and Pesse and all our friends,*

---

* Source: Ellis Island Passenger Records. Barney is listed as a redhead on the document; later documents state his hair color as brown.

† Nechame was the paternal uncle of Itzie Stumacher, the husband of Molly Cutler.

‡ Nechame's undated letter was most likely written and smuggled out of Belaya Tserkov sometime after the end of August 1919 and received by his son Barney in America no later than July 1920. It was used in Barney's passport application and is on record at the National Archives.

§ Basse was also called Bossie.

and come and save us. We cannot live here any longer. We are not sure from hour to hour with our lives, for every now and then a gang appears and they kill and plunder. Many of our friends were killed. I cannot write any more. The children will add whatever they wish. Mother and the children send their greetings. Do not forget us. Be well and happy.

From your faithful parents who hope to see you,

Nechame Stumacher

Dear Brother Benny and Dear Sister and Brother-in-law, Father writes you of everything. To live through another time such as we have is beyond our strength. The only hope is in you, and if you will not do anything for us, we will be entirely wiped out. We are without clothes or food and the rest, you can imagine yourselves.

From your sister, Dvoira,

P.S. Nissel and the children send their greetings.

After reading the urgent pleas from his father and sister, Barney instantly knew what he had to do. Years later, he recalled his gut reaction to his father's letter. "I came back from the First World War without a scratch, and I realized that I had a job to do. I never did anything for my parents since I was in this country, and realized that I had to go and help them. My sisters agreed with me."[*]

Barney, now an American citizen, desperately set out to obtain a passport from Washington, DC, that would permit him to travel to Warsaw, Poland, where he hoped to make arrangements to bring his family from Belaya Tserkov. Conditions in Ukraine made direct entry into the country an impossible task.

On July 23, 1920, Barney Stumacher, while sitting at a desk in his new residence in Bronx, New York, drafted the following letter to Bainbridge Colby, who served as the third secretary of state under President Woodrow Wilson:

Sir:

I am attaching, hereto, formal application for passport to go to Poland, in order to bring to this country, my family consisting of my father, 55 years of age, my mother, 50 years of age, my three sisters and my brother-in-law. I wish to inform you that I am a veteran of the United States Army, having

---

[*] The quotes in this chapter (that involve Barney) are Barney Stumacher's own words, and many stories are from his recollections.

served about one year during the recent war. My record while in the army is without flaw; after I had been in the army for several months I was promoted to First Class Private, and my service was satisfactory in every way. The case in connection with my application is as follows:

I had not heard from my people for about six years. In spite of my repeated attempts, I could not reach my people in any way, either to help them or to get into communication with them. I had given up hope of ever hearing from them again, when several weeks ago, I received the enclosed letter from them, which was brought to me by an American citizen who had been in the city where my parents live. As you can readily see by the translation, they have lost everything they had and are in extreme want, and yet can find no way out of the situation. They implore me to come to them in order to bring them to the United States. I, being the only son, it is quite natural that they should appeal to me, as they have always looked to me for help and advice. I have two sisters in the United States, also American citizens, and it was decided among us, that I take the trip and bring our people here. <u>Realizing that conditions at the present time are such that it will be impossible for me to go to the city of Belaya Tserkov, where my people are, I have, therefore, decided to go to Warsaw and from there make arrangements to have my people meet me there and bring them back to the United States with me.</u>^{*} I also know that conditions in Poland at the present time are not of the best, and that the Department of State uses a great deal of discretion in granting passports to Poland, but I am ready to stand all hardships so as I may alleviate the condition of my parents and other members of my family. Knowing of the state of affairs in Poland at the present time, I would not for a moment think of taking this trip, if the reason for my journey were not such an urgent one.

I, therefore, request that a passport be granted me in order that I might proceed to Warsaw, Poland, at once, and carry out my duty to my parents and other members of my family. My sisters in this country are also most anxious that this passport be granted me, as we are all greatly upset over the unhappy plight in which our people now are.

Respectfully Yours,

Barney Stumacher

---

*   The underline is Barney's own emphasis. Source: National Archives, general records of the department of state/passport applications.

Despite a flurry of letters that were collected from prestigious business owners in New York City in support of Barney's application,* dire conditions stemming from the ongoing Polish-Russo War (February 1919–March 1921) forced the honorable secretary of state to politely decline Barney's request for a passport to Poland. On July 31, 1920, Barney responded to the denial:

> *Sir:- In re: PC 7-20-14522*
>
> *Replying to your letter of July 28th, in connection with application for passport filed by me on July 23rd, I wish to say that if your decision at present is final in connection with granting me a passport to Poland, that I shall be willing to have this passport made out for the British Isles, France, Switzerland, Czecho-Slovakia and* [name of country crossed out, possibly Bessarabia]. *This is with the understanding that if conditions in Poland change, either before I have started upon my journey or after, that my passport be amended to read Poland.†* *As I have made all arrangements to start at an early date, I would request that you kindly give this matter your further consideration, and send me the passport as outlined above without delay.*
>
> *I am returning the $9.00 fee which you returned to me, and trust that you will give this matter your early consideration and grant me a passport without delay, so that I may start upon my journey at once.*
>
> *Thanking you very kindly for your prompt action in this matter, I beg to remain,*
>
> *Very truly yours,*
>
> *Barney Stumacher*

On August 4, 1920, the Department of State finally issued Barney Stumacher a passport to travel to the above-mentioned destinations, as well as to "other

---

* Mr. Alex Rabinowitz from Starr Display Fixture Company signed an affidavit swearing that Barney was the same person he claimed to be on the passport application. Three prominent New York City business owners, Philip Cohen of P&B Cohen, wholesale jobbers in woolens, silks, and dress goods; Mr. Louis Klausner of Up-to-Date Silks, Woolens, and Dress Goods; and J. Biller of Biller & Lindenbaum Company, wholesale and retail dealers in paper and paper bags, wrote letters to the secretary of state urging him to grant Barney's application for a passport to Poland.

† Conditions would only become more complicated after the United States declined Barney's request for a passport to Warsaw. Within a few short weeks, on August 13, 1920, the Battle of Warsaw began with a Russian attack across the Vistula River.

necessary countries" en route to assist his parents. Despite all his efforts, though, Barney still didn't know how to get into Ukraine.

Sixteen days later, on August 20, the spirited young war veteran boarded a ship that would sail from New York to Paris, where he met another American along the way who befriended him and showed him a map of Europe. His new acquaintance wisely advised him to take a train from Paris to Romania, pointing out that the nearest entrance into Ukraine was through Bessarabia.

Once in Bucharest, Romania, Barney arranged to be taken by horse and carriage to the city of Khotin. On a Sunday morning, he was met at the carriage by an American group whom he referred to as "delegates," who asked why he was in Bessarabia. When Barney confided in them his plans of traveling to Belaya Tserkov in order to save his family, they laughed and said that he could not possibly enter the country without official permission.

"Look, we've been waiting here for more than two months and we didn't get into Ukraine. You can wait here with us until we all get permission," one of the delegates told him.

Barney agreed and even paid for his hotel room one week in advance so that it would appear to the delegates that he intended to wait with them in Khotin. In reality, he didn't want to attract any attention to his real plan. When everyone in the hotel had retired to their rooms at ten o'clock that Sunday evening, they asked him why he wasn't going upstairs to sleep. Barney answered that he couldn't sleep and wanted to sit around for a while.

Barney Stumacher was anxious to leave Khotin that evening; he knew if he stayed any longer, he'd be lingering at the hotel forever. He made arrangements to be led by a young guide who was experienced in crossing the dangerous body of water that separated the two countries. While literally thousands of persecuted Jews were desperately trying to cross over the Dniester River in order to flee Ukraine, Barney was the only one trying to get in.

The two men met at midnight at an embankment by the river. For two and a half hours, a dog barked relentlessly at Barney while he sat waiting impatiently for the shadowy figure to return after paying off soldiers who were guarding the Romanian side of the river. They boarded a rowboat with an old-fashioned rounded bottom. As the men rowed across the Dniester, water poured into the boat, and their clothing and shoes became soaked. On the other side, they arrived at an open field with no houses in view.

The guide, who was beginning to panic, whispered to Barney, "Walk slowly and pray that nobody meets us, or we'll be shot." As they rested briefly on a pile of hay, the guide confided in Barney that life was both meaningless and miserable for him and his parents.

Barney tried to boost the spirits of the young guide. "Look, we are both young," he reassured him, "and we have a lot of years ahead of us; things will get better."

The two men resumed walking and found themselves in a little village. Once they reached a house, the guide knocked on a window with a closed shade. An old man answered, "Who is it?"

"Pop, it's me—open the window," the young man whispered.

"I told you not to come here—they're looking for you," the old man responded. "They are going to kill you. I told you not to come here!"

"Pop, just open the window!"

The window opened, and Barney, who was tall and lanky, dove through it, followed by his young friend. The old man quickly closed the window after them and pulled down the shade. It wasn't believed to be safe in the city, so the men kept a low profile for the next few days and stayed inside the house until they could figure out a plan. The guide had a younger sister who was concerned about protecting her dowry, which was comprised of Old Russian rubles. She decided it would be prudent to hide them in the floorboards of her sister's house in the nearby city of Kamenetz-Podolsk. It was agreed that she would be the one to accompany Barney into the town.

Barney took a good look at his new female guide and suspected that the next leg of his journey would not go as smoothly as he had hoped. The young woman suffered from a disfiguring medical condition called kyphosis, an abnormal forward bending of the spine, causing a bowing of the back: his new companion was a hunchback and therefore was automatically conspicuous.

Trouble in Kamenetz-Podolsk

Barney gave the young woman a lift onto a peasant's wagon, where they sat in the hay with a few others who were also heading into the town. Barney was smoking, and one of the men sitting on the wagon asked him for a cigarette. When Barney obliged and handed him one, the man realized that it was a Romanian cigarette, one which had been bought in Czernowitz; he became suspicious. Meanwhile, the group heard rumors from passersby that soldiers were confiscating horses in Kamenetz-Podolsk. The peasant driver became nervous and insisted that everyone get off his wagon so that he could turn back to the village. As Barney and the female hunchback walked toward Kamenetz-Podolsk, he tried to convince her that if they were stopped, she should claim not to know him.

"If anything should happen, say that you never met me," he said to her. "Save yourself; I can take care of myself."

Just as Barney had suspected, the man who had asked for a cigarette pointed two Communist soldiers in his direction, and they promptly asked to see his papers. The hunchback ignored Barney's advice and tried to intervene on his behalf by telling the soldiers that she was his cousin, so they took her by gunpoint, too. The soldiers led the two travelers to a room inside a small wooden structure on the side of the road and held a revolver to Barney's head, ordering him to empty his pockets. They confiscated everything that he had carried into Ukraine: about seventy-five American dollars, a few cans of sardines, some Romanian cigarettes, and a fountain pen. They then wanted to physically search the girl, but Barney objected.

"It's not a nice thing for men to search a woman," he protested.

The men, still holding a gun to Barney's head, brought in a woman to frisk her. The hunchback's dowry money was quickly discovered strapped to her deformed back. The two were released unharmed, but the girl was crying. "That's all of the money that I had in the world for my dowry," she cried. "Now I'll never get married."

Barney, feeling sorry for her, gave her a letter to give to her brother that would ensure that her money would be replaced by one of his contacts when her brother returned to Romania. In Romania, Russian rubles from the old regime could be bought very cheaply, and Barney knew where to get them. At this point, she parted ways with Barney and left for her sister's house.* Now free, broke, and alone, Barney had nearly two hundred miles to cover before reaching his destination of Belaya Tserkov. As he was finally about to enter the city of Kamenetz-Podolsk on foot, he encountered two more bandits, who pointed a gun at him. Barney laughed when they demanded that he remove his shoes, but he soon realized that the bandits were not joking and took them off. Now shoeless and

---

* Her brother was later able to replace her dowry money with Barney's help.

penniless, Barney walked into Kamenetz-Podolsk in his stocking feet, where he soon found a group of Jewish men who directed him to the doors of the Jewish Joint Distribution Committee. The JDC helped local Jewish communities in Europe establish relief programs in Ukraine following the Revolution. They assisted Barney by finding him an old pair of Russian boots. Years later, Barney remarked that the boots were so large that he felt like he was "walking on mountains" with them, but he was very grateful to have something covering his feet.

While he was a guest of a Jewish family in Kamenetz-Podolsk, Barney overheard the disturbing news that "the soldiers are catching girls here." At first, he misunderstood the locals' concerns. "My God, that's wonderful that they catch girls here," Barney remarked, laughingly. "In America, it's the girls who have to catch the boys!"

He was soon set straight as to the meaning of "catching girls." Communist soldiers were grabbing innocent girls off the streets of Kamenetz-Podolsk and taking them back to their barracks to scrub their floors and wash their clothes.

The Polish army was advancing rapidly and planned to occupy Kamenetz–Podolsk. Barney's hosts advised him that he should immediately take a train to Belaya Tserkov and offered to accompany him to the station. When they arrived, the very last train was about to leave the city. It was a large freight train bursting with men, women, children, and soldiers. Barney was about to give up hope of getting on the packed train when, through the open doors, an unexpected hand extended outward and pulled Barney inside.

For two hours, the train traveled slowly at a pace of about fifteen miles per hour. Barney was gazing out of a window when, to his amazement, he saw the Polish army advancing on horses toward the train. Suddenly, soldiers began shooting at the train, but their horses could not keep up with the speed of the locomotive. Finally, the damage from the gunshots took its toll: the train derailed, crashed, and then overturned into an embankment. Barney and the young man who had helped him onto the train fell through the doors and rolled down a ditch to safety. While at the bottom of the embankment, they could see smoke rising from the engine of the train that soon burst into flames; many passengers either died or were injured.

The train wreck left a trail of disaster in its wake: children screamed for their mothers and the injured cried for help. Barney and his newest acquaintance spent the next hour and a half pulling hurt passengers to safety. After a while, the two men decided that it would be wise to leave before authorities happened upon the scene. Barney's mysterious new friend spoke Russian fluently and told Barney to come with him; he knew how to get out of the area.

From a distance, they spotted a farmhouse and a lone peasant who was plowing his land with an old horse. Barney's latest ally unexpectedly pulled out a revolver and threatened the peasant that if he did not give up two of his horses, he would be forced to kill him. The farmer cried to him, "Please, I've only got a few plow horses and I work alone in the fields."

Barney's companion aimed his weapon at the peasant. "We've got to have two horses, or you know what's going to happen to you; I'm going to kill you!"

The farmer, in tears, was left with no choice but to comply with the man's wishes; he brought over two horses without saddles. Barney wasn't a horseman, but out of desperation, he climbed onto the horse bareback, as did his companion. They rode for about an hour until Barney's body ached so badly that he could no longer continue; instead, he opted to part ways with his new friend and headed toward the train station in Miringchuk.*

Tired, filthy, and starving, Barney arrived at the crowded train station that evening and found himself a small vacant spot on the floor among many others who were sleeping. He hoped that he would be able to travel the rest of the journey north to Belaya Tserkov by train. Barney dozed off while waiting for a train to arrive but was brutally awakened minutes later when a soldier with hard leather boots kicked him. "Get up, comrade," the soldier barked in Russian.

Pressing a revolver to his temple, two Communist soldiers demanded to see his papers. But the only document that Barney could produce was his American passport. The soldiers promptly accused him of being an American spy and brought him by gunpoint to see their superiors at the police station.

Barney was paraded before a group of soldiers who were sitting around a table at the station house. The soldiers spoke among themselves in Russian while passing around the American passport. One soldier said, "Yes, he's a spy; the only thing to do is to shoot him." Barney had forgotten much of his Russian, but he remembered enough to understand that his life was hanging in the balance.

Barney could hear gunshots outside the station house and became very nervous. He recalled:

---

* It is believed this was the name of the city with the station, but it might have been another similar name.

I woke up [to the severity of the situation] . . . I started crying, as
big as I was. I couldn't explain myself well in Russian so I asked
if there was a soldier among them who could speak Yiddish. One
man sitting at the table said, "Yes, I can understand Jewish; what is
it that you want to tell us?"

Barney tried his best to explain in broken Yiddish that he was not a spy; he
had not seen his family in many years and was simply trying to get to Belaya
Tserkov to see them.

"When was the last time you were in Belaya Tserkov?" the Jewish soldier
asked.

"1910," Barney responded.

"When you left Russia back in 1910, do you remember anybody living in your
city of Belaya Tserkov?" he asked Barney.

Barney named some of the more prominent figures that he could recall from
his childhood in Belaya Tserkov. The soldier turned to the others and said, "No,
I don't believe that he is a spy, because the people that he mentioned are people
that I knew; they were in that city. So he's not a spy, and there's no use in killing
him. We should send him to the prison and let them keep him there until we
find out who he is."

The soldiers agreed to send Barney to the prison instead of taking him outside
and shooting him on the spot.

They called in another soldier, a commissar, to escort Barney to the prison.

Although Barney was a tall young man, this soldier was at least two heads
taller than he was.

"He was an army by himself," Barney recalled years later. "He wore a rifle on
his back, a revolver on one side, and a sword on the other side. He had bullets
all over him and wore a tall hat. He told me to come with him."

The two men walked through the darkness for quite some time until they
reached a house, where the soldier took Barney into a back room. "Sit down,
comrade," he said to Barney in Russian. "Are you hungry?"

There was a loaf of black bread sitting on the windowsill. The commissar
broke it across his foot and offered a quarter of the loaf and a drink of water to
a starving Barney. Although Barney had enjoyed many fine meals in America,
this piece of black bread mixed with straw was the most appreciated meal of
his life.

"You know, I am a Jew, too," the soldier said in a conspiratorial tone. "You know that I know what you are planning to do; you are going to take your people out of Belaya Tserkov and bring them to America."

Barney remained silent, fearful that the soldier was setting a trap for him, and that he would possibly find himself charged with more crimes.

"What could you give me if I was to put you on a train and hand you a paper that would ensure that nobody bothers you, so that you could get to your hometown to see your people?" the soldier pressed.

Barney began answering his captor in broken Russian. "What do you want? I don't have anything; they took all my money in Kamenetz-Podolsk. All I can give to you is the coat that I'm wearing."

"I don't want your coat; I want a promise from you."

"What promise do you want?"

"I want a promise that on your way back, when you pass through here, that you take me and my young daughter with you to America. I come from Grunzia, and my people were Jewish and they killed them; we are the only ones left from our entire family. If you promise me this, I will help you."

"Commissar, I can promise you this only if I'm able to go through; there is a lot of fighting here. I hear that there is a lot of trouble with the Poles, the Denikins, Petliura's gang, and all the other bands. So if there is any possibility, then I give you my word of honor that I'll take you both along with me."

That evening, when Barney laid down and tried to rest, he wondered what was in store for him the next morning. The situation was beyond his control now, he thought to himself as he drifted off to sleep. Whatever would be, would be.

❖

At five thirty the following morning, the commissar was true to his word. He put Barney on a train with falsified papers, which the conductor read aloud: "This officer is traveling on orders to ride the train on a special mission to the front."

Before a large crowd of witnesses, the commissar did all the talking. In Russian, he put on an act pretending to give Barney orders not to waste any time; he should return right away from the front after his mission was completed. There was a board hanging on the wall, and the commissar pulled it down and instructed Barney to lie on it and rest up for his mission because he was needed back as soon as possible.

The people on the train presumed that Barney was some kind of big shot, and they tried to strike up a conversation with him, but he faced the wall and didn't turn around until the train stopped at the town of Fastov, which was just twenty-two miles from Belaya Tserkov. He would have to wait in Fastov until ten o'clock in the evening for the next train into Belaya Tserkov.

Barney vaguely recalled Fastov from his youth. As he exited the train, people stared at him—it was obvious by the way he was dressed that he wasn't one of their own. Yes, the boots were Russian, but his clothing did not look native to the shtetl. He walked into the Jewish quarter of the city, hoping to find a family that would be kind enough to feed him. The quarter was strangely deserted, with the exception of a young girl who was playing alone on the street. After taking a closer look at her features, he approached the girl and asked, "Are you Jewish?"

"Yes."

"Where is everyone? I would like to speak with some Jewish people," Barney asked her.

"You're Jewish and you don't know?" the girl answered.

"Know what?"

"You don't know that today is Yom Kippur?"

"No, I didn't realize," Barney answered. What he did realize at that point was that his chances of getting a meal were considerably reduced.[*]

"Who are you?" the girl asked.

"I'm an American who is going to see his family in Belaya Tserkov."

"What, are you kidding me? If you're an American, what are you doing here? Anybody who comes here in these times should have his head examined. I don't think you're right [in the head], mister."[†]

The little girl wandered away in disbelief.

Barney walked aimlessly around Fastov for many hours, finally hearing the familiar sound of the *shofar* blowing in the distance. He recognized the traditional long blast of the ram's horn signaling a symbolic end to the Yom Kippur service.

> Then you shall transmit a blast on the horn; in the seventh month, on the tenth day of the month, the day of Yom Kippur, you shall

---

[*]   Many observant Jews fast on this Day of Atonement.

[†]   Many of the quotes regarding Barney's arrival are from his own recollections, see Notes.

have the horn sounded throughout the land. . . . And proclaim
liberty throughout all the land unto all the inhabitants thereof.[*]

A couple of hours later, at nearly ten o'clock in the evening, Barney Stumacher finally boarded the train that would take him to his long-awaited
destination—the city of his birth, Belaya Tserkov.[†] The train was so crowded that
the conductor couldn't even get close enough to him to ask for the fare, which
was a blessing since he was penniless. It was less than an hour's ride, and Barney
met a few Jews from Belaya Tserkov on the train. From them, he learned that
his parents and sisters were still alive and well in Belaya Tserkov. He asked if he
could stay with them that evening, as it was getting late and he didn't want to
shock his parents by waking them up in the middle of the night.

While Barney caught up on some much-needed sleep in Belaya Tserkov,
his hostess made her way over to the residence of sixty-five-year-old Nechame
Stumacher and his sixty-three-year-old wife, Miriam, and asked the couple if
they had a son in America.[‡]

"Yes, sure, we have a son who went to America, but we don't even know if
he's alive," Nechame answered. "Why did you come over here in the middle of
the night to ask me about my son?"

"I heard that he is coming from America to see you."

"You're out of your mind! It's impossible for anyone from America to get into
Ukraine now!" Nechame exclaimed.

One of Nechame's daughters, who had overheard the conversation, quietly
slipped out of her father's house and ran over to the home of her older sister
and brother-in-law, Dvoira and Nissel Ravicher. She repeated the story of how
the old Jewish woman arrived late in the evening at their parents' doorstep and
told them that Barney was coming from America. Stunned by this news, Nissel

---

[*] Leviticus 25:9–10.

[†] Belaya Tserkov was also the birthplace of Cantor Yossele Rosenblatt (1882–1933), who is still
considered to be the king of cantorial music. Rosenblatt, a gifted tenor, is remembered for singing a
religious melody while appearing as himself in the 1927 hit *The Jazz Singer*.

[‡] Passenger records confirm that in 1921, Barney's parents were sixty-five and sixty-three years old,
not fifty-five and fifty years of age, as he had stated in his letter when requesting a passport in order to
go and save them.

insisted that they all walk over together to the elderly woman's house to find out more information.

"Now look, where did you get this information?" Nissel confronted the old woman in her home. "Who told you that Barney is coming from America? Is he here or not?"

"Yes, he is here; he's sleeping."

When Barney woke up, he was greeted by the sight of his brother-in-law, Nissel, standing over the bed. After the two men had embraced, Nissel urged his brother-in-law to get dressed so they could walk over to see his parents. As they were walking, the entire street congregated outside their houses, as if they had just heard news of the arrival of Eliyahu the Prophet.[*]

"As I was walking with them," Barney recalled, "the entire street and all of the people living there were outside, and my own father and mother were both running together in front of me and they were hollering words that I never heard in my life."

Shrieks of happiness reverberated throughout the neighborhood. All the neighbors gathered on the street to witness the joy of their reunion. Miriam and Nechame were reunited with their dear son after a tortuous ten-year separation, during a time when it was close to impossible to get in or out of the country. Barney overcame harrowing obstacles while possessing stunning determination in order to come and save his family. He had entered Ukraine illegally, was held and robbed at gunpoint, shot at by the Polish army, and survived a fiery train derailment. He was arrested and accused of being an American spy and was brought to a police station and was nearly executed. His arrival on foot in Belaya Tserkov was miraculous.

The Caprove family ran outside to see this American who had arrived late in the evening after sundown on Yom Kippur, September 22, 1920. Channa saw her older cousin Ruby talking to his parents.

"Who is he?" Channa asked Ruby while tugging on his shirt.

"He's my father's cousin, Benzion Stomachin. He's come all the way from America to save his parents," Ruby answered. "It's unbelievable!"

"I have come to take you to America," Barney assured his stunned parents, in front of a growing crowd of curious neighbors. From that moment on, everyone's

---

[*] According to Jewish legend, Eliyahu (Elijah) the Prophet mystically appeared in times of trouble to promise relief. His rare appearance is believed to have planted hope in the hearts of the downtrodden.

thoughts were occupied with the Goldene Medina, a place where you can pick gold from its streets. It was a place where everyone could live in peace.

Miriam held her son tightly, fearing that if she let go she would lose him again. "You are my son, and the house here and everything in it belongs to you."

"We're leaving everything—we're all going to America as soon as we can," Barney informed her.

❖

During his first morning in Belaya Tserkov, Barney saw for himself the devastating living conditions that his father had described in his letter: residents of the town roamed the streets in starvation. He strolled over to the market that he had remembered from his childhood and noticed an old man with a long white beard selling fish. Two Communist soldiers casually picked up a large carp from his stand without paying for it, and the old man promptly ran after them, hollering that he wanted his fish back. One of the soldiers turned around and struck the elderly man in the neck with the butt of his gun. The old Jew instantly fell to the ground. Upon closer inspection, the soldiers realized that the old man had died as a result of his fall.

Shocked by the murder he had witnessed, Barney tried to clear his head by walking around the yarid. He found that peasants wouldn't take any money for their goods; the Russian ruble was almost worthless, and farmers only wanted to barter their items for other products. Exchanges such as, "You give me salt; I'll give you milk," were commonplace.

Barney Stumacher told his parents that they should be prepared to leave Belaya Tserkov within a month—he would bring them all to the United States. He planned to hire wagon caravans to help his family escape from Ukraine.

But not all of Barney's relatives were enthusiastic about his plan. Nissel Ravicher, who was Barney's cousin as well as brother-in-law, was initially determined to remain in Belaya Tserkov, despite the fact that his dry goods business had been torched. When the oldest of his two children, a daughter Estelle, who was endearingly called Filia,* was no longer permitted to go to school, Nissel decided it was time to leave.† He then assisted Barney with his plan to escape to America.

---

* Filia is the mother of Elizabeth Holtzman, who became a New York congresswoman.

† Source: Holtzman, Elizabeth, with Cynthia L. Cooper. *Who Said It Would Be Easy? One Woman's Life in the Political Arena.* New York: Arcade, 1996.

Barney later explained, "I got together all my relatives, cousins, first cousins, second cousins. I had an aunt (that joined us); she was eighty years old and blind in both eyes. My brother-in-law's partners whom he said he didn't want to leave were asked to come along with us. All in all, we had fifty-eight people. We left everything behind; we sold nothing."

Barney's cousin Itzie Stumacher added an additional twenty people to the group of fifty-eight, bringing the total to nearly eighty. The add-ons were mostly his wife Molly's extended family members, who would begin the first leg of the journey with Barney's group of refugees. Isaac, Rebecca, and their daughters would be among the additional twenty to travel on wagons in this caravan, as well as Esther and Yunkel Cutler's family, and Avrum Cutler and his family. The family of Avrum's wife, Slova, which included her father, Myer Ova Denka, the Tarashcha boot maker who once impressed Tsar Nicholas II, and his wife and children, would also accompany the expanding crowd.

Itzie wrote to his brother Julius, a wealthy plumber who lived in Brooklyn, and asked that he send money and passports for his own family of five. When Molly heard this, she insisted that her sister Bessie be included with them; if not, she would refuse to leave Belaya Tserkov. Julius had no choice but to agree to send a passport for Bessie.

The entire group, an entourage of fifty-eight of Barney's people plus the Caprove, Cutler, and Ova Denka families, planned to travel together through the rough terrain from Belaya Tserkov to Kishinev, which was then a part of Romania. After arriving in Kishinev, Barney's group and a few others would move on and spread out in hotels across the cities of Bucharest and Galatz as they waited for their visas. Isaac, Rebecca, and their girls would remain in Kishinev because they did not have the funds or visas to travel to America. They were depending on Molly, Itzie, and Bessie to send for the rest of the family.

Although his family did not have passports, Isaac decided that they would all travel together in the large caravan to Romania, from where it was their eventual goal to reach the Port of Constanta. The border of Romania was at least two hundred miles south of Belaya Tserkov, but he knew that having the power of numbers when traveling together was the safest and only way to get there. Each family planned to set out in their own uncovered wagon, and there were over a dozen wagons in total.

At the helm was their adventurous young leader Barney, whose stunning entrance by foot into Belaya Tserkov only strengthened their faith in his resourcefulness to lead them out of there. Barney's uncanny ability to always land on his feet, combined with a chutzpah that attracted those that he randomly met to rally for him, enabled him to lead the group forward. Without that charismatic quality, which was so apparent to all upon his miraculous arrival on Yom Kippur evening, the lives of nearly eighty people would have surely taken a devastating turn.

Knowing that it would only be a matter of days before they would all be leaving for Romania, Isaac made one final trip, with Channa in tow, to the shop of the tombstone-maker. Isaac explained to him that he would not be around for his baby daughter's unveiling, so the man there promised that he would put the stone on for him. With this assurance, there was nothing else keeping the family in Europe. It would not be long before Barney Stumacher would lead them on the first step of their journey toward the Golden Land.

The group would, however, encounter many bumps along the way.

CHAPTER SIXTEEN

THE GREAT ESCAPE:
THE WAGON TRAINS

Last week of October, 1920

They were all desperate and eager to leave Ukraine. Everybody that is, except for Shalum, the husband of Rebecca's oldest sister, Hiya, who shared the same first name as their older brother. Despite Hiya's entreaties, her domineering husband refused to allow their family to leave Europe. Shalum's business took precedence over everything, and he was not about to give up his comfortable life. Despite his insistence, however, he was no fool. He realized that to remain in Ukraine as a Jew was a death wish.

At that time, Jews were escaping the smaller towns as pogrom after pogrom exploded throughout the countryside. Shalum decided that their only option was to convert. The village priests promised Shalum and Hiya emphatically that they would be safe after their conversion to the Russian Orthodox faith.* Shalum did not hesitate. He gave the village priests the go-ahead to enroll their children in a Christian school. In short, he chose his grocery store over his faith and ignored his wife's desperate pleas to leave with her family to America. Hiya continued

---

* Twenty years later, with the Holocaust upon Soviet Ukraine's doorstep, Channa prayed for her mother's sister Hiya and her family that their Jewish blood would not be remembered.

to beg her husband to change his mind and only gave up when her sister Bessie packed up to join the rest of the family on the wagon caravans.

As a single act of defiance, Hiya secretly took Bessie to the grocery store that she owned with her husband. Without her spouse's knowledge or approval, Hiya sent her youngest sister away with a bag of much sought-after groceries, including a large sack of wheat, which was worth a fortune. When the rest of her family saw Bessie arrive in Belaya Tserkov dragging the large sack behind her, they were excited. Wheat was food, and they all needed food.

Sol Moser

Although he was not departing with the large caravan, news of Channa's friend Sol Moser spread as members of the group were preparing their own wagons for the journey. In the upcoming months, Sol would also be preparing to leave Belaya Tserkov for the port in Romania. His aunt had finally obtained visas for her son and daughter to immigrate with her to America, but one child was drafted into the army, and the other died tragically during the long waiting period. Their aunt chose to pluck the orphaned Sol and his sister, Goldie, from the streets of Belaya Tserkov and take them with her to Boston in her children's place.

When word reached Sol and Goldie's older brother, Schmuelik, that his two youngest siblings were leaving, he walked the twenty-eight-mile journey from his home in Stavishche to Belaya Tserkov to say goodbye to them. Seeing his little brother standing before him in his pitiful stocking feet, Schmuelik took off his only pair of Russian leather boots and insisted that his younger brother wear them on his journey to America. They were two sizes too big, but he assured the ten-year-old that he would soon grow into them. More important, Schmuelik insisted that Sol should be wearing a pair of boots when he first stepped foot on the streets of the Goldene Medina.

On the morning of their planned departure, Channa was sitting with her mother and aunt Bessie in a wagon preparing for their journey; they were hiding jewels and money by sewing them into the linings of their winter coats. While the women stitched, Bessie's eyes filled up with tears. Rebecca and Channa assumed that she was thinking of a young Jewish man that she had met after the murder of her husband. He had fallen in love with her and wanted to be with her, but could not bear to watch Bessie suffer so deeply as a result of the pogroms. He had to try to do something to fight back and put a stop to the endless Jewish suffering around him.

In 1920, Bessie's boyfriend decided to join the Red Army, which he considered to be the only band at the time coming to the rescue of his people. Bessie begged him not to enlist, but even his own mother's pleas were fruitless. That day, as she sat with her sister and young niece and sewed in preparation for the journey, Bessie revealed to them her love for this man. He was never seen or heard from again.

However, there may have been yet another man who was occupying Bessie's thoughts. She was harboring a well-guarded secret that would not be revealed until one of her young grandnieces overheard a conversation between Bessie and her sister-in-law Esther Cutler two decades after the family fled Europe.

Following the brutal murder of her young husband, Bessie fell in love with a count—a landowner whom she called "Graf Paul." Not much is known of their relationship, but from what was inferred years later, the nobleman kept a proper distance, loving the pretty young widow from afar. When a dangerous bandit attack ensued in Bessie's village, Paul could no longer keep away. Sensing that her life was in imminent danger, he literally swept her off her feet and carried her to the safety of his estate, where he was still living after the war. When Graf Paul placed her down lovingly on his elegant sofa, he had every intention of consummating their relationship.

Despite her great affection for the nobleman, Bessie harbored mixed feelings about becoming involved with him romantically. To avoid his advances, she pretended to fall asleep on the sofa. After waiting for the handsome count to doze beside her, Bessie sneaked away and left the estate. She knew that Paul would wake up the next morning and find her gone; they would never see one another again.

Bessie sat solemnly in the wagon, waiting to leave for Romania, reflecting on her tragic past while wondering what the future would hold for her; in this she was not alone.

Deep in thought, the family huddled closely together. The carriages were open, and everyone dressed in many layers to keep warm. What little valuables they had left were strategically hidden between the iron wheels of the wagons. Jewels that were not sewn into the linings of their coats were instead baked inside the loaves of bread that were carried in baskets. The men, who bought weapons for protection during the journey, were prepared to fight any bandits who were hiding in woods in search of prey.

There were no paved roads, and the terrain was expected to be rough and bumpy. Mostly young families boarded these wagon trains, with the exception of a few elderlies, including Barney Stumacher's parents and his nearly eighty-year-old aunt Frieda Ravicher. Blind in both eyes, she was determined to make it to America to be with two of her sons who had left for the United States fifteen years earlier, in 1905.

Nearly eighty refugees had loaded onto these wagons, ready to begin a nearly two-hundred-mile trek toward Romania. They had abandoned their homes in Europe forever. Each shared the same prayer: to survive the treacherous journey ahead of them. On a bitterly cold October morning, the families set out on a dozen wagons, almost blindly, traveling in a southerly direction through the most ravaged part of the civil war–torn Ukraine.

Zeyde Kalman (Carl Cutler)

There was one person of great importance who was noticeably absent on the wagon trains as the Cutler families set forth on their journey. Rebecca's father, Carl Cutler, whom the children lovingly called Zeyde Kalman, was still alive, living and hiding among his Gentile friends in Skibin. After the death of his wife, Fay, three and a half years earlier, Carl's children all wanted him to come and live with them, but he was determined to remain independent. Zeyde Kalman vehemently insisted that he didn't want to become a burden to his grown children.

Carl's children sent a letter by messenger asking him to join them, but they weren't optimistic that he would receive it on time. Carl was in hiding, and the messenger that they finally found going in his direction had a difficult time locating him. His children knew that they were racing against the clock to get word to him; they could not travel without the group to Romania and would be forced to leave whenever Barney's entourage decided to depart.

Rebecca's oldest brother, Shalum Cutler, had by this time left Belaya Tserkov and had moved his large family north to the larger city of Kiev. Their family was well-established and successful, and they did not want to leave. Word was sent out to Shalum so that he could send his oldest daughter to look for Zeyde Kalman, in the event that he turned up in Belaya Tserkov after the family's departure. His children and many grandchildren all counted the days and then the hours, praying that the old man would arrive in Belaya Tserkov on time to leave with them. Unfortunately, their worst fears materialized: he never showed up. His two sons and three daughters were all devastated.

Soon after they left Belaya Tserkov, Zeyde Kalman arrived at their departure spot, possessions in hand, only to discover that his five youngest children, along with his grandchildren, had already left without him for the Goldene Medina. When he reached Belaya Tserkov and realized that he would never see most of his family again, he dropped to his knees and was inconsolable for days. Somehow, he found his way to the grave of his baby granddaughter Fay and then cried over the little girl that he'd never known. Carl Cutler never had the opportunity to visit his children and grandchildren in Belaya Tserkov, since the country was in chaos, and travelers were often robbed and killed. The visit would have required an entire day and night's travel by wagon—far too much unrest and exertion for an elderly man.

Shalum Cutler's married daughter, who still lived nearby in Belaya Tserkov, heard what happened and went to fetch her grandfather. She brought him to Kiev to live with her father. Zeyde Kalman stayed with Shalum for a while but eventually chose to return by himself to his home in Skibin. Soon afterward, his children heard the news that he had died there alone of a broken heart.

The Destruction of Tetiev

During the course of their journey, the wagon group stopped in Tetiev, a town not far from Stavishche and about thirty-four miles from Belaya Tserkov.[*] Once upon a time, Tetiev had a Jewish population of thousands, but now there were barely any remnants of Jewish life left in this city of ruins. Rubble and ashes remained where the old, somewhat oriental-looking wooden synagogue, the bet hamidrash, once stood.

Just seven months earlier, in March 1920,[†] a horrible massacre had occurred. The entourage sat in their wagons on the very spot where between 1,500 and

---

[*]   See Notes.

[†]   The widespread massacre appeared over a few days, March 24–26, 1920.

2,000 Jews had sought safety hiding in the temple's loft. Several former Petliura officers, headed by Ataman Kurovsky, stood by the side of their colleague Ostrovsky[*] as he incited hate in a speech, calling for the extermination of every Jew. He demanded the crowd take an oath not to spare any Jewish life, even in exchange for a payoff. The carnage began on Wednesday, the fifth of Nissan, when screams of men, women, and children could be heard across Tetiev. Executioners broke into houses and businesses and murdered every Jew they could find.

Young children were snatched from their parents and thrown violently against the pavement as their blood covered their attackers.[†] A woman in labor was jabbed in the abdomen, killing her baby before it was born.

At night, the murderers neared the synagogue. The entryway to the attic there was well hidden. Bandits, headed by Colonel Kurovsky and two others, brought logs and hay and lit the synagogue on fire. Smoke quickly filled the attic and the Jews who were hiding there started to cough and choke. They quickly realized that they would all die and sent a three-man delegation out to save them. Rabbi Simon Rabinovitch, Yosef Kaliches, and a third congregant made a desperate plea and offered all the Jews' assets in exchange for their lives. The rabbi tried reasoning with Kurovsky,[‡] a son of Tetiev, but was unsuccessful in his negotiation. The bloodthirsty band of murderers killed the two men who accompanied the rabbi on the spot.

As the temple was engulfed in flames, bandits fought between themselves as to what to do with the rabbi. The forty-three-year-old spiritual leader of thousands began screaming in a crazed state as nearly two thousand of his followers were deliberately smoked out and burned alive in the loft where they were hiding. The rabbi stood near his wooden desk in the shul, reciting psalms by memory to himself—as trouble loomed—until he went mad.

Velvel, a fourteen-year-old boy, along with the rabbi's seven-year-old daughter, Lena, were among a dozen to miraculously survive the carnage. Velvel bore

---

[*] Source: Committee of Jewish Delegations. "The Pogroms in the Ukraine Under the Ukrainian Governments 1917–1920." Historical Survey with Documents & Photographs. Bale & Danielsson, London, 1927.

[†] Committee of Jewish Delegations, page 112.

[‡] Kurovsky, a former Petliura officer, was placed at the murderous scene with seventeen other bandit leaders by the Committee of Jewish Delegations, in their report, "The Pogroms in the Ukraine Under the Ukrainian Government, 1917–1920," by five eyewitness testimonies, Annex No. 49. In Annex No. 50, the same committee reported testimony of Ch. Kuperchmiid, stating that Kurovsky and twenty-five former Petliura officers were responsible for the massacre.

witness to the last minutes of the heroic rabbi's life. The rabbi's daughter most likely heard it, too.

"Leave him as is!" one side argued, as the murderers watched the revered rabbi delve into madness.

"He is their leader: kill him!" others demanded. The killers won out: the esteemed leader of thousands was brutally shot.

After they murdered the rabbi, Velvel escaped the massacre by jumping out of a window as he was chased by bullets. Young Lena feigned death on the floor as one of her father's killers walked over her tiny body with his leather boots.[*]

Few survived; almost everyone was burned alive. The majority who escaped the brutal heat of the flames by jumping out of synagogue windows were viciously shot and stabbed by bandits, who stood outside armed with guns and pitchforks.

Later that year, Barney Stumacher's group looked around at the devastation in shock. They had heard about the massacre, but nothing prepared them for the sight that met their eyes. The great synagogue in Tetiev was gone, as were those who once worshipped in it. Shortly after the destruction, human remnants were seen scattered in piles about the ruble.

Isaac, whose grandfather Rabbi Meer Caprove knew of the great rabbi who had served Tetiev since his youth in 1895, was well aware of Rabinovitch's prestigious place among the spiritual leaders of Kiev Guberniya. Rabinovitch's paternal great-great-grandfather was the righteous Rabbi Gedalia of Linets, author of *Teshu'ot Chen*[†]; on his maternal side he descended from the brilliant Rabbi Aryeh Leib of Sudikov in Wolyn. The latter claimed marital ties to the noted scholar Rabbi Moshe Chaim Ephraim, one of the most important Hasidic leaders in Russia who wrote the book *Degel Machaneh Efraim*, a commentary on the Torah.

However, such an impressive rabbinical pedigree could not save the beloved Simon Rabinovitch,[‡] who in the end suffered the same doomed fate as his wife, and most of their many children who perished in the burning synagogue. His death was reminiscent of another martyred rabbi, Reb Pinchas'l Rabinowitz of Sokolovka Justingrad, whose father, Reb Gedalya Aaron, also hailed from Linets.

---

[*]   Source: Lena's son, Jerry Cutler.

[†]   Rabbi Gedalia's (Gedaliahu ben Rabbi Yitzhak) book *Teshu'ot Chen* (Teshuot Hen) is an 18th-century commentary on the Torah. *Teshu'ot Chen* (Teshuot Hen) means "applause; shouting of grace." The het-nun is also the abbreviation of Hochmat ha'Nistar, which is another name for Kabbalah. The rabbi was a Hassidic Kabbalist.

[‡]   In an obituary of one of the rabbi's grandsons in America, the family's surname is spelled Rubinowitz.

Out of about six thousand Jews living in Tetiev, only two thousand survived the massacre that continued for multiple days and encompassed not only the synagogue, but many Jewish houses and establishments around town.* The survivors fled to other cities. The morning after the massacre, Thursday, was a market day. Local peasants assisted the murderers in looting the remaining Jewish homes and businesses, and then loaded the pillaged goods into their wagons. They torched all Jewish properties. Many of the local peasants became concerned only after the fires spread near Tziprivka Street, where their own houses were in danger of burning down. As the Jewish quarter of Tetiev burned, Kurovsky's vicious gang of hoodlums headed toward Stavishche.

When news of the massacre reached Kiev, a small group of Jewish men rushed to Tetiev—a whole day and night's journey—with horses and wagons. Shocked at the decimation they found before them, they desperately called out, "Yidden! Yidden!" It was a call that was safe for survivors. A young girl, Ruschel, and her mother came out of hiding by the river; her father was shot and killed days earlier. The Kiev rescuers were shocked to find such little signs of life.

During their very brief layover in Tetiev, Barney's entourage chose not to drink the water, as rumors spread that for many weeks after the massacre, Jewish corpses filled the wells. It was horrifying to behold the destruction of this once-vibrant Jewish community, and everyone was extremely relieved when it was time to leave the piles of ashes that was once Tetiev. The journey continued, and they hoped to find a surviving synagogue in another town where they could rest for the night.†

They sought refuge at a synagogue south of Tetiev, along with hundreds of others who were in the same predicament. The accommodations were communal, with no privacy and poor sanitary conditions. The day's journey had been rigorous,

---

*   These numbers are guesstimates from survivor testimonies (see Notes).

†   Although Barney's group did not pass through the nearby village of Pogrebishche, nineteen miles north-northwest of Tetiev, they later heard of the devastation that had hit there more than a year earlier, in August 1919. The Jewish dead in that attack numbered four hundred; half the victims were defenseless women. During the pogrom, two hundred unfortunate Jewish women took refuge in an open park where, without mercy, they were ruthlessly attacked with knives and sabres by Zeleny's troops. Less than one month earlier, Rabbi Pitsie Avram had courageously saved Stavishche from Zeleny's fury, but the Jewish populations of both Pogrebishche and Sokolovka Justingrad were subsequently massacred.

and after finding some chairs and benches to rest on, it didn't take long for the travelers to fall asleep.

As everyone began dozing, Channa's seven-year-old cousin, Paul Cutler, suddenly stood up in the room filled with two hundred sleep-deprived Jews and screamed, "Do we have to get up now and run?" It was the sad reality of the times that no child ever expected to sleep peacefully through the night without having to get up and run for his life.

The next day, a few hours into the journey, Barney Stumacher signaled for everyone in the wagon caravans to pull over. Barney's stop at a small village was intentional: he went in search of the Jewish commissar who had released him from custody a month earlier. In return for his assistance in securing him a railway pass to Fastov, Barney had promised to take the commissar and his daughter with him to America. He intended to keep his end of the bargain.

Shortly afterward, Barney returned alone to his wagon, looking very solemn. He had found the commissar sitting *shiva* for his daughter, who had recently died during a cholera epidemic.* The commissar's dream for his only child to experience freedom and happiness in the Golden Land would never come to fruition. Shattered by the devastating loss of his last family member, the commissar lost any desire to save himself and chose instead to remain in Ukraine.

Throughout the remainder of the journey in Kiev Guberniya, it was expected that bandits would attack at any moment. One did boldly approach the wagon caravans on horseback, brandishing a gun. He wore a smile on his face, making his thoughts transparent: he was going to have a ball with all these Jews, who were known to the peasantry as a group of people who didn't fight back. The peasants used to say in Russian, "The Jews are like sheep; they let you do what you want with them." This solo bandit thought that he would get rich by holding up a caravan full of Jews.

Some of the men—among them, Isaac, Avrum, Yunkel, and Itzie—bravely stepped down from their wagons and faced the bandit. They were armed and outnumbered the cocky peasant. Avrum Cutler, the tallest of the men at six feet five inches, stood squarely next to his brother-in-law Isaac, as he threatened the bandit, "It's either you or us; you can't possibly kill all of us before one of us kills you." The bandit sized up his opposition and saw that he had no way

---

*   Some family members believe that the commissar had hoped to marry off his pretty daughter to Barney.

out, so he backed off peacefully. For many of the Jewish children sitting on these wagons, it was the first time that they witnessed Jews fighting back and actually winning.

Their travels also took them through southern Kiev Guberniya, and then through Podolia. At times, during blizzard conditions, they "forged across icy rivers and ponds." It was a tiring and troublesome journey, lasting nearly a week. At one point, Molly was almost lost when she stepped off a wagon and fell through a thin patch of ice into the freezing water. After a lot of pulling by everyone, though, she was finally lifted to safety.

Relief came when the travelers discovered a few abandoned cottages where they could all rest, and where Molly could recuperate. But the relief was short-lived. When Itzie wandered outside in search of food, three Cossacks grabbed him and wanted to shoot him. A recovering Molly, who did not have the stereotypical Jewish appearance, yelled out from an open window, in her perfect Russian, "Spare that man!"

The Cossacks, assuming that Itzie was a Jew who worked for a beautiful Ukrainian lady, backed away and apologized profusely to Molly.

It was a tremendous hardship just to travel through so many of these towns. The caravan would often be stopped and taken to what Rebecca mockingly referred to as a "Confiscate Court." The so-called authorities in these villages would arrest the refugees by gunpoint, forcing them to abandon their wagons; they'd then be taken to a room inside of an old building, where those in command would attempt to confiscate their valuables. It was understood that in exchange for handing over something of value, the group would be permitted to pass through their town. These were all poor people, and what little they possessed was hidden.

Before leaving Belaya Tserkov, Bessie had refused to take off her wedding band when the women were sewing their jewelry into the linings of their coats. One day, though, Bessie made the decision to take off her ring. She gave it to one of the men at a Confiscate Court who had been eyeing it so that the group would be allowed to pass through. Even Channa, at the tender age of eight, understood how painful it was for Bessie to let go of her wedding band. To the thieves, it was just a ring, valuable only for its gold content, but to Bessie it represented so much more. Her husband and baby were gone, and now she had lost her wedding band, the last physical reminder that she had of her life with her beautiful family in Konela.

❖

When the group rode through a small town in Podolia Guberniya in 1920, they arrived at the tail end of a pogrom just minutes after murderous thugs had vacated the area. The mothers of the caravan, including Rebecca, Molly, and Esther, tried hard to cover their youngest children's eyes, but they witnessed the carnage anyway. Entire families, including young children, had been slaughtered, and their houses were set on fire. Corpses were lying before them on the barren ground. This was a year after Petliura's gang was responsible for the greatest loss of Jewish life in Podolia Guberniya. In 1919, the towns of Felshtin and Proskurov suffered catastrophic losses, adding to the many thousands of Jewish victims of the pogroms in Ukraine.

After eight exhausting days, the next formidable, yet welcome, challenge was finally reached: the risky crossing of the Dniester River. Behind them, the shtetls of their homeland were in flames: some literally, others figuratively. Before them were the icy waters of a river that could ultimately lead to freedom. The river was not yet frozen, and each family faced the challenge of making the daring journey across the river on a small rowboat. This was safer than by foot, the mode of transportation used by other Jewish refugees who'd crossed over the winter before. Holding hands, families walked together across the frozen Dniester River to freedom, while some unfortunates fell through the thin ice and were never seen again.

CHAPTER SEVENTEEN

THE PERILOUS CROSSING
OF THE DNIESTER RIVER

First Week of November, 1920

From 1918 to 1940, the Dniester River[*] formed part of the border between Russia[†] and Romania. Its boundaries originated in the Carpathian Mountains and flowed in a southeasterly direction and emptied into the Black Sea through an estuary. The Dniester meanders for about 840 miles, and its width south of Mogilev-Podolski measures anywhere from five to ten miles. The water usually freezes from sometime in November to January each year.

Crossing the Dniester to enter into Romania illegally was a scary proposition. Some refugees believed stories that if they were caught crossing the border illegally, they would be arrested, shot, or nailed to a tree. After traveling nearly two hundred miles from Belaya Tserkov, sometimes through blizzard conditions, the prospect of having to cross the river to eventually reach the Port of Constanta was horrifying. To survive the experience, smugglers, who commanded large fees, were left in charge of rowing the families safely over to the other side. The

---

[*] Channa called the river "Nester."
[†] Author note: At times, the border was Ukraine.

pilgrimage would have to be done under the cover of darkness and carefully timed to coincide with the changing of the guards.

So how did this band of eighty poor Jewish refugees know just where along the approximate 840 miles of the meandering river to cross? Barney once again saved the day. He and another gentleman traveled over the Dniester River the evening before the rest of the group in an attempt to secure a safe crossing. Smugglers on the other side of the border quickly saw dollar signs when the young American leader approached them requesting their unique services. Finding himself in an impossible situation, Barney reluctantly agreed to their outrageous demands of five hundred dollars[*] per head to cross over the river; he promised to settle with them after the job was done. Of course, once his entourage was safely in Romania, Barney had no intention of paying the full price demanded by these greedy smugglers.[†]

If not for Barney's lead, his followers would never have pinpointed the most accessible spot to cross the river, which was of great importance for two reasons. Not only was it imperative to find a narrow crossing point, but also crucial to cross through a valley to avoid having to climb over frozen hills and mountains. Mountains randomly neighbored the other side of the Dniester River, making entry into Romania a daunting task.[‡]

Within a week or two of Channa's group, at different points along the Dniester, two other families from Stavishche, both with daughters Channa's age, were forced to travel over those treacherous peaks after crossing the nearly frozen river. Channa's neighbor Rose Lechtzer later wrote about her family's parallel struggle to cross over the mountainous border.[§] "Then [we] began the climb up the other side . . . I was numb from the cold. I sat down on a rock and begged to be left to freeze to death."[¶] She later added, "Our pace [across the mountains] was too slow and it was unbearably cold. Many years have now passed but I still shiver when I think of trudging along on top of that bare mountain with no trees to shield the sharp, cold wind that went through me like a knife."

---

[*]   This is today's equivalent in US dollars for the amount Barney was quoted in Europe.

[†]   After he arrived in Bucharest, Barney did have a few hundred dollars sent to the smugglers.

[‡]   Bernard Sanders, once a resident of Stavishche, wrote in his memoir that a hill approximately two miles steep had to be climbed in order to enter Romania.

[§]   These personal recollections were extracted from family stories that Rose wrote and later shared with the author in an interview before her death at the age of ninety-seven in 2007.

[¶]   Her brother-in-law carried Rose the rest of the way.

Rochela Faynzilberg and her family also faced the same unmerciful mountain climb, closer to the location where Rose and her family had traveled. She would later write that branches used as walking sticks helped with the trek, and every few minutes she would look up, hoping to see the end of the mountains. People threw away their precious belongings to make the climb lighter. Mothers struggled to hold their babies. Everyone kept stumbling, but fear gave them the strength to continue.

Barney's entourage split up into many different groups in order to make the dangerous voyage across the border. As they all waited together in the small room of a house owned by a smuggler near the river, fear set in. What if Molly's baby, Fay, let out a loud cry, revealing their hiding place? The family also worried about Daniel Cutler, who had fallen ill with bronchial pneumonia. His father, Yunkel, had no choice but to carry him down to the river by piggyback.

Isaac, Rebecca, Channa, and Sunny were all insistent that Bessie travel with them in their wooden rowboat. They all loaded into the small boat, carrying with them their personal belongings, including clothing and bedding. The smuggler was constantly checking his pocket watch, timing the expedition to the minute.

"Hurry up and get in," he snapped. "We have to move quickly."

The smuggler surveyed his group and declared to Isaac, "There are too many people; you should leave someone behind."

"No," Isaac answered firmly. "We're all going to cross together."

The smuggler shrugged his shoulders and began to row the boat into the cold darkness of the Dniester. The rowboat felt very heavy and was moving at a slow pace. As they paddled toward the middle of the river, Bessie realized that something was terribly wrong.

"Isaac, look, my feet are wet!" she whispered.

Channa looked down to find water gushing into the rowboat.

"Papa," she asked quietly, "do you think we're going to drown?"

As they continued rowing slowly toward the middle of the river, water began pouring into the tiny boat, causing it to rock. The boat flipped sideways, throwing its occupants overboard. It was early in November, and the water was so cold; Channa was sure she was going to die. If the man had rowed any farther into deeper water, they would have certainly all died.

Miraculously, Isaac found that he could still stand in the river, and he and his wife were able to grab Channa and Sunny and hold their heads above water. After Channa coughed up a mouthful of water, Bessie took her from her father's arms, and gently whispered into the child's ear to stay calm and quiet. She didn't want the guards to be alerted. Isaac and the smuggler were somehow able to tilt the boat over on its side and pour the water out, and then turn it back upright. Although lucky enough to survive the ordeal, most of their clothing and some of their bedding sank in the Dniester.

The family climbed back into the boat anxiously; valuable time had been lost, and the smuggler informed them that they would have to return to the Ukrainian side of the border. Soaking and shivering, they were disappointed that they were not able to make it over to the other side, as the others from the caravan had done that evening. The smuggler took the sodden refugees home with him so that the family had a place to dry off and rest before attempting once more to cross the river the following night.

"It looks like we'll be traveling with a much lighter load tomorrow," Isaac remarked sardonically, referring to the loss of some of their possessions in the river. The smuggler turned to Isaac, looking him seriously in the eye. "God must have been watching over you and your family. A few more minutes, and we would have been in deeper water and we all could have drowned . . ."

Fortune shined upon them that they were not apprehended that evening by the border guards. Later that evening at the smuggler's house, Rebecca and Bessie moved to a corner of the room where they were less likely to be seen and opened up the linings of their winter coats. They were all soaked from the fall into the Dniester, and the sisters wanted to make sure that their money and jewels were not ruined. Relieved that there had been no damages or loss, Rebecca handed the smuggler's wife a ring, paying her off for sheltering them. While fate forced them to stay on the Ukrainian side of the border that evening, the other members of their group congregated together in a Romanian synagogue.

The following night, during the changing of the guards, Isaac, Rebecca, Bessie, Channa, and Sunny were rowed over the Dniester without incident. Late that evening, the last members of Barney's entourage were taken to the house of another smuggler who lived on the Romanian side of the river. The following morning, the smuggler took them by horse and wagon to a large city located above the Dniester Valley on the river's tributary. They were now in Kishinev (Chisinau).*

---

* Some of Channa's older cousins believed that the family crossed over the Dniester River near the town of Sguritsa, in the district of Sorocki. This town is located eighty-six miles north northwest of Kishinev. If true, it may have taken more than a day to travel from Sguritsa to Kishinev by horse and wagon. However, since they were children and unfamiliar with the area, the exact crossing point remains unconfirmed.

CHAPTER EIGHTEEN

ADVENTURES IN ROMANIA

Can you believe that there was once a city where no Jew went hungry or went about poorly clothed? A pauper need only apply at the shul and there he would find matrons clamoring to take him home to share the dinners they had cooked. A beggar was treated as the most honored guest. After he had been filled with delicious food and wine, if there was an extra bed he was invited to stay—and if not, he could return to the shul and sleep on one of its benches.

It is true such a city existed. And its name was Kishinev.

—From *The Journeys of David Toback**

1920–1921

When first arriving in Kishinev in November 1920, some thirty years after David Toback's described visit to the city in 1890, the new refugees were taken aback by the sight of long lines of desperate people waiting for food. Soup, which had been prepared in large buckets, was being doled out to the poor Jewish immigrants. This most heavily populated city and capital of Bessarabia could no longer afford to offer the special treatment that former visitors used to enjoy from the once-prosperous Jewish community. The Jews from Russia and

---

* Malkin, Carole. *The Journeys of David Toback (as retold by his granddaughter).* New York: Schocken Books, 1981, page 71.

Ukraine who flocked to Romania were all stranded there without permission; likewise, most were destined for America.

Though many called this land "Romania," just two years earlier it was known to the world as Bessarabia, a historical region of southeastern Europe that once belonged to the Ottoman Empire and to Moldavia. It has been a long-disputed territory between Russia and Romania. This area is physically bordered by the Dniester River on the north and east, the Prut River on the west, the Black Sea on the southeast, and the Kiliya arm of the Danube delta on the south.

Bessarabia remained an integral part of the Russian Empire until 1917. After the Russian Revolution, a national council (Sfatul Tarei), composed largely of Moldavians, was formed. The council, in fear of terror and disorder, appealed to Romania for protection. Little did the council members know that the government of Romania wasn't much more stable than its neighboring country.

In 1918, the council proclaimed that Bessarabia was an Independent Moldavian Republic; in the fall of that year, it voted to unite with Romania. The Soviet government did not recognize this land as part of Romania. The Romanians, on the other hand, argued that like the people of Latvia, Lithuania, and Estonia, Moldavians had the right to choose their own fate. However, all negotiations between the two countries soon fell apart.

Meanwhile, on October 28, 1920, just days before the caravan group illegally crossed over Bessarabia's northern border, the Treaty of Paris confirmed this union. Many of the world's great powers recognized Bessarabia as a part of Romania. In 1940, however, Bessarabia reverted back to Russia.

There were tearful goodbyes as Itzie, Molly, and their children, as well as Bessie, prepared to leave for the next chapter of their journey to the Goldene Medina. Like many other members of Barney's group who had traveled together from Belaya Tserkov, they had their passports and the funds necessary to immigrate to America. The Caprove family, however, did not, and Channa's two aunts and uncle parted with the promise that when they reached America, they would send for the rest of them.

With Barney Stumacher heading the group to the United States, they continued on to Galatz, Romania, where they resided for a few months. Barney's closer family members received preferential treatment and were accommodated in hotel rooms across Bucharest. While delayed in Bucharest, Barney ran into a familiar face: the American he had met on board the ship on his way to Europe who had showed him the map of Bessarabia, was now also in Romania. His friend eagerly recounted to Barney the colorful details of his run of good fortune: he had "come into possession" of Romanian money plates and was printing what looked like legitimate bills at random. He gave Barney a private demonstration of how he printed the new Romanian tender and then lined his pockets full of cash. Finally, he extended a dinner invitation to Barney and the members of his family to be his guests for a meal at an upscale café in Bucharest.

While the Stumacher family feasted on dinner and wine, their new American friend disappeared to the back of the café to speak with its owners. Barney sat himself down on the bench at the café's piano. Although he had never learned to read music, he could play by ear as well as any seasoned pianist. Minutes later, his friend returned to the dinner table and announced grandly that he had just bought the café—piano included. Barney could now enter the establishment at will and eat, drink, and play tunes on the piano as often as he desired. This was not the first café Barney's friend had purchased—he had bought many throughout Bucharest and in different cities across Romania with cash that he himself had printed.

Barney and Bossie's Arrest: Bucharest, March 1921

While Itzie Stumacher had his own family's passports provided to him by his brother Julius, a wealthy plumber from Brooklyn, Barney was still waiting to receive about twenty passports that he needed in order to get the rest of the group out of Romania. Tired of wading through five months of red tape, Barney heard of a forger selling false Romanian passports in Galatz. Wasting no time, he provided the forger with the twenty names, ages, and photographs of the refugees from Belaya Tserkov and falsified their country of birth as Romania. With the new passports in his hand, Barney was about to travel back to Bucharest when he heard a female voice behind him call out his name. He turned around and was taken aback to see his twenty-year-old sister, Bossie.*

---

* Bossie was identified as the sister of Barney who assisted him with the passports by Allen Avery in a letter to the author in 2004, after he confirmed it with Filia Holtzman. Barney did not mention which sister accompanied him on this mission. Much of the dialogue regarding Barney and the passports is from his own recollections.

"What are you doing here?" he asked her.

"They sent me to carry the passports into Bucharest."

"I don't need anyone to carry the passports for me. I travel all over Romania; nobody knows my business. They know I'm an American, and you didn't have to come here."

Of course, it was obvious why the family had chosen to send Bossie, a glamorous singer with the Kiev Opera Company, to help her older brother smuggle the passports out of Galatz. Her physical attributes would surely throw off any suspicion of wrongdoing, and her calm demeanor under pressure could only assist Barney on his travels.

Bossie was a strong and resourceful woman who had known a lot of pain and heartache in her short life. Just eighteen months earlier, her husband, Boris Weinschel, a well-known Jewish writer, poet, and actor, had died from pneumonia.* Just nine months before her husband's death, Bossie had given birth to the couple's daughter, Blossom, who was also traveling with the family under the Stumacher name.

Barney's striking sister took the twenty passports and hid them in her brassiere. The siblings then boarded an all-night train back to Bucharest with standing room only. There was a small compartment on the train where six men were seated in first class. When they eyed Barney's stunning sister standing on the train in her fashionable dress and hat—and now very well endowed—the men offered to move over and make room for her to sit with them. The young woman smiled as she walked confidently toward the cabin, but as she bent down to take a seat, the passports moved around and began to stick out of her clothing. A few of them fell out onto the floor.

Unfortunately for Bossie, seated directly across from her were two police agents who had noticed the passports sticking out of the bosom of her dress. She cried out to her brother, who was still standing outside the compartment, "They want to see my passport, but I don't have one for myself."

Barney peered in and saw that the passports had been gathered and spread out on a table; he knew that he and his sister were in deep trouble and quickly emptied his pockets. The policemen told Bossie, in German, that they were arresting her for having false passports in her possession. Barney tried to bribe

---

* In an interview with the author, Bossie's daughter, Blossom, stated that she believed her father, Boris Weinschel (Weinshell), had died from pneumonia. However, according to her grandfather Nechame's letter to Barney, Bossie's husband, a Jewish stage actor, was murdered (probably during a pogrom).

the agents, but it was useless: holding false passports in Romania was a serious matter. Bossie began to cry as she and her brother were arrested, taken off the train, and brought to a prison.

In the Bucharest jail, Barney called upon an old family friend named Gross* to help them out of their difficult predicament. Mr. Gross was apparently a powerful ally to have in Romania. He was the type of man to have connections all over Bucharest: he knew the police, jailors, the chief, judges, and officials—everyone of importance in the city. Gross came to Barney's jail cell and asked him, "What do you want me to do?"

"Gross, you see I am in trouble—what do you mean what do I want you to do? I want you to get us out of here!" Barney told him.

"I can get you both out now without the passports. But if you wait until the morning, I can get you, your sister, and the passports out, too. I can have them validated legally as official Romanian passports. So now I'll ask you again: What do you want me to do?"

Barney looked at his younger sister, who was determined not to leave the jail without those twenty official passports. "Look, we need the passports; it is better that we stay overnight," she said to him. Barney and Bossie endured a dreadful and sleepless night in jail, in the unsavory company of pickpockets and burglars.

At ten o'clock the following morning, just as Gross had predicted, Barney and Bossie were led upstairs to a room where they faced the police chief of Bucharest. In German, the police chief questioned Barney.

"You didn't make these passports, did you?"

"No."

"You just wanted to take them?"

"Yes."

"Did you know that these passports were false?"

"No."

"Suppose that I make them good for you; how soon will you all leave Romania?" the chief asked.

---

* On their Ellis Island passenger manifest, eleven of Barney's close family members, including his parents, listed a David Gross as their closest family member or friend left in Europe. One entry has David Gross living on Maria Street in Galatz; the other entry has him listed as living in Czernowitz. It is possible (but unconfirmed) that the man whom Barney refers to as "Gross" in his story is David Gross. We do know, however, that Barney bought cigarettes in Czernowitz before arriving in Belaya Tserkov, an indication that he may have stopped there first for assistance.

"As soon as we get our visas, we're going to leave Romania," Barney assured him.

The police chief took the passports out of a drawer and began stamping them one by one with an official seal, making each one legitimate. He placed them back inside the newspaper that had been used to carry them into the station and handed them over to Barney. The two men shook hands, and the chief wished him luck.

Barney Stumacher and his sister Bossie left the police station that morning along with Mr. Gross and twenty official Romanian passports.*

Unfortunately, Barney's misfortune did not end with his arrest. When he returned with the passports, Barney was disappointed to learn that, in his absence, the American consulate had discovered that he had entered into the country illegally while holding his American passport. There was a law at the time that one had to leave their passport with the nearest consulate when entering the country. Barney was unaware of this law, and while he was in Belaya Tserkov, his passport had been handled by others and blue ink was splattered all over the stamp.

The consulate in Bucharest repossessed Barney's passport, forcing him, on March 10, 1921, to apply for an emergency United States passport from Washington, DC. Since Barney needed a new passport before he could reenter the United States, the group's departure was delayed in Bucharest for a few more weeks.

The refugees from the small shtetl in Ukraine gathered together in Bucharest for a historical photograph taken on March 25, 1921, just before they departed the country to set sail to the Golden Land.

With visas and passports in hand,† Barney Stumacher's group of refugees from the village of Belaya Tserkov left Romania in their wagon caravans. By April, the group—which included Itzie, Molly, the couple's three young children, Bessie, and Itzie's three much younger half-siblings—was diverted to Germany via Poland. Somewhere along the journey, they abandoned their wagons and boarded a train to Hamburg, Germany.

---

* The author discovered that on the outside cover of a passport belonging to a close relative of Barney's, the name "Gross" was scribbled in ink in an upper corner. In the opposite upper corner, a letter *G* was written and underlined in pencil. This would seem to confirm Barney's story that Gross paid off the court and had the passports stamped.

† Barney's parents met privately with the vice counselor at the American embassy in Bucharest, who issued them their visas.

On April 21, 1921, the Jewish refugees set sail from the Port of Hamburg on a 1,300-seat passenger steamship called the *Mount Clay.*[*] It was the day before the eve of Passover (Erev Pesach), a Jewish holiday commemorating the deliverance of Jews from slavery in Egypt three thousand years earlier. Adhering to the strict dietary tradition of this festival that marks both the physical and spiritual freedom of their ancestors, the group ate only eggs and matzah during the next eight days of their journey.

Meanwhile, back in Kishinev, Isaac, Rebecca, and their daughters faced an indefinite waiting period for their passports. They were, however, in good company: stranded with them in Kishinev were Esther and Yunkel Cutler and their four children. Avrum Cutler, his pregnant wife, Slova, and their baby daughter, as well as his in-laws, the Ova Denkas, had also remained behind.

On May 3, 1921, Barney's group of Jewish refugees, who had risked their lives to pursue the American dream, sailed (with legitimate stamps on their passports) into the free waters of the New York Harbor, docking at Ellis Island.[†]

Barney and Uncle Itzie's eighty-year-old aunt, Frieda Ravicher, who was blind in both eyes, had miraculously survived the entire ordeal. From the anchored ship, she was excited to speak with her two sons, whom she had not seen since they had arrived in America more than fifteen years earlier. Frieda hollered down to her beloved sons in Yiddish, "My only wish is to look at your faces once more before I die."[‡]

---

[*] Less than three months before their journey, a deadly outbreak of typhus cases resulted in voyages of the *Mount Clay* to be diverted to the Boston Harbor.

[†] Source: Ellis Island Passenger Records.

[‡] Frieda's sons soon rushed her to a New York City ophthalmologist, who removed a cataract from one of her eyes, restoring her vision. (She is seen in photos taken in America wearing eyeglasses). For the first time in a decade, she not only saw the faces of her two sons but also the faces of her many grandchildren. She then went on to live for another ten years with her daughter and son-in-law in Tulsa, Oklahoma!

CHAPTER NINETEEN

LIFE IN KISHINEV

Despite the presence of the monarchy in Romania in 1920, its government was weak and impotent in the face of the organized bands of robbers that were wreaking havoc on the country. The rich were constantly watching their backs, expecting to be attacked and robbed at any moment.

Poverty had its advantages. Isaac and Rebecca owned nothing that could possibly be of any value to thieves, and therefore didn't have much to worry about. During their three-year layover in Kishinev, they resided in a poor housing complex,* but directly across the street lived a wealthy family who owned a beautiful house surrounded by a large gate and a number of ferocious guard dogs. But all the security measures in the world did not provide the family peace of mind. The wealthy family ended up selling the house to others who were not as fortunate to have the protection of guard dogs.

One day, the couple and their daughters watched helplessly as their new neighbors were brutally threatened and robbed by a band of vicious criminals. Under normal circumstances, one would call the police, but there was no police presence or form of control.

The government may have turned a blind eye to the wave of crime that was sweeping the area, but they wasted no time in dragging Isaac and his wife out of their dreary housing project one day and into a dingy-looking courtroom in Kishinev. Their family, like thousands of other Jewish refugees from Ukraine and Russia, was living in the country illegally. The Romanian government had

---

* It is believed that the Caprove family may have lived at Strada Tzasovnea 8 in Chisinau (Kishinev). In Russian, the name of this small street, which no longer exists, was pronounced "Chasovenny."

little sympathy for the plight of these people, and their Jewish status didn't help matters. Jews were a minority in Romania and were disliked by many. Up until seventy-two years earlier, Jews enjoyed few rights in Romania.*

The court gave the couple the equivalent of a lecture; it was essentially a warning to leave their country. Rebecca stood up defiantly in front of the court, throwing her hands into the air and proclaiming to the magistrate, "Believe me, when we're finally able to go to America, nobody will be more thrilled than us . . ." It was fortunate that the judge didn't understand her heavily accented Yiddish.

The humiliation that Channa saw on her mother's face was something that the young girl had never witnessed before. For the first time since fleeing Stavishche, Rebecca publicly verbalized her disgust over the entire matter and expressed frustration over her family's predicament. That evening, Channa and Sunny watched their mother break down and cry to their father, "We always had trouble, and we still have it. The way it looks, we'll always have it. They don't let us [Jews] live; wherever we go, they knock us. They let us live for a while, and before you know it another one [some type of pogrom] comes along."

Perhaps the largest blow to the family while living in Kishinev was the implementation of the immigration quota put into effect in America in the spring of 1921, just two months after Barney's group departed. The new quota system limited the number of immigrants from any given country to only 3 percent of the people from that nation already living in the United States during the Federal Census of 1910.

The total number of immigrants that the United States was allowing into the country in 1922 was 355,825. The quota limits for those from Russia were 34,284 and from Romania 7,419. Massive numbers of hopeful immigrants from the former Russian Empire were stranded in Europe. Many chose instead to sail to Palestine and South America, but others remained in limbo in Kishinev.

Jews in Kishinev in 1920 were grateful recipients of the assistance offered to them by the Jewish Federation and Hebrew Immigrant Aid Society (HIAS). These relief programs were established after an attack on the Jewish community of Kishinev back in 1903. When a fourteen-year-old Christian boy who had gone ice skating in a nearby town was found murdered by the Dniester River, false rumors of a Jewish blood libel murder circulated around a city that was already beginning to exhibit anti-Semitic sentiment.

---

* On June 9, 1848, the Islaz Proclamation was adopted in Romania, providing "Emancipation of the Israelites."

In reality, the boy had been stabbed by a family member over an inheritance. However, encouraged by rumors published in *Bessarabets*, the local newspaper, the common belief was that he had been murdered by Jews. According to rumors, the Jews had drained the boy's blood by piercing all his main arteries, and used it for ritual purposes, most specifically in the making of Passover matzahs.

Following these unsubstantiated accusations leveled against the Jews, tensions flared in Kishinev. The prosperous Jewish community suffered a vicious pogrom over a three-day period beginning on Easter Sunday. The attacks left forty-nine Jews dead and more than five hundred injured. Hundreds of Jewish homes and businesses were looted and destroyed by bandits, leaving two thousand families penniless.

A young Jewish poet from Odessa, Chaim Nahman Bialik, who years later would become one of Israel's most famous writers, was sent to Kishinev to report on the massacre.[*] His haunting poem "The City of Slaughter" drew worldwide attention to the tragedy. His epic work chronicled the bloodbath that left Kishinev's Jewish community crippled.

As a result of the Easter pogrom of 1903, American Jewry put aside any differences they may have had and became united in their common goal: to help their unfortunate brethren abroad. Knowing that most of the Jews who were stranded in Kishinev in 1920 had endured similar tragedies and pogroms, they reached out to lend a much-needed helping hand. Their assistance with food, clothing, and education, as well as their guidance in completing the paperwork necessary for immigration to the United States, was invaluable.

A Silver Lining

It was thanks to the Jewish Federation that Channa and Sunny were able to attend school in Romania. Unlike many schoolchildren who dread going to school each day, the girls began their days merrily as their father walked them to school. It was the first time that the young sisters felt safe.

---

[*]   Chaim Nahman Bialik (1873–1934) moved to Tel Aviv in 1924 after living most of his life in Russia. He was soon recognized as Israel's national poet. In 1927, Bialik became head of the Hebrew Writers Association, a position that he held until his death.

One morning, at the makeshift Kishinev school, Jewish delegates arrived in Channa's classroom as the students were singing Hebrew songs. They asked all the children in the class to walk with them to a large warehouse. The relief workers knew that the families of these children literally owned nothing, and they wanted to help prepare them with a warm wardrobe as winter approached. The warehouse was stacked with gently used garments, and the relief workers outfitted all the students with clothing. A nice female delegate took Channa aside and tried her best to judge her size; she then looked around for clothes that might fit the skinny girl. She found a little coat with a fur collar as well as a pair of shoes and a dress.

When Channa returned home from the warehouse that day, her mother was heartbroken at the sight of her daughter in her new fur-trimmed coat. Rebecca's pride was so great that despite their desperate financial situation, and Channa's urgent need of clothing, she refused to be the recipient of charity. So the next day Channa was forced to return the items. The young girl secretly envied the other children who were lucky enough to keep their new clothes.

Channa was allowed, however, to attend camp that summer, which was also sponsored by the Federation; they called it a *datcha*. She rode a trolley to the outskirts of Kishinev to the day camp, which was near a lake. There were bunks there for the overnight campers, but that waiting list was too long, so she attended during the day, when they put on shows for the children. They had games and toys for the kids to play with and for just a short while, the poor refugees felt like any other carefree children in the world. To Channa, that was heaven on earth.

A Royal Celebration

In 1921, King Ferdinand of Hohenzollern and his wife, Queen Marie, a grand-daughter of Queen Victoria and a cousin of the late tsarina Alexandra of Russia, sat on the throne of Romania. Just four years earlier, their eldest son, Prince Carol, had fallen in love with a beautiful Romanian girl named Jeanne "Zizi" Lambrino. She was a Romanian general's daughter and an indirect descendant of Prince Cuza, a mid-19th-century monarch. While the present king and queen disapproved of their son's match with a civilian, it is possible that their six or seven million subjects would have accepted the marriage.

In 1917, Prince Carol and Zizi eloped without his parents' consent. Queen Marie forced her son to annul the marriage. After seeing to it that the couple's son had no rights to the Romanian throne, Queen Marie then handpicked a "suitable" bride for her impetuous son.

On March 10, 1921, the same day that Barney Stumacher found himself filling out tedious paperwork for an emergency passport at the American consulate in Bucharest, Prince Carol married Princess Helen of Greece, in Athens. She was the pretty daughter of the Greek king Constantine and his wife, Queen Sophie. It was the second union between members of these royal families; the first marriage was between Princess Elizabeth of Romania and Prince George of Greece.

The couple was married in a civil ceremony held in the Grecian palace; an elaborate wedding in the cathedral followed. The procession to the cathedral was led by Carol and his bride in a golden carriage. Princess Helen was wearing a white satin gown trimmed in gold and a veil fit for a queen.

After the ceremony, the royal couple was greeted in Athens by cheering crowds. In Romania, it was hoped by the masses that their prince had finally settled down and was ready to serve his country well. So when he married the Greek princess, the celebration in Kishinev, as in all of the country, was immense, and one that its witnesses would never forget.

For four days and nights, Romania indulged in constant festivities. Right outside Isaac and Rebecca's housing complex, free food was being passed around liberally, and people were drinking and dancing drunkenly in the streets. Free performances and shows in the theaters were open to anyone who could find a seat. Young children looked on as men passed around wine from large jugs while waiting on lines to enter the theaters.

Of course, there were those who took advantage of the drunkenness of the Romanians and the relaxed nature of the celebrations. While celebrating with neighbors on a street in Kishinev, Channa eyed a few young pickpockets, whose victims were too inebriated to notice. Many homes were robbed and vandalized in the more affluent neighborhoods.

The Gypsies

Most noticeable among the villagers on the streets of Kishinev were the Gypsies.[*] Standing in the crowd in their bright, multicolored clothing, they were both

---

[*] Today we refer to Gypsies as the Romani people or Roma.

distinctive and conspicuous. The Gypsies, an ethnic minority enslaved in the country for centuries, were probably the only group of people disliked as much as the Jews in Romania. Until 1856, most Gypsies in Romania were slaves or serfs, usually for boyar families. Even after they were freed, their financial condition didn't improve much.*

Traditionally, the Gypsies in Kishinev made their living as artisans or by tinkering, telling fortunes, or playing the fiddle. However, unfounded rumors spread among the locals that they were kidnapping small children and forcing them out on the streets as beggars. Isaac, disturbed and angry at such ignorant claims, sat his young family down to explain that the rumors were groundless. He told his wife and young daughters that there were many in the country who disliked the Gypsies, just as there were many who disliked the Jews, and it was these people who encouraged such horrible rumors. He assured everyone that there was nothing to fear from the Gypsies, just as the Gypsies had nothing to fear from the Jews.

Consequently, as these groundless, vicious rumors spread around town, many didn't feel safe in the streets. The newly arrived Jews in Kishinev, who were naïve immigrants, didn't know which stories to believe. So parents tried to be more vigilant and watched their children more closely, but it was difficult keeping track of them. And it became virtually impossible to keep the children close to home when posters announced a traveling circus coming to town.† All the children in the city begged their parents to see it, and Rebecca and Isaac's oldest daughter was no exception.

Channa had never experienced going to a circus before and was afraid that her mother wouldn't let her go. In fact, when she finally mustered the courage to ask permission, Rebecca didn't even know what a circus was.

One of the older boys from the group, Moshe Ova Denka, invited her to accompany him. He was the son of the tsar's shoemaker from Tarashcha as well as the younger brother of her uncle Avrum's wife. On the way to the circus, Moshe admitted that his father had only given him enough money for standing-room-only tickets at the back of the tent to watch the show, but Channa didn't

---

* It is difficult to detail the history of this area's artisan Gypsies because of the changing borders between the countries. In 1897, a census indicated that there were 8,636 Gypsy Rom living in the region of Bessarabia. In 1920, an analyst named Elemer Illyes estimated that there were 133,000 Gypsies in all of Romania including this region, which made up 0.8 percent of the total population.

† The traveling circus became very popular in Europe after World War I.

care. She was so excited to experience the circus for the first time that it didn't matter to her that she would not have a seat.

That evening, the children never sat down once. From the moment the ringmaster first stepped out onto the floor, Moshe and Channa were captivated; beautiful horses and animals performed tricks in the ring, followed by the entrance of an amazing acrobat, who performed double somersaults on a flying trapeze. On the tightwire, women were dancing and men were juggling. What made Moshe and Channa laugh the most were the theatrical clowns that captured the crowd's attention. They were thrilled to be at the circus and loved every minute of it.

At the end of the show, instead of walking Channa home, as he had originally agreed to do, Moshe complained that he was tired from standing the entire evening and was too exhausted to go out of his way. Channa understood and agreed to make the return trip by herself, even though Moshe originally promised that he would be by her side on the return walk after dark. She was now left alone to find her way home.

The girl ran as fast as she could, without stopping, until finally reaching the housing complex. In the distance, Channa heard faint sounds of fiddling, but never stopped to look around her. Her father's calming assurances made her feel safe among the Gypsies, but the young girl was petrified to be alone in an unlit part of the large city in the pitch dark. She never ran so fast in her life.

Sunny loved listening to the band that played in the park across the street from where her family lived. She didn't realize it until years later, but it was Gypsy music that she loved. When a young man from Kishinev committed suicide by hanging himself from a light, this Gypsy band led the funeral procession on the road outside of the housing complex. None of their neighbors knew the deceased, but they all found themselves caught up walking along with the procession. The Jews whispered among themselves that the deceased was an Italian who had died young. The truth was that the Jewish refugees unknowingly found themselves in the midst of an elaborate Gypsy funeral.

A huge send-off is the rule rather than the exception in Gypsy society, and this funeral was considered to be a traditional one. Channa and Sunny enjoyed the musical performance: the band comprised of a fiddler, a clarinet player, a cellist, and a flutist. Behind them, a wagon pulled the coffin, trailed by hysterical female mourners who wailed loudly and unselfconsciously. It appeared as if these women were professional criers who were paid to perform. The screaming was so loud that even the young girls questioned the sincerity of their dramatic displays of grief. The parade of Gypsies headed toward a cemetery outside of town, with the sobbing of the women growing louder and louder. It was an emotional display; the Jews were perplexed, but no one seemed particularly surprised by it.

Isaac Gets a Kaddish

It was a surprise to the Romanian masses when just seven months after the wedding of Crown Prince Carol and his bride Princess Helen, an heir to the throne was born. The October 25, 1921, arrival of Prince Michael (later Mihai I) provoked much talk among Romanians, as well as a lot of finger counting. However, it was another reason for the masses to celebrate, and celebrate they did.

Prince Carol was not the only one to celebrate the birth of a son during that time. *Or chadash al tzion ta'ir.* A new light is lit. Seven months later, on May 25, 1922, Isaac's thirty-second birthday, he celebrated the birth of his first son in Kishinev.* After fathering three girls, Isaac finally had a boy.

It was of great importance to Isaac to finally have a son. He called the boy "My Kaddish."† Kaddish is the traditional prayer for the dead, and a son was given the honor of repeating Kaddish during the eleven months after the death of his parents and also on their yahrzeit.‡ A son, after his thirteenth birthday, could be counted as a part of a minyan. In a sense, a man's son was in fact his Kaddish, and without one, his name would not carry on and a branch in Israel would end.

Channa and Sunny's Papa finally had a "Kaddish." He named his firstborn son Beryl after his own father. Beryl was a big baby, weighing over eleven pounds at birth. Rebecca always bore large babies, but she had a terrible time delivering him. The doctor who attended her performed an episiotomy, but he didn't suture her up properly. She was so torn from the delivery that years later she would

---

* Family records have Isaac born on the same day as his son in 1890, although other documents show different years. In 1986, his great-great-grandson was also born on the twenty-fifth of May.

† Anne Caprove Kravitz mentions this in her 1990 letter to the author, page 24.

‡ Kaddish is recited for the dead, yet it never mentions death. It is a prayer dedicated to praising God.

be hospitalized from complications stemming from the birth. She had so much trouble, in fact, that after Beryl, she was unable to have any more children.

Channa was ten and Sunny was six when Beryl was born. He was a beautiful baby and a joy to his family. A large celebration was held in the yard for his *brit milah* (ritual circumcision). As Abraham had circumcised his son Isaac some four thousand years ago, another Isaac would now ask a *mohel* to do the same for Beryl on the eighth day of his life. The rabbi repeated the words that God told Abraham in Genesis: "This is my covenant, which you shall keep, between me and you and your offspring after you: Every male among you shall be circumcised . . . when he is eight days old."*

The celebration that afternoon in the yard wasn't fancy, as the family was very poor, yet everyone in the housing complex was invited. There were so few causes for celebration in those days, so many attended the party. As the proud papa told his *landslayt* that Beryl was his father's namesake, Rebecca took their oldest daughter aside and said, "I had a dear aunt named Channa, who lived to a very old age; you were named after her."†

Channa and Sunny had adopted a cute little dog that was with them in the yard that day. Their neighbor, however, was always complaining about the mutt to the girls' parents. He was raising pigeons in the next yard and was obsessed with racing them. He disliked the dog because he would start chasing after his pigeons in the middle of his races.

On the day of Beryl's bris, this man was among the guests in the yard. During the party, Rebecca noticed the dog chewing on something and suddenly saw him darting into the woods. As hard as they searched, the girls never saw their dear pet again. Their mother always swore that this neighbor must have poisoned the dog's food at some point during the party.

Times were trying for the members of Rebecca's extended family who remained in Kishinev. Yunkel and Esther Cutler were forced to hire out their twelve-year-old son, Daniel, for manual labor. They were naive to the hardships that their child would face in such a situation. Daniel worked from 5:00 A.M. to midnight

---

*   Genesis 17.

†   Years later, the author discovered on the Russian Revision lists that Rebecca's grandmother may have also been named Channa.

in a shop in Kishinev. After midnight each evening, he grabbed a blanket and slept in the shop as mice and rats jumped over him. During the colder months, with no indoor heating, that same blanket froze like a tent over him. Needless to say, Daniel was mature beyond his years.

In 1922, sometime after the birth of their second child, a son, Avrum and Slova Cutler were given the opportunity to sail to Eretz Yisrael with her family, the Ova Denkas. Tired of the endless waiting in Kishinev, they embraced the opportunity to travel to France, where they boarded a ship to the Holy Land.[*]

In preparation for the arrival of their passports, those in the group who remained in Kishinev underwent physical examinations that were required before leaving for America. The doctors knew that immigrants would be put through a battery of exams at Ellis Island, and, if they failed, they would not be permitted to enter the country. Naturally, everyone in Channa's family was examined, and she was the only one to have a problem. When the doctor simulated the Ellis Island eye examination on her, he folded her upper eyelids back over a special instrument that resembled a buttonhook. She was diagnosed with trachoma, an extremely contagious eye disease that prevented many immigrants from realizing their dream in the Goldene Medina. It is a conjunctivitis infection that begins slowly; if the eyelids are severely irritated, the lashes may turn in and rub against the cornea. It is easily passed from child to child, and eventually, if left untreated, can cause blindness later in life.

If an Ellis Island doctor suspected trachoma, he would be forced to mark a "CT" (symbolic of trachoma) or an "E" (which indicated eye problems) across the immigrant's coat in chalk. On most occasions, the poor souls who bore these letters would find themselves sent back to Europe.

Channa visited a doctor twice a week in Kishinev to remove the white puss from the inside of her eyelids. Eventually, he cured her so that she would be able to pass the exam in America. The day of Channa's last appointment she had a long wait because the doctor was busy talking to a family that she recognized from her neighborhood. The couple had their little boy with them who clung tightly to his mother's leg. He was a cute little kid, a mongoloid child.[†] Channa overheard the doctor speaking with the parents about him and saw the distress

---

[*]   Once there, however, Avrum suffered greatly from an eye condition that was triggered by the climate. His family eventually ended up joining the others in America.

[†]   *Mongoloid* or *mongolism* was the term used during that time period referring to a person with Down syndrome. Down syndrome has been used as the accepted term since the 1970s.

on their faces after the physician explained that their son's condition wasn't going to improve.

Bucharest, July 1923

Finally! After spending over two and a half years in Kishinev, the journey to Bucharest began. It was the last stop where immigrant families waited for their ship to arrive. The Caprove family always remembered Bucharest for the inn that they stayed in that first evening. With their limited funds, it wasn't the finest motel, but the inn still provided a roof over their heads. The excitement soon wore off, however, when they discovered that the inn was infested with bugs, and Rebecca, a very meticulous housekeeper, was going crazy. They were everywhere. As soon as she set eyes on the bugs, she complained to her husband that she wanted to go to another hotel. Isaac knew just what to say to change her mind: "Are you going to let a couple of bugs chase you out of here?" he teased her.

That evening, just a couple of minutes after settling down in her bed, Channa was the first to feel itchy. She started scratching herself, and soon noticed that she was not the only one in the room suffering from itchiness. Looking up nervously from her bed, she saw hundreds of bugs—on the ceiling, on the floors, in her bed . . .

"*Vanzen!*" her mother yelled in Yiddish, referring to the bedbugs. "We're getting out of this inn, Isaac—tonight!" So in the dark, the family of five—Isaac, Rebecca, Channa, Sunny, and Beryl—wandered through the dimly lit streets of Bucharest in search of another inn. Rebecca did eventually find one.

The next day, Channa woke up early and slipped out of the new establishment without telling her parents. The girl was curious and eager to explore the busy streets of Bucharest. In Kishinev, she had heard the women raving that Bucharest was the "Paris of Romania," with its magnificent stores and huge display windows.

As a young girl, she wasn't impressed by the shops, but was completely mesmerized by the beautiful, pale-faced women who modeled the fancy dresses in the display windows. One was smiling, so Channa waved at her, but found it strange that she didn't wave back. An old man standing behind her broke out in laughter at the sight of a little girl waving at a mannequin.

He had no idea what an odd sight it was for her, the daughter of a Russian-born seamstress, to see a mannequin that not only had a head, but whose face appeared so lifelike!

Channa's exploration of the city continued; she enjoyed the music that was playing during lunch hour at the outdoor cafés. Adults congregated in groups and laughed as they drank. Channa watched with envy.

Another unusual discovery that she made while wandering the streets of Bucharest was how Romanians went about selling things. Beautiful ladies walked down the streets carrying heavy baskets filled with hot corn on their heads. Channa was in complete awe of these women and was amazed that they were able to balance the baskets so steadily without ever dropping them.

Hot water was a novelty. Women walked past her down the street hollering, "Hot water! Hot water!" Doors flew open from every direction—people ran out of stores, inns, and houses to purchase the basins of hot water before they were all sold out.

Despite the glamour and excitement of Bucharest, the family was both happy and relieved, after just a few days, to be leaving the city. The appearance of bugs wherever they turned was proving unbearable.

From Bucharest, they traveled to the port city of Constanta, Romania, which was on the western coast of the Black Sea. Constanta was the site of the ancient city of Tomis, and acquired its current name from the Emperor Constantine I.

In Constanta, the family was held up an extra week because Sunny was sick. Landslayt from Stavishche urged them to go ahead and set sail for America, assuring the young parents that they would bring Sunny with them on the following ship that was scheduled to depart for America. However, Isaac would hear none of this and insisted they wait and travel together as a family. Daniel Cutler, who was once again ill with pneumonia, also delayed his parents' departure, although they ended up boarding a Greek ship, the SS *Byron*, which left Constanta four days before the others.

At last, on a beautiful sunny morning, Thursday, August 9, 1923, the family set sail for America on a cargo vessel from the Fabre Line named the SS *Braga*. Before the voyage, Isaac insisted on buying a color picture postcard of the ship. He wanted to send it to Itzie Stumacher in America, either hoping to impress him or to forewarn him of his impending arrival. However, Itzie already knew that they were coming, and Isaac never did get around to mailing it.

CHAPTER TWENTY

JOURNEY ON THE SS *BRAGA*

PRAYER DURING A STORM AT SEA

May our prayer be acceptable in Thy presence, O Lord, our God and God of our forefathers! and for the sake of Thine attribute of mercy, cause the waters to cease from their raging, and still the waves of Thy great deep. Conduct us speedily to our destined port, for the issues of life and death are in Thy hands. Hearken unto our supplication, even at this present hour when we are praying unto Thee. Calm the storm, and conduct us with kind and gentle breezes. Guard us from the tumultuous billows, and from all the perils of the sea; guard us from the lightning and the tempest, and the confusion of darkness; guard us from dangers by water and fire, and from every obstruction, injury or fear.

From the treasury of the elements, O God, send forth a favorable wind. May all who have charge of the vessel be faithful and vigilant, active and skillful in directing or obeying, that so we may speedily and safely be brought to our destined port. Thou who madest the sea canst still the waves thereof; Thou who didst create the winds, canst allay their rage. O Lord! guard our souls which depend upon Thee, and deliver us from evil. As we put our trust in Thee, let us never be confounded. And as for us all, we will bless Thy name, O God! from henceforth and for evermore. Amen.

—From "Hours of Devotion," a similar prayer that Isaac Caprove read from his own Hebrew prayer book during the first storm of the voyage

❖

August 9, 1923–September 1, 1923

The year 1923 might be remembered by historians as the year that the conflict between Greece and Turkey officially ended with the signing of the Treaty of Lausanne. To those who were traveling on the lower deck of a cargo ship that year, however, that particular war did not occupy their thoughts in the slightest. They were more interested in curing their seasickness. Who could blame them? The waves of the Black Sea were powerful and forbidding, and the journey was turbulent and rough.

The Black Sea became stormy, and jagged streaks of lightning illuminated the dark sky before violently attacking the sea. The SS *Braga* swayed relentlessly, back and forth, back and forth.

It was so damp and miserable on the lower deck that most of the passengers became ill. The people who suffered most from seasickness were grown-ups. Children watched as their parents threw their heads out toward the water when they became ill. Others clung to the railing, supporting their bodies upright while the ship rocked.

In the midst of the commotion, Channa looked at her poor mother, white as a ghost, calling out to her in desperation.

"Channa," she cried, "take this with you to the kitchen, and bring me back a spice cure."

She took a cup from her mother's unsteady hand and walked toward the kitchen. Channa had learned a little bit of English while attending school in Romania, so her mother always sent her to fetch the onion and garlic remedy.

When she opened the ship's kitchen door and was greeted by the sight of Black chefs, the terrified girl let out a scream. Although Channa was already eleven years old, she had never seen a Black man before. In an instant, she recalled rumors she had heard from the women in Kishinev. "If a Black man places a ring on a girl's finger," they would say, "he could take her away with him forever."

As her body trembled, the girl cast nervous glances at the American cooks. She was petrified that one of them would attempt to place a ring on her finger.

Of course, they never did; they simply smiled at each other in amusement. In fact, as Channa was leaving the ship's kitchen, she overheard one of the men telling the others, "If the little girl was so scared to see just three of us," he laughed, "I can't wait to see her face when she lands in America!"

The SS *Braga* was a cargo vessel capable of holding 1,480 passengers: all but 130 were in third class. The Caprove family was among those in the lower deck because it was the cheapest. From Constantinople onward, Channa's parents lined up to get off at every port, anxious for a reprieve from their constant seasickness. Channa was left on the ship to take care of seven-year-old Sunny and baby Beryl. As she watched Rebecca and Isaac leave them behind at each port, Channa could not help but feel envious.

It wasn't all bad, though. The children took advantage of their time without parental supervision to play with the other kids and explore their new surroundings. At the beginning of the voyage, Channa and Sunny used to see animals on the boat—the livestock would pass right by them, and cows could be heard mooing on the bottom deck—but as the trip progressed, the girls saw less and less of them. Sunny asked Channa in all innocence, "What did they do with these animals?" Her older sister didn't have the heart to tell her that the animals were slaughtered right on the ship to be used as food.

The Dardanelles

Traveling through the Dardanelles, the narrow waterway connecting the Aegean Sea with the Sea of Marmora, was surprisingly calm. One of the old Jewish passengers explained to Channa and Sunny that it was the same famous strait that separated the legendary lovers Hero and Leander. He recounted the tale of how Leander lived on the Asian side of the Dardanelles, and his love, the maiden Hero, lived on the opposite shore. In the evening, Leander swam across the strait (presumably at its most narrow point, about one mile) guided by the torch atop a tower lighted by his love. One evening, a storm extinguished the light as Leander was halfway through the Dardanelles, and he drowned. Tragically, in response to his death, Hero threw herself into the water.*

The SS *Braga* sailed forty miles down the Dardanelles, which separates the Gallipoli Peninsula of European Turkey from Asia Minor.† On the western shore the spectacular hills and cliffs framed the coast of Europe. In the waters below, the scattered wreckage of different vessels that were destroyed in a naval battle was visible. Passengers on the ship questioned whether the shipwrecks were due to the recent fighting between Greece and Turkey; some believed that they were remnants of sinking vessels that were lost in the Gallipoli Campaign years earlier.

Rumors spread that the ship might not be able to pass through the Dardanelles because of the fighting. On July 24, 1923, just a couple of weeks before setting sail, the Treaty of Lausanne officially ended the conflict in the area.‡ Turkey recovered several lands and the internationalized Zone of the Straits, but it was to remain demilitarized. In times of peace, the Straits were to remain open to all ships. Likewise, it would also remain open to all ships if Turkey was neutral during times of war. If Turkey was at war, it could not hinder the passage of neutral ships. The passengers were grateful to pass through the Dardanelles without any trouble. It would be while passing through the waters at Athens, in Greece, that they would suffer their most humiliating experience.

The soon-to-be immigrants could not understand why it was that the Greeks didn't have the proper facilities to allow their ship to dock at their port. In hindsight, the reason may not have been, as they had first assumed, that the water was too shallow for the ship to pull in. For health reasons, the Greeks may not have wanted the vessel to reach their shoreline. Instead, the passengers were piled in like cattle on small tugboats, manned by oars.

---

* Later, Channa learned that many poets and writers were inspired by this folktale. Homer, Keats, Marlowe, and Byron all wrote poetic verses about the tragic lovers. Lord Byron took the matter one step further. As an amusement, on May 3, 1810, he swam across the Dardanelles in emulation of Leander's legendary swims to visit Hero.

† Since the Renaissance, Europeans have called the strait the Dardanelles, after the vanished city of Dardanos. Dardanos was said to have been built by the founder of the Trojan dynasty on the Asian side of the strait. It was also once known as Hellespont. In Turkey, it's referred to as Canakkale Bogazi.

‡ The world formally recognized the country of Turkey that the Turkish nationalists had built for themselves. However, in their war of independence, the Turks had lost ten thousand men during the fighting and more than double that number from disease. Greece's casualties amounted to about ten times that of Turkey's.

The sea was so rough that it took all their effort and strength to stop themselves from tumbling over.

The small tugboats led the confused passengers toward the city of Athens, where they got their first and only glimpse of Greece. While lucky enough to reach land without falling into the water and drowning, they soon found themselves quarantined. Faced with the indignity of delousing, officials in Athens separated the travelers into groups of men and women and demanded that they take off all their clothing and shoes, which were sent through a massive heating and sterilization process.

They were then taken to huge, public showers where they were instructed to wash away the most feared thing of all: lice. Some of the authorities there really made it miserable for them; every minute of that day was humiliating. Their clothing, which for many was all that they owned to wear, was returned ruined. They then piled everyone mechanically once again onto those small tugboats, returning them to the ship.

At the time, no one could understand why the Greek authorities had put them through such a demoralizing experience. As far as they were concerned, they were simply passing through their waters. However, the fear and concern of the Greek authorities regarding the problem of lice was a justified one. Just a few years earlier, lice that transmitted typhus rickettsiae had claimed the lives of between two and three million people in the Russian Empire. Typhus had almost taken Rebecca's life in Belaya Tserkov. With poor hygiene conditions on the ship, and little access to bathing, the immigrants could potentially spread lice among the passengers, causing a life-threatening epidemic.

The humiliation didn't stop at Athens. While on the voyage, passengers were also subjected to degrading searches. No one was spared examination: men, women, and children were searched for lice. Even if just one nit was found, the refugee would be immediately directed into another room and their hair would be cropped short without hesitation. It happened to some of the most beautiful women and children. Channa never imagined it would happen to her.

On one particular search, conducted after she had been running around the ship with other children who were not chaperoned, a woman found nits in her long, beautiful brown hair. Her mother tried frantically to get them out, but it was too late. Without hesitating, they pulled the girl into a room and cut her hair extremely short above the ears. As Channa's long locks dropped to the floor, she cried and cried. Her home and possessions had been brutally stolen from her, and now her hair, too. It was too much.

Rebecca tried to console her, but she could not undo the hurt and embarrassment that her daughter felt.

The heartbreak of her own ordeal could not compare with the despair of a woman on the ship whom Channa recognized from the doctor's office in Kishinev. She was the mother of the child with Down syndrome, whom the doctor had been examining just prior to her last eye appointment. Channa looked for the little boy, but he didn't seem to be on the ship with his parents.

"We couldn't bring him with us," her husband explained to Channa's parents. "The doctor told us that they would never admit him through the medical inspections at Ellis Island."

"Where is he?" Rebecca asked him.

"We paid a woman in Romania to take care of him."

The mother of the little boy who had clung to her leg in the doctor's office in Kishinev was inconsolable.

As his eyes welled up with tears, the father told them, "The doctor warned that if we brought him with us, we'd all be sent back to Europe. I had to think of our other children; I had to decide what's best for our family."

Before that day, Channa had never seen a mother so tormented at the loss of a child. Perhaps for this woman, the emotional pain was greater knowing that her beloved child was living, but that she could only wonder about his condition. If he had died as baby Fay did, at least his mother would know that there was nothing more that she could do for him. Only God knows if that child ever survived or if the woman in Romania that they paid ever really showed him kindness and took care of him. Times were so bad, and people so desperate, that they often abandoned handicapped children they loved. People were fleeing to America in order to save their lives and were forced to do so under any pretense and at any price.*

Watching the distraught couple, Channa forgot all about her hair. There was no doubt that with hair, or without hair, she was among the lucky ones since

---

* The name of the family who faced the heart-wrenching decision to leave their child behind—a child they truly loved—is the only piece of information that Channa ever refused to share with her granddaughter.

her immediate family was still together and would soon meet up with her other loved ones in the Goldene Medina.

A Taste of Freedom

The journey across the Atlantic lasted three weeks, and the weather that summer after leaving the Black Sea was gorgeous. On that glorious evening, as the ship was entering the New York harbor, the crew told the people, "If you look outside, you'll see such lights."

This was the first time that the young family saw electric lights. Channa and Sunny stood out on the deck together on the evening of August 31, 1923, and watched as the *Braga* sailed toward the harbor. The sight of the entire harbor glowing was truly breathtaking; they never felt more thrilled in their lives. Their ship would dock on September 1, 1923, and they would not leave it until daylight.

Early the next morning, Molly, Bessie, and Itzie sent up a beautiful basket of fresh fruit filled with bananas. No one knew what they were or even had the slightest idea how to eat them. Isaac held a piece of the foreign fruit up to his nose to smell it, trying to imagine what it might taste like. He then tried to take a bite out of it, but he quickly spat it out! None of the refugees on the ship knew that bananas had to be peeled before they could be eaten!

Channa and Sunny looked around and scanned the harbor with their eyes to see if they could find their aunts and uncle. Molly and Bessie had talked Itzie into renting a small rowboat so that they could row out to greet them.

Channa spotted them before her on the rowboat; she and her family were way up high on their newly docked ship and waved to the others in the water below. They were deliriously happy to see them; the pain of being separated for more than two and a half years was finally over. Itzie, Molly, and Bessie had never seen their sister's baby boy before. Isaac was hoisting him up on his shoulders, showing off his new son. Rebecca cried as she watched her sisters' faces light up when they got their first glimpse of Beryl.

Tears of joy soon gave way to laughter as the first thing Itzie thought to ask Isaac was about his generous gift of fruit. "Isaac," he yelled up to him in Yiddish, "*Di glakhst di benenes?*" ("Did you like the bananas?")

Isaac looked down at him with a puzzled look on his face.

"*Di glakhst di benenes?*" Itzie once again asked, this time making it clear that he was referring to the yellow fruit.

Together, they all let out a hearty laugh.*

Sunny held Channa's hand as they continued waving down to their aunts and uncle in the small boat below them. The little girls knew that when they first eyed the statue of the lady in the harbor, they had finally made it to the Goldene Medina. Channa and Sunny had reached the land where people could pick gold from its streets, and where everyone could live in peace.

---

* It seemed like almost every immigrant had a banana story to tell. Channa's cousin, Ruby Stumacher, who had landed at Ellis Island about two and a half years before her, was given that same fruit basket by his uncle Julius, a plumber in Brooklyn. Ruby initially thought that you had to eat the skin and throw out the inside of the banana; needless to say, it didn't take him too long to realize that he had it backward.

CHAPTER TWENTY-ONE

AMERICA:
THE FIRST YEARS

1923–1925

When the rowboat carrying Itzie, Molly, and Bessie disappeared from the shoreline, they didn't realize that all of New York City, and perhaps the entire country, also knew of their family's arrival. Splashed across the front page of the *New York Times* on September 2, 1923, was the headline, "Aliens on Four Ships Too Soon to Enter." It was followed by the harrowing news blurb, "Most of the 1,896 Who Arrived Before Instead of After Midnight Must Go Back."

The United States implemented not only an annual quota for immigrants entering the country, but also a monthly one, making the first day of each month the most desirable time to arrive at Ellis Island. Once monthly quotas for each country were filled, steamships were forced to return any excess immigrants back to their original ports, at the expense of the company.

When the ship's crew advised all passengers to go to sleep early on the evening of August 31, 1923, so that their eyes would look rested for the medical examinations scheduled for the following morning at Ellis Island, Rebecca and Isaac could not have predicted the chaos that would follow. A strong flood tide caused the stern of a steam liner to drift over the imaginary line, leaving Gravesend Bay too early; three other ships, including the SS *Braga*, raced in afterward.

An official observer looking through a pair of binoculars claimed that a steamship, the *Esperanza*, was the cause of three other ships entering before midnight. By recognizing the arrival time of their ship before midnight, the *Braga*'s passengers would be counted in the already exhausted August quota.

According to the *New York Times*, "The four steamships which the official observer says crossed the imaginary line between Fort Wadsworth and Fort Hamilton before midnight on Friday were the *Esperanza* of the Ward Line, 11:55 P.M.; the *Braga* of the Fabre Line, 11:56; the Greek steamship *Byron*, 11:57; and the *Estonia* of the Baltic-American Line at 11:59.45, fifteen seconds before midnight." At that moment, Isaac and Rebecca's entire future, as well as that of their children and (future) grandchildren, hung in the balance by a mere four minutes!

The captains of the four ships fiercely disputed these times, insisting, during a meeting on September 1 with Commissioner of Immigration Henry C. Curran,* that they followed the ships' chronometers, which must be exact to the second or else their navigation would be off. Both the Western Union observer and the postal observer agreed with the captains of the ships, and recorded the *Braga*'s entrance as seven minutes later at 12:03 A.M.

Captain Jurgensen of the *Estonia*, the fourth ship accused of entering into the harbor too early, insisted that he called out each half minute from 11:55 P.M. to midnight to the pilot. Jurgensen stood by the wheelhouse door, carefully observing the chronometers that were in their boxes, which could not be wrong.

Yunkel and Esther Cutler and their four children also found themselves in the same precarious predicament—they were sailing aboard the SS *Byron*. On their ship were a large number of Greek girls whom the media referred to as picture brides, whose marriages had been prearranged. They were traveling to meet their prospective bridegrooms in America for the first time and openly wept when they were told that they would have to return to Greece without ever getting a glimpse of their future husbands.

The new immigrants were fortunate to have an important advocate on their side. Commissioner Curran, although agreeing with the early arrival time of the official Ellis Island observer, sympathized with the plight of the immigrants. He agreed, in conjunction with the decision handed down by the Department of Labor, to allow the passengers to enter America, and apportion the blame

---

* Henry Curran, who had only assumed his position at Ellis Island two months earlier, had been defeated in the New York City mayoral race in 1921 by incumbent John F. Hylan.

instead on the steamship companies. A tremendous fine was imposed on the four steamship companies, amounting to two hundred US dollars per immigrant. In addition, the liners were ordered to return the passengers' fees which amounted to approximately one hundred US dollars per passenger. The ships would not be allowed to leave Ellis Island before posting a bond for the fines.

The liners paid the first part of their fines before returning to Europe. However, it is not known whether they ever informed the passengers on the SS *Braga* that a problem ever occurred. Channa never knew if the steamship company ever returned the fare money to her father as they had been ordered. As far as she knew, Isaac left Ellis Island with the same meager thirty-five dollars in his pocket that he had traveled with across the ocean.*

Ironically, as the new immigrants desperately sought entrance into the Goldene Medina, after fleeing atrocities in Ukraine that most people could never imagine, a large number of sophisticated and prominent Americans were readying themselves to leave New York City to set sail for Europe. On September 8, 1923, one week after their controversial arrival, eight liners left New York with important passengers aboard, including Colonel George Harvey, the US ambassador to Great Britain, and Will H. Hays, a prominent politician. The liners were traveling across the ocean for the end of the summer tourist season; several Americans were headed for England and Scotland for pheasant shooting season, which was set to begin in early October.

As these ships carrying their respected first-class passengers sailed back to Europe, Isaac, Rebecca, and their children, as hopeful new immigrants, were soon subjected to the much-anticipated medical examinations and other tests at Ellis Island. They felt sympathy for the poor sick souls, whose clothing was marked in chalk with coded letters, labeling them as undesirables. Even they knew that those immigrants would be subjected to further examinations,

---

* On the same day that the SS *Braga* sailed safely into the port of New York, disaster struck on the other side of the world. On September 1, 1923, just before lunch hour, devastation hit Japan in the form of a catastrophic earthquake that measured 8.0 on the Richter scale; 140,000 lives were lost, including 30,000 in downtown Tokyo, who were incinerated by a firestorm.

Following the disaster, violent pogroms broke out in Japan targeting Koreans who were living in Tokyo. *The People's Korea* reported the vigilante murders of approximately six thousand ethnic Koreans (and a lesser number of Chinese) living in Japan. The pogrom started after military forces believed unfounded rumors that Koreans in Tokyo deliberately started fires and poisoned wells to start an uprising after the earthquake.

The Caprove and Cutler families were unaware of the disaster that hit the other side of the earth.

quarantines, hospitalizations, and sometimes deportations. Channa even noticed one slick character turn his marked shirt inside out before proceeding among the others to live a new life in America.

The family knew they were fortunate to pass all their medical examinations. Channa's parents were particularly relieved that she had made it through the dreaded buttonhook exam of the eyelids. In the end, this awful day ended on a more pleasant note as they were at last fed sandwiches in a large mess hall in Ellis Island. The girls and their parents were famished; this was the first decent meal served to them since departing the Port of Constanta. The long tables, each covered with white rectangular cloths and set with food, were the most vivid memory that Channa's little sister Sunny had of the entire journey.

Subway

It was the first time Channa had ever seen a subway, and it cost only a nickel to ride from one end of New York City to the other. You'd put a nickel in a slot, and then you'd go through the turnstile. Channa stared intensely as the guide inserted nickel after nickel to let the immigrants through. Her papa wanted to be the first in their group to get on the subway, and he thought he'd be a sport and pay for it himself. When he pulled a penny from his pocket and put it in the slot, it got stuck.

Chelsea

Since their passports stated "Destination: Chelsea, Massachusetts," that is where the Caproves were sent. Grandpa Carl's (Zeyde Kalman's) nephew Harry Wise, a well-respected Jewish philanthropist, had settled there back in 1892, and he and his family became prominent members of the Jewish community.*

The invitation wasn't exactly Harry's idea, but Bessie Cutler was running out of viable options. She had worked for two years to save up enough money to bring her family over, but she hadn't lived in America long enough to sign for them herself. So a year before the remainder of her family left Europe, she

---

* The Wise (formerly Weiss) and Cutler families of Chelsea were successful in the textile, cotton waste, burlap bags, rags, and junk businesses.

made the trip to Chelsea, Massachusetts, to ask a favor of her father's relatives. When Harry Wise saw the lovely namesake of his mother—the original Bessie Cutler—he could not turn her away. Her sisters often wondered if Bessie had confided in Harry the details of her awful ordeal in Konela, perhaps to make him aware of the gravity of the situation in Europe. Harry rose to the occasion, and instructed his oldest son, Robert, a successful cotton waste dealer on Arlington Street, who was also the bearer of an American birth certificate, to sign visas for the entire extended family. For that, the Cutlers and Caproves have always been grateful to the Cutler and Wise families of Chelsea.

And so it was that upon their arrival during the first week of September in 1923, the family stayed at the modern Orthodox home of Harry Wise and his wife, the former Ida Fastofsky, who had suffered a partial hearing loss after the great fire of 1908. When nearly half of Chelsea was engulfed in flames, Ida ran outside into the cold air and caught a fever, which left her hard of hearing.

Harry and Ida were well-known in Chelsea circles for their charitable contributions to Jewish causes. Harry was an active Combined Jewish Appeal worker and devoted his time and money to the Hebrew Home for the Aged, the Chelsea Hebrew School, the Chelsea Hebrew Free Loan Association, and the YMHA. He was also an active member of the Cemetery Association in Chelsea and later served as president of both the Elm Street and Walnut Street Synagogues. Harry, who was once the president of the Zhashkover Society in Boston, also took part in assisting many new immigrants.

Zeyde Kalman's (Carl Cutler's) New England relatives came out in droves to visit his children at the Wise household. Hertz, Zeyde Kalman's brother, the peddler from Zhashkov who often sold his goods at the market in Stavishche, brought his large brood over to see their "pilgrim" relatives from Kiev Guberniya. Hertz immigrated back in 1911 with the help of his son Jacob, who sent him a steamship ticket. After settling near relatives in Chelsea, he Americanized his name to Harry Cutler and became a burlap bag merchant. Hertz was with his brother back on that fateful day in 1875 when Zeyde Kalman had first laid eyes on his future wife, Fay, as she wandered into the town yarid.

The newest arrivals were embarrassed and self-conscious about their appearances in front of their American relatives. Not only were they physically weakened from their arduous voyage, but their clothes left no doubt in anyone's mind that they were European Jews from the shtetl. One of Rebecca's American cousins, Fannie, pitied the little girls and took Channa and Sunny into downtown Chelsea to buy them each two new dresses. Even though the girls were relieved to say goodbye to their old dresses that had disintegrated into rags, the new ones that she bought didn't exactly fit. Fannie, who was single and never had any children of her own, was inexperienced in buying clothing for young girls, and the garments that she chose were two or three sizes too big. That didn't diminish their excitement over the new clothing.

Channa and Sunny couldn't stop thanking Fannie, as they tripped over their new dresses. But Channa took a few minutes to take a closer look at herself in the long mirror in the dress shop. Her hair was butchered with a brutal haircut that left patches of skin showing; her new dress was so long that it would surely take a year or even two to grow into. She heard others in the shop call her and Sunny "greenhorns." Embarrassed, she decided then and there that she would never again be mistaken for a "greenie."

As for sustenance, the new immigrant relatives were fed tomato herring every day in Chelsea; it was served for each meal . . . breakfast, lunch, and dinner, until they couldn't look at the stuff anymore. A tall can of tomato herring must have been cheap; perhaps it cost a nickel or a dime back in 1923. The family couldn't understand it; did Americans really believe that Europeans loved tomato herring that much? They only visited for a week but ate enough tomato herring to last a lifetime. Never again in their entire lives would Channa or Sunny be able to look at or eat tomato herring!

Finally, the Caproves left Chelsea for Brooklyn, New York, to join Bessie, Molly, and Itzie. Channa was so embarrassed over her shortly cropped hair that she always wore a kerchief or a hat to cover it. Strangers on the street would point at her and whisper. At that time, a disease was spreading where people would lose clumps of hair due to sores on their head, and Channa was sure that's what people thought she was suffering from.

Bessie wore fashionable hats that she designed to match her beautiful dresses. She was a young woman now in her twenties who delighted in dressing up and going to social clubs; it was at one of those functions that she befriended a young couple who were divorcing soon after their marriage. They lived in a three-room apartment that they had just completely furnished, and they were now dividing up the entire household. Bessie came along and paid them three hundred dollars in cash for the whole works.

The apartment was located in the back of a butcher shop in Brooklyn, complete with beautiful furniture, dishes, pots, pans, carpets, and even window treatments.* Rebecca, Isaac, and their family felt as if they were now living like royalty. Bessie, who had been living elsewhere, moved in with them that first day.

Channa loved playing ball with the kids on the stoop. In the evenings her mama and her two aunts enjoyed meeting out on that same stoop to sing Russian folk songs and harmonize as Molly played the balalaika. Many nights, Bessie sat and talked with her sisters; the young beauty had a hard time finding a place for herself in this new world. She was still young and pretty, but she had been married before and had lost a child, and was still in pain from her tragic loss.

Many young fellows belonging to that generation refused to marry someone who had been previously married. Every time a boy would get serious with her, she would confide in him that she had been caught in the pogroms, and her husband was murdered and her baby had died. Shortly after hearing this revelation, the young men would invariably cool off and disappear from the picture. Bessie felt they didn't want a "Second-Hand Rose."

Channa often overheard Bessie asking her mother's advice out on that stoop. "What shall I do?" she'd ask, her head buried in her hands. "Every time I find a man I like, who is also interested in me and wants to marry me, he hears my story and says, 'I don't want anybody who's been married before.'"

But Bessie's fortunes did change. In 1925, she met a young furrier named Ben Baker. He was handsome and fell head over heels in love with her. Nervous to share her background with Ben, she debated whether to tell him the truth after he proposed to her. "Should I tell him or not?" she asked Rebecca. Finally, she told her sister with a sigh, "If he really loves me, he will accept me as I am." She did tell him. Ben was grateful that Bessie was honest and trusted him enough to share the painful details of her past. He made her promise not to think of or talk about the unhappiness that she had suffered; he wanted her to only focus on happy thoughts.

Bessie Cutler and Ben Baker were married in August 1925 and moved into their own apartment. They eventually became the parents of three children.

---

* A November 1923 document signed by Isaac had the family living at 4310 Thirteenth Avenue in Brooklyn.

ABOVE: Isaac Caprove is on the right, with unidentified friend, 1910, Stavishche. RIGHT: Rebecca Cutler Caprove with her daughter Channa Caprove, circa 1914–1915, Stavishche.

ABOVE: Rabbi Pitsie Avram (far right, with white beard) with his wife, Sara, and son, Nissan, Gaisinsky (center), 1920s. *Courtesy of Esther Goldman Grossman.* BELOW: Post card of the steamship *Braga*, which brought the Caprove family to America. Isaac purchased it in 1923, signed his name across it in Russian, and intended to mail it to his brother-in-law Itzie Stumacher.

Moishe Caprove, the older brother of Isaac, as a decorated soldier in the tsar's army during WWI.

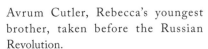

Avrum Cutler, Rebecca's youngest brother, taken before the Russian Revolution.

The wedding of Bessie Cutler and Ben Baker in August 1925, New York City. Top row, from left to right: Avrum Cutler, Ben Baker, Bessie Cutler Baker, Ruby Stumacher, Daniel Cutler. Second row from top, left to right: Channa (Anne) Caprove, Isaac Caprove, Fay Cutler, Slova (Sluva) Ova Denka Cutler, Max Kaplan, Sheva (Bessie) Cutler Kaplan, Sarah Cutler, Itzie Stumacher. Third row from top, left to right: Beryl Caprove, Sunny Caprove, Rebecca Cutler Caprove, Yunkel (Jacob) Cutler, Esther Moser Cutler, Molly Cutler Stumacher, Kolman Stumacher. Bottom (front) row, left to right: Paul Cutler, Fay Stumacher, Moe Stumacher.

LEFT: Bossie Stumacher (Berta Weinshell in America), Barney's stunning sister, in a town hall opera program in New York City, dated January 23, 1926. Bossie was arrested with Barney for holding false passports in Bucharest, Romania. *Courtesy of Blossom Batt Linder and Lisa Linder Danziger.* BELOW: Itzie Stumacher's house in Belaya Tserkov, 1911. The second door was a rental apartment where the Caprove and Cutler families stayed after fleeing Stavishche during a 1919 pogrom. *Courtesy of Marsha Kaufman.*

ABOVE: Channa "Anne" Caprove in America as a teenager during the Roaring Twenties. BELOW: Esther Moser Cutler and Yunkel (Jacob) Cutler, shortly after their arrival in America, 1920s. *Courtesy of Hy Kaplan.*

Passport of the Caprove family, 1923.

Russian writing on the Caprove family's 1923 passport.

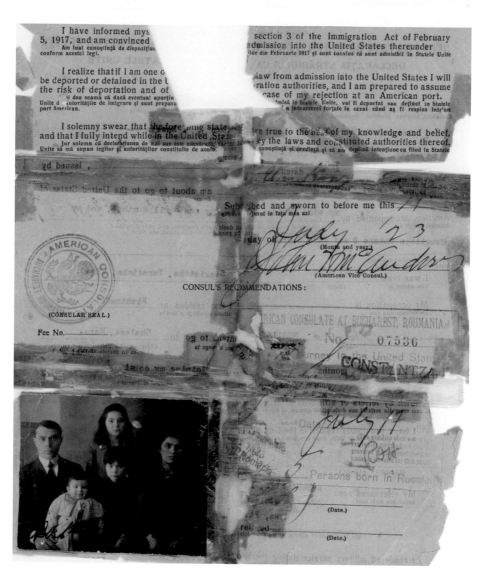

ABOVE: Passport photo of the Caprove family, 1923. BELOW: detail from passport.

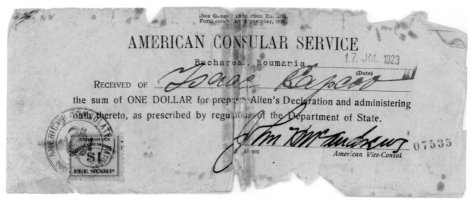

ABOVE: Isaac Caprove's receipt for one dollar, for preparing the Alien Declaration and administering the oath. Issued by the American Consular Service in Bucharest, Romania, and dated July 17, 1923. BELOW: Isaac Caprove in New York City, circa 1924–1925.

ABOVE: Rebecca Cutler Caprove in
New York City, circa 1924–1925.
RIGHT: Barney Stumacher in 1921.
Courtesy of the National Archives.

From the List of Jews in Tarashchansky Uyezd.
The list was compiled in 1882 and updated in 1893, because there were severe restrictions for Jews living in rural areas such as Skibin, where the family was living illegally. Updated in 1893, it states: Urban Commoner of Skvira, Kelman Shimonov Kotlyar, his wife, Feyga Berkova. Their children: Shalum, Jankel ("Yunkel"), Hiya, Sura, Rivka ("Rebecca"), Mariyam ("Molly"). (Daughter Sura died as a child; the two youngest children in the family weren't born yet.)

Rebecca's sister Molly Cutler (Stumacher) with
Isaac's sister Rosa Caprove, Stavishche, before WWI.

Bessie Cutler, circa 1921–1922. The inscription on back reads in Russian: "I am sending you my picture. Keep it, and never forget. From me, Bessie Cutler."

Avrum Cutler (pictured on the right) in his Russian army uniform, circa 1916. At left is believed to be his oldest brother, Shalum Cutler (Kotlyar), who remained in Kiev. *Courtesy of the Cutler family of Los Angeles.*

ABOVE: Anne's only child Marcy (in the center) with Anne's two granddaughters: Mindi (at left) and Lisa, the author (at right, with long hair), 2016. *Courtesy of Russ DeSantis Photography.*
BELOW: Cousins Sol Moser and Daniel Cutler (on right, with mustache), who fled Stavishche during the pogroms. They immigrated to the United States in the early 1920s; later that decade they found themselves as American soldiers in the Panama Canal Zone. *Courtesy of Vivian Flamm.*

Murder victim Elek Stepansky. The young blacksmith's murder was witnessed by his cousins Sol, Daniel, and Sarah as the children watched through a window during the Denikin raids in Stavishche in 1919. His widow and two surviving children fled to Argentina. *Courtesy of Elba Muler de Fidel.*

Sunny Caprove and Harry Usatch on their wedding day in 1938.

Max "Little Moshe" Zaslawsky holding the Stavishche Torah Crown in 2005. In 1920, his grandfather, Rabbi Pitsie Avram, saved the crown from the ark of the burning synagogue in Stavishche that was torched by pogrom bandits. *Courtesy of Marcy Brahin.*

Isaac Caprove as a soldier in the tsar's army, 1911.

ABOVE: Anne and Ben, taken at Sunny and Harry's wedding in 1938. LEFT: The author Lisa on her wedding day with her grandmother Anne, 1983. *Courtesy of Allan Goldberg, Coachman Studios.*

ABOVE: Anne and Ben in Philadelphia, late 1940s. *Courtesy of Marcy Brahin.* RIGHT: Anne and Ben on the day of their marriage, 1936.

The headstone (left) and footstone of the heroic Stavishche rabbi Yitzhak Avraham Gaisinsky ("Pitsie Avram"). The grave is located at the Old Montefiore Cemetery in Queens, New York, in the First Stavishter Benevolent Association Section. He died in March 1942 after being struck by a taxicab while crossing the street in the Bronx. *Courtesy of Dr. Ira Levitan.*

ABOVE: Rebecca Cutler Caprove and daughter Channa, Stavishche 1912–1913.
BELOW: Birth record of Sunny Caprove in the Stavishche metric book of 1916.
Born July 22, 1916, in Stavishche. Father: Ayzik Berkov Koprov, urban commoner of
Talnoe, mother Rivka-Kelmanova. Child Sura Leah. Marriage certificate not submitted.

Pogrom Death List (partial) in Hebrew found in the original manuscript *Megilat Ha-tevah* by Eliezer David Rosenthal. Listed are murder victims of Zhelezniak's gang in Stavishche, June 1919. Translation into English appears in Appendix D. *Courtesy of Gnazim Archive.*

Isaac Caprove's three sisters, from left to right: Shifka, Rosa, and Piya (Pollya) with their sister-in-law, Rebecca Cutler Caprove (seated at right), Stavishche, 1911.

ABOVE: A likeness of a childhood portrait from the 1850s of Count Wladyslaw Branicki, the last Branicki nobleman to own Stavishche, known for his generosity and kindness. *Courtesy of Count Paul Potocki.* BELOW: Haika Stepansky Moser and Itzie Moser, parents of Sol, who owned the bakery in Stavishche. Haika was the aunt of the famous blind cantor, Leaper the Blinder. Taken in Stavishche before the Revolution. *Courtesy of Vivian Flamm.*

UPPER LEFT: Channa (Anne) Caprove as a teenager in America. BELOW RIGHT: The Stavishche Torah Crown, discovered in a New Jersey Synagogue in 2005. Rabbi Pitsie Avram saved the antique relic from the ark of the Stavishche synagogue as it was burning after being torched by pogrom bandits in 1920. *Courtesy of Marcy Brahin.*

LOWER LEFT: Cantor David-Yosel Moser of Stavishche, circa 1916. The chazzan died beside his burning Torah during a 1920 pogrom. *Courtesy of Hy Kaplan.*

ABOVE: Back row, left to right: Isaac, Rebecca, and Bessie. Front row, left to right: Beryl, Channa, and Sunny, circa 1924, New York City. BELOW: Chiah Sura Postrelka Spivack of Stavishche, at left, circa 1910. She was a healer, schmaltz maker, and goose feather collector (for bedding) of the shtetl. At right is her son Leib Spivack, who was drafted into the Russian army during WWI and taken Prisoner of War in Germany. His heartbroken family never saw or heard from him again. *Courtesy of Emily Bayard.*

Isaac got a job as a baker's assistant, working the evening shift helping bake doughnuts. He was paid thirty-five dollars a week, which, to him, was a fortune. Soon, he learned how to bake them himself, and in the mornings he and another man would go out delivering the doughnuts to their customers. Isaac never had a night off, but his family enjoyed enough doughnuts to feed an army—powdered, jelly, and chocolate. At first they could not get enough of them, but after a while, they were as unappealing as the tomato herring, and the family begged him not to bring home any more doughnuts!

Channa and Sunny loved going to school—they attended PS165 in Brooklyn. At first, the teachers didn't know where to place eleven-year-old Channa. She began the year in the first grade, but after just six months, she was quickly moved up to the sixth grade. The teachers kept an Italian boy after class with her, and they'd drill both children on how to pronounce the letters w and v so that they'd sound more American. Channa was fortunate to have had such dedicated teachers.

Her favorite part of school was recess. The kids were taken to an empty lot to play dodgeball and pegs. When she returned to the apartment one afternoon after a dodgeball game, Channa found her father sitting at the table, looking very solemn. It had been a year and a half, and his boss could no longer keep him on as an apprentice; he would have to join the union as a baker. A union man would have to be paid twice the salary as an assistant, and his boss didn't want to pay the higher salary. He'd found a new immigrant to take over her father's job; Isaac was crushed.

Shortly after losing his job, a letter arrived from Kiev from Rebecca's brother Shalum Cutler; the timing couldn't have been worse. He wrote to Isaac that he had an opportunity to come to America with his wife and all their children, and he wanted to ask his brother-in-law's opinion if he should come to the United States or stay in Kiev. Shalum knew that he would not get an unbiased answer from his own siblings; over the years he had grown to deeply respect Isaac and knew that he would be truthful with him.

It is ironic that Isaac's first experience with Shalum began with that fateful letter back in 1909 that Shalum had written to Rebecca, warning her against marrying him. Fifteen years earlier, he had meddled in the love affair of his sister and her fiancé; now Shalum was putting the future of his own family in the hands of Isaac. Isaac, who was going through a terrible time in his life after losing his job, wrote back to Shalum, saying that if things weren't so bad in Kiev, he'd be better off staying there.

Shalum Cutler never did come to America, and nobody in his family ever saw him again. When Rebecca's siblings discovered that Isaac had advised Shalum to stay in Kiev, there was a terrible rift in the family. Eventually Rebecca's family forgave her husband, as they came to understand how rough his life had become since losing his job. A certain ache remained in all their hearts, though, as they truly longed to be reunited with their family from Europe.

Isaac continued to worry about how he would support his family and reached out to his cousin Sonny Vinokur, who had immigrated to Toronto, Canada. Sonny's father was the brother of Isaac's mother, Sarah Leah Vinokurov Caprove. He received a six-page reply in Yiddish from his cousin, as well as good wishes from a group of old friends from Stavishche who sent him encouragement and apparently an invitation to move to Canada. Only the last page of this poignant letter has survived, which had the Toronto addresses of his cousin, who by then called himself Mr. S. (Sayner) Winniks, and his friend from Stavishche, Mr. Mirotchnik.

On the other side of the addresses was the last page of the letter, written by his cousin and his friends from the Old Country. The translation read:

> . . . my speech is easier (in Yiddish). Be well, all of you. May my letter find you all in the best of health. . . . This is your friend Yankel Mirotchnik and my wife Frehme and our son Kharving (Irving). I greet you, Isaac, and your wife Revka and your dear children. My wife and I wish you the same as we do for ourselves and our husbands and wives and children, and your Sayner (Sonny) and his wife and children; also (sending regards are) Halle Riven and his wife and children. All send greetings. You will not be embarrassed when you come to Toronto. I am sending you my address so that you can write to me.

As it turned out, though, Isaac and his family were not destined to move to Toronto. Avrum Cutler's father-in-law, Myer Ova Denka, once the famous boot maker for the tsar of Russia, had resumed his business of manufacturing shoes in Philadelphia. When he heard that Isaac, once a shoemaker in Stavishche, needed a job, he offered him employment. Rebecca packed up everything that they owned, and in just a few days, at the end of August 1925, they set out for Philadelphia. Money was so tight that Rebecca had to borrow funds from her landslayt to pay the movers. The family rented a tiny house located at 627 Mercy Street. This is where their new life began.

PART IV

REBECCA AND ISAAC'S CHILDREN

SELECT STORIES IN PHILADELPHIA 1926–1941

CHAPTER TWENTY-TWO

STRUGGLING IN
THE GOLDEN LAND

1926–1930

More than anything, Channa, Sunny, and Beryl longed to be Americans. Like thousands of other young Jewish immigrants who fled Europe, they strived to become "Americanized." They did not want to be associated with the Old Country: their desire to blend in as Americans took precedence over everything else. Sunny and Beryl, who were only seven and two when they first arrived in the United States, had an easier time learning English than Channa did at eleven. But so determined was Channa to master the language, she took special elocution classes at night. She wanted to sound like a natural-born citizen.

"I want an American name," Channa proclaimed to her English teacher. "From now on, call me Anne." From that day forward, Channa began permanently using this Americanized version of her name.

Anne's greatest fear, aside from her claustrophobia, was being identified as a "greenhorn," a new immigrant who was unfamiliar with American ways. She and her siblings didn't converse in Yiddish with their new American friends at school, because that was the language they used in Stavishche, where they had suffered a great deal. And Anne certainly didn't want to be fixed up with a green-horn, despite her mother's best efforts. In fact, she almost died of embarrassment the time that her mother set her up on a blind date with the son of one of her new immigrant friends. As a dutiful daughter, she felt obligated to go, but was embarrassed to be seen out with him. She was only interested in American boys.

Her parents were not successful in integrating into American society. Rebecca deliberately chose to socialize with people with whom she could converse with in Yiddish. She befriended and played cards with a group of Jewish ladies from Russia and Ukraine. Rebecca even shopped on an Old World street in Philadel-phia, reminiscent of the open marketplace in Stavishche. There, she walked by rows of wooden cages crammed with live chickens. Like her mother before her, she stopped to feel the *pulkies** beneath their feathers, to see if they were plump enough to eat. The kosher butcher would then remove the bird of her choice and take it in the back and slaughter it.

Isaac did not integrate any better than his wife. Every morning on his way to work, he walked alone to shul, where he enjoyed the company of his fellow landslayt. The men prayed together in Hebrew and kibitzed in Yiddish. In busi-ness, he learned to communicate with his American customers by using ges-tures. Like many other Yiddish-speaking immigrants, he playfully coupled any English words or names that he learned with nonsensical ones. The silly rhymes were endless: crazy-schmazy, bird-shmird, ridiculous-smikulus, blood-shmud, Masha-kasha, here-shmere, vodka-schmadka.

In Philadelphia, Isaac's new job didn't last. So he opened a little shoe repair shop of his own and worked long hours. Most of his business came to him on weekends, so for the first time in his life, he had to give up observing the Sab-bath. For the grandson of a Stavishche rabbi, working on Shabbos, the day of rest, was a huge sacrifice. His morale was not helped by the fact that despite working on the Sabbath, his family barely survived living above the poverty line.

Isaac's Saturdays were only made brighter by the arrival of his skinny nine-year-old daughter, Sunny, who walked the few blocks to his workplace carrying a pail filled with sandwiches. Sometimes she would surprise him with a small slice

---

* *Pulkies* refers here to the drumsticks of chickens, although some use this Yiddish word to describe the legs of chickens. Others use the word to describe a person's thighs, usually with affection when referring to chubby babies.

of *kapchonka*, his favorite smoked whitefish, which was salty and bony.* To Sunny, it looked something like haddock, but to Isaac it was a popular Sabbath treat from his boyhood that was fished from the many ponds surrounding Stavishche.

Sunny was content spending Saturdays by her father's side, often sharing both lunch and dinner with him. She performed menial chores, like sweeping the shoe shop, probably hoping to avoid spending her days with her mother.

Living in America was hard for Rebecca. There was never enough money, and she carried the burden of scrimping and saving from what little she was given to run the household. On Shavuot of 1926, the constant stress of having to stretch a dollar finally caused her to snap. Rebecca was looking forward to baking her holiday specialty—cherry *varenikes*. While preparing to fill the *kreplach*-looking dough pockets that were shaped like half-moons, Rebecca discovered that the pound of cherries she had saved up for was half gone. Sunny was hungry and had helped herself to the luscious fruit, causing her mother to explode and run after her. Isaac, who was now thirty pounds lighter than his wife, was forced to intervene.

Channa, now calling herself Anne, had seen enough. Witnessing her mother's meltdown coupled with the vision of her empty kreplachs abandoned on the kitchen table sealed her decision. As the oldest daughter, she would go to work. Anne had always been tall for her age, and at five feet five inches, she knew that she looked older than thirteen. The young teen saw an ad in the newspaper for a summer position. They needed someone to sew tickets onto clothing using a Singer sewing machine at a men's clothing factory. Her mother had an old Singer machine, and Anne had seen how it worked, so she applied for the job.

When she got there, their Singer machine was a factory model and was nothing like her mother's. They handed her long strips of paper with numbers on them to sew onto the garments that came from the same dye lots. The suits were in pieces and piled forty or fifty high. There were stacks of front lapels, back lapels, pockets, sleeves, and pants, and she was expected to sew numbers on each section so that the exact shades would match when they finally pieced the garments together. Anne made lots of errors but was so determined to get it right that a few of her new coworkers took pity on her and showed her what to do. She'd use both hands—one to hold the garment down and put the

---

* Some refer to kapchonka as a specific type of whitefish, while others say it's the way in which the fish is prepared.

ticket on, and the other to press and tear it off. She'd then move very quickly on to the next piece.

When Anne turned fourteen, she decided not to return to school. Before leaving, she had to fill out paperwork to prove her age. Her devoted teacher, who already knew the dismal life that she would face as a young factory worker, begged her not to drop out. She told her favorite student that she had so much promise. "Don't leave school—finish," she pleaded with her. "You have so much to live for, and you're still so young." But Anne was determined. She had learned how to make a dollar, and that was all that mattered.

The law required young dropouts to attend a continuation school every Thursday evening. It was a vocational school at Thirteenth and Spring Garden Streets. There, the teenagers learned personal hygiene and home economics. They were even given some classes on grammar and art.

Anne worked at a number of factories, but always longed for a better job. There was an opening at the Middishade Clothing Company that manufactured men's suits. The *Saturday Evening Post* used to run impressive ads for the company's specialty, Blue Serge Suits. It was a large firm with many departments, and they hired the girl to print all their tickets. Anne eventually became the head of their ticket department.

She soon had friends in every department, including the forelady of the pants division upstairs, who had a lot of pull in the company. She was an attractive blonde divorcee who was having an affair with one of the bosses. Each day over lunch Anne caught an earful of the lurid details of the goings-on behind the scenes. However, what interested her most was the forelady's advice on how to make herself indispensable to the firm by learning how to manage everything in the company.

Anne took her friend's words to heart. By the time the Great Depression hit, she had landed a position in the main office as head of the payroll department. From there, the teenager moved on to the shop office where she learned how to operate all the machinery. Soon after, she became an expert on working the dreaded tabulating system. Anne could shoot the cards out so fast that the bosses amused themselves by using her as an example to others how quickly a pair of human hands could move. She'd then sit down at a desk to print out and divide the long sheets of paper and start comparing all the numbers. Staring at those figures day in and day out made her crazy.

In 1930, the Depression took its toll on the once-prosperous Middishade Company. The firm began the year with 120 employees on their payroll and ended it with eight. Anne was one of the eight. They shipped her from place to place within the business: she could run everything. Anne didn't understand why one of the big bosses, Sonny, always enjoyed needling her so. There was a list of people being laid off, and he called her into his office.

"So and so is going," he said to her. And he ended it with, "You're lucky; you've got a job."

She said right back to him, "Look, I'll always eat. If I can't work with you, I'll be a waitress. In fact, I'd like to be a waitress."

And he answered her, "A waitress—that's a maid!"

Anne retorted, "I don't give a damn what it is. I'm going to make a living, and I'm going to eat. You don't threaten me."

There were times that the workload was so great that the teenager slept there in the bins. They never paid her overtime, but she was desperate to hold on to the job. Anne's father earned a dismal income from his shoe shop, and he depended on the couple of dollars that she would contribute each week. Even though Anne later felt that she should have been more generous and given him more, he was so proud of his oldest daughter.

After the layoffs, those who remained were spread across the building. Anne's desk was downstairs, where she worked under a light most of the time. Behind her was the shipping department. The doors opened constantly while they were shipping orders, and the wind constantly blew on her. As a result, she became ill. The fourteen-year-old menstruated for a month straight.

Anne went from doctor to doctor. Finally, an elderly practitioner was the first doctor to take down a complete history of her life and where she worked.

"Were you out with a man?" he asked. "Maybe you had a miscarriage."

She said, "I've never been with a man."

The doctor finally concluded that Anne was severely overworked and that her young body needed a rest. "Go to the country for a month and do nothing but relax. It's the only way that you'll get better."

Anne spoke to Mr. Johnson, who was the head of the department, and told him that she was ill and needed to take some time off. She asked, "Is my job secure when I come back?"

He said, "Of course, without a doubt."

So, she took her doctor's advice and went away to a friend's house in New Jersey to recuperate. After a few weeks, she was feeling better and went back to work. Anne didn't call in advance to tell them that she was coming in and was shocked to find upon her return another girl sitting at her desk.

She went to see Mr. Johnson. "Anne, I don't know anything. You didn't call and give me any notice that you wanted to come back to work." She was then called to the main office. There was a new general officer named Winston. She didn't know him; he didn't know her. He said to her, "Are you Anne Caprove?"

"Yes."

"You worked here?"

She said, "Yes, for years."

Anne guessed that he knew the story behind her leaving. "You just can't go off and then come back in and say that you want your job. You should have given us notice. You went away, and we have someone else replacing you."

Anne said, "So what does that mean—that I don't have a job?"

He answered, "I can't promise you anything. We'll let you know."

When Anne left, she couldn't stop crying. She ran the few short blocks to her father's shoe shop and cried in his arms. Her papa's soothing embrace was a familiar place of comfort to her. Even during the worst times in Europe, his loving words always gave her the strength to go on. Isaac knew how to exude calmness; whether they were fleeing for their lives or burying baby Fay, he was Anne's rock. Now, at the age of eighteen and just four years after dropping out of the eighth grade, she suddenly found herself out of a job along with many others who suffered during the Depression. Once again, she sought comfort in his arms.

As always, Isaac's gentle words reassured her. "Don't worry, my child," he told her. "We'll eat; you'll eat, too."

CHAPTER TWENTY-THREE

THE STORY OF ANNE AND BEN

1935

"The ad says the millinery department is up on the fourth floor," Anne said to her friend Matilda. Dressed to the nines, the two young women turned heads as they walked through the main floor of Strawbridge & Clothier. When Anne looked up from the first level and eyed the moving stairway, her body began to shake. Her face turned pale and her breathing became labored: she knew it was the start of a panic attack.

"Anne," Matilda asked, "are you all right?"

"When did they replace the stairs?"

"They put in an escalator a few years ago."

She took a moment to regain her composure but couldn't bring herself to set foot on it. "How about we go over to Bonwit Teller and take a look at that other hat? We can use your employee card and get a discount."

"The hat at Bonwit is twenty-five dollars, even with my discount. You'll have to use all of your winnings. But you'll sure look swell when Ed takes you to the wedding."

"I'm not going with Ed."

Matilda was startled: this was news to her. For two years Anne had been dating Ed Silverglade, a handsome champion wrestler from New Jersey in the 175-pound class. As a three-state Ping-Pong champion of New Jersey, New York, and Pennsylvania, Ed was also well-known on the table tennis circuit, which is how Anne, also an accomplished Ping-Pong player, met him.

Why did they separate? One of Anne's girlfriends was getting married. Anne was asked to be a bridesmaid and Ed an usher. Scheduled on the same evening as the wedding was a table tennis tournament in Asbury Park, New Jersey, chaired by Ed. She told him that he should let someone else take over the tournament that night, but he refused. Anne was extremely upset and gave him an ultimatum: if he attended the ping pong competition that evening, they were over. She made him choose between their relationship and his commitment to sporting events: Ed chose the tournament.*

Matilda, however, eyed this as an opportunity to set Anne up with her friend Ben Kravitz. Matilda was like a sister to Ben, and she decided it was time that he settle down and find a wife. She introduced the couple on the night of the big table tennis tournament at the Adelphia Hotel, where Anne was scheduled to compete in the finals for the Women's Championship of Philadelphia. Matilda, knowing that Anne's anxieties prevented her from learning how to drive, called her friend to tell her she was going to pick her up to take her to the hotel.

Matilda had Ben drive, and it was in her father's borrowed car that she introduced the couple. Ben took an instant liking to Anne; he told her that she was a beautiful Russian girl. Anne thought he was presentable, but she wasn't looking for romance; she was on the rebound. Ben, too, had suffered heartbreak a number of times: he had abandoned a prestigious scholarship at the National Farm School near Philadelphia in search of his first sweetheart Bebe, the love of his life who married another man for his money as soon as the Depression

---

* Ed had an elderly relative who did attend the wedding, and being an immigrant, she was unfamiliar with American customs. That night when the bride and groom opened their gifts, they found that she had taken one of Ed's prized state trophies, wrapped it up, and gave it as a wedding present. She probably thought that Ed would never miss it.

Long after Anne's public engagement to Ben, the phone continued to ring; Ed Silverglade was calling, but she never acknowledged him again. Anne had cared for him deeply but felt that she could not depend on him. After her marriage to Ben, the sports section of their morning newspaper often mysteriously disappeared; Ben would see Ed's picture in the paper and didn't want his wife to read about her former flame.

Years later, Rebecca heard that Ed had married and became a Trenton police officer. His unyielding dedication to sports paid off as he became the director of health, education, and welfare for the city of Trenton, New Jersey, and a founder and the executive director of the Police Athletic League. Later he became an Olympic boxing official and the manager of the US Boxing teams in the 1980 and 1984 Olympic Games.

hit. His heart was soon warmed, rebroken, and then warmed again by a bevy of beauties, including Myrtle, a fashion model who appeared in newspaper ads. Ben was actually quite fond of her, but her dysfunctional family played a significant role in their breakup. It was this relationship that had just ended before he met Anne in the fall of 1935.

Ben was twenty-seven and running the meat and delicatessen department in a supermarket on Friday and Saturday evenings. He worked there as a bookkeeper and cashier and was making twenty-five dollars a week, which, in the height of the Great Depression, wasn't bad.

He was also a former athlete but was forced to give up a promising baseball career that began well before his fifteenth birthday, when he was a star pitcher for two semipro teams owned by the Reading Railroad in Atlantic City and the Yellow Cab Company in Philadelphia. In the mid-1920s, scouts from the Baltimore Orioles were interested in signing him, but his Jewish immigrant mother, Pearl, refused to allow her underage son to attend training camp for the champions of the International League. In her mind, education was far more important than sports. If Pearl had allowed her son to pursue his baseball career, he might have made it into the record books as their youngest player and would have pitched from the same mound where Babe Ruth had briefly gotten his start a decade earlier.*

The week following their introduction, Ben called Anne, now the new Ladies Table Tennis Champion of Philadelphia, and asked her out on a date. It would have to be on Sunday because he worked late on Saturday nights. On that particular Sunday, however, Anne's mother was preparing to go to Brooklyn, New York, to help her sister Bessie, who was expecting a baby. Anne told Ben that she was sorry that she couldn't meet him, because as the oldest daughter, it was her responsibility to run the household in her mother's absence. He asked if he could call her again and she said, "Sure."

Just as she put the receiver down, the phone rang again; this time it was her friend Belle Jacoby. "Anne, what are you doing tonight?"

"Nothing special, I'm staying home."

"Why don't you join me—there's a dance tonight close to where I live."

Reluctantly, Anne went with Belle to the dance, but immediately regretted her decision. She wasn't accustomed to these types of socials where a man would

---

* In 1914, Babe Ruth was briefly signed to play minor league baseball for the Orioles before heading to the Red Sox.

walk right up to a woman and ask her out onto the dance floor. The men and women didn't have a chance to meet and talk first. All the older and shorter men were asking her to dance; she wasn't interested and kept saying no.

Belle met a nice fellow who spent the entire evening by her side. Anne was about to give up hope of finding a suitable dancing partner, when a good-looking young man approached her and asked for a dance. She finally agreed.

As they took a spin on the dance floor, Anne couldn't help but notice that he was grinning from ear to ear. Unable to contain her curiosity, she asked him why he was so happy.

"Because I just won five dollars," he answered.

"What do you mean?"

"All of these men have asked you to dance, and you didn't want to dance with them, but you danced with me."

As her face became red with indignation, she retorted, "Well, if I had known, I wouldn't have danced with you, either!"

A couple of days later, Ben called again and asked for a date the following Sunday. When Sunny first met him at the front door, she immediately thought he was the perfect man for Anne. On their first date, the young adventurer took her on an airplane ride. She was absolutely terrified, but he dared her to board the plane. The couple took off at the Philadelphia airport, and in a panic, Anne, who had never seen the inside of an airplane before, grabbed hold of Ben's tie so tightly that she nearly choked him to death. She clung to him during the entire flight, and he felt like a hero. Letting her date take her for an airplane ride was scary enough. But it was 1935, before modern safety regulations were implemented . . . what would her mother say?

One evening, the couple was taking a walk on Ritner Street when Ben stopped and pointed to a house, remarking that it was his. He suggested that they go inside. Through the window, Anne could see his mother, Pearl, sitting on the sofa, preoccupied with her knitting. Anne was hesitant to meet Ben's parents—they didn't even know that the couple was dating—but Ben wouldn't take no for an answer. He introduced a very nervous Anne to his mother and told her to take a close look at the young beauty.

Pearl looked up at him questioningly, "What do you mean?"

"Take a closer look. I'm going to marry this girl."

His mother was so taken aback by the sudden news that she dropped her knitting needles.

After she got over her initial shock, Pearl decided that she wanted to learn more about her perspective daughter-in-law's family, and who better to pump for information about a Jewish European family than from their kosher butcher. So, unbeknownst to Ben, his mother went clear across town to pay the butcher a visit, asking questions about the Caprove family. Luckily, the butcher happened to like Rebecca, and not only did he say nice things about the family to Pearl Kravitz, but he also tipped off Rebecca, telling her, "There was a lady here inquiring all about Channa, who must now be calling herself Anne, and your husband, your family and what kind of people you are . . ."

Pearl meant business. In the Old Country, she was a modern woman living in an antiquated world. She was the daughter of Hersh Mindes Saltz, a prominent landowner in Pochayev, in the province of Wolyn. While Hersh devoted himself to the people and charities of his shtetl, including taking on an active role in the Chevra Kadisha,* he was also the owner of a bar. He smuggled goods, including alcohol, from Galicia into Russia with the help of hired hands.

Pearl often assisted the smugglers by distracting the guards at the border. When Ben's mother was not involved in such daring activities, she was a well-respected money lender in her shtetl, continuing with her business even after divorcing her first husband. When Pearl later married Ben's father, Israel Kravitz, a handsome scribe in the tsar's army,† she continued to dabble in her profitable business.

Within a month of their introduction, Anne and Ben found themselves sitting and talking on the parkway in Philadelphia when Ben turned to her and said, "Let's get married."

"What?"

Ben's mother was not the only one to be taken aback by talk of marriage.

Ben was the first man to show such serious interest in Anne. In general, men tended to be intimidated by her. She was twenty-three years old, it was the

---

* Hersh was a member of Pochayev's Chevra Kadisha, a private organization comprised of Jewish men who acted as the shtetl's burial society. It was the responsibility of the Chevra Kadisha to see to it that the bodies of Jews were prepared for burial according to Jewish law. Since tending to the dead is a favor that the recipient cannot return, it is considered to be the greatest *mitzvah* that one can fulfill.

† Israel, who was born in Trostyanets in Podolia, was stationed in Pochayev with the Fifth Group of the Yakutzker Regiment when he met Pearl.

Depression, and she liked to take care of herself. She held a steady job at an ink factory, but it was not enough to support her love of high fashion. To supplement her income, she entered and won two local beauty contests and cashed in on the winnings. Men were scared that they couldn't afford to support her, but Ben wasn't afraid.

Anne weighed her options. She barely knew Ben, but in order to get to know each other more intimately, they had to get married first. Anne was disgusted with all her previous boyfriends, and Sunny was praising Ben to the Lord when he uttered those magical words, "Let's get married."

And so it was that Anne agreed to become Mrs. Kravitz. The couple settled on a date: Thanksgiving Day, November 28, 1935. Most of the country celebrated the holiday at home with their families as President Franklin D. Roosevelt carved the turkey with First Lady Eleanor looking on in Warm Springs, Georgia.

Anne and Ben celebrated rather differently. On Thanksgiving Day, he pulled up in his father's car and they secretly drove to Elkton, Maryland, the elopement capital of the East Coast. Famous for its fast and convenient marriages, they stood in front of the justice of the peace and got hitched. Anne was wearing her elaborate twenty-five-dollar hat as Ben quietly slipped a five-dollar ring on her finger. The justice's wife witnessed the nuptials. They then drove to Atlantic City and only stayed half the night. Afterward, they separated: he went back to his house and she returned to hers. Anne made Ben promise not to tell anyone about their elopement, and he agreed that they would not live together until they had a proper Jewish wedding.

Sunny kept their secret as the couple formally announced their engagement.

In honor of the impending marriage, Rebecca prepared a formal dinner for her future *machatunim* (in-laws). As she served her famous Russian strudel, God only knows what Pearl and Israel Kravitz were thinking when they got their first glimpse of Anne's poor immigrant family. Their humble rental on Mercy Street was so tiny that they didn't even have enough room to invite Ben's siblings.

Pearl and Israel had immigrated to America two decades before the Caprove family and had already established themselves financially in Philadelphia. There were awkward moments between the two families until Israel shared a story over dinner that would break the ice.

"Thirty-five years ago, I left Russia in hopes of making my fortune in America," he said. "For four years, I could not convince my wife to leave Pochayev. Out of desperation, I decided to write her a letter and give her an ultimatum."

"What did it say?" Isaac asked with great interest.

"I threatened that if she didn't come right away to Philadelphia, I would take the first ship to Camden!"

Everyone laughed: Camden was just a short ferry ride from Philadelphia.

"I panicked that I would never see him again," Pearl continued. "I collected as much money as I could that was owed to me by my customers before leaving Europe."

"I had slipped a Blitzstein passenger ticket inside my letter," Israel added.

"Once I landed in America, I took a look around," Pearl said. "What modern, conveniences—it was a new world! I decided to stay awhile."

Anne and Ben's second wedding, which, of course, everyone assumed was their first, was planned for Sunday, March 22, 1936. It would be one of those affairs that no one would brag about. There were many nice restaurants in Philadelphia where they'd feed you a meal, but they were expensive, and Isaac couldn't afford it. Anne's papa wasn't making a decent living as a shoe repairer and was forced to borrow one hundred dollars just to throw the party. He booked a downstairs hall located at Eighth and Mifflin Streets and hired a three-piece band.

The weekend of the festivities, Rebecca's family, the Cutlers, and the Stumachers, arrived in carloads from New York City, and the tiny house was filled to capacity. They all slept on the floor as nobody could afford a hotel room.

Disappointed that the wedding would not be the elaborate affair she dreamed of for her son, Pearl Kravitz decided that she would throw a party herself. The evening before the wedding, Pearl threw a big reception in her fancy house, to which she invited all her own wealthy friends and relatives. Ben, however, had a demanding job and was disappointed when his boss at the supermarket refused to give him Saturday night off. That didn't stop Pearl—she threw the pre-wedding bash without her son, the groom.

In the end, Ben's employers were generous in providing all the potato salad, corned beef, and cold cuts for the fifty wedding guests.* Ben arranged a three-day honeymoon package in New York City. At one of the big nightclubs, the

---

* Now that he was a married man, Ben's employers gave him a raise of two dollars per week.

couple watched comedian Milton Berle perform, followed by radio star Rudy Vallee and his orchestra.*

When Anne and Ben returned home, they were faced with the dilemma of where to live. There was no room at Anne's parents' house, so the newlyweds went to survey the situation over at Ben's house. Pearl and Israel Kravitz owned a large, beautiful home that was well furnished, but their older daughter, Ida, already lived there with her husband and daughter. Ben's younger brother, Milt,† who would often bring around his steady girlfriend, Beatrice Kaplan, also lived in the household.‡

When Ben's father returned home that evening after making the rounds to collect rent from his tenants, Pearl asked him in front of the newly married couple, "Did you get anything today?" She could see on his face that not only did her good-natured husband forgive his tenants' monetary obligations to him, but he also gave them cash out of his own pocket. When he showed up at their doors asking for the rent, he saw firsthand that these families didn't have enough food to eat. It was a typical scenario: Israel Kravitz would rather lose his properties than let his tenants starve. In the United States, Pearl and Israel Kravitz owned a great deal of real estate but lost most of it during the Depression years.

Times were pretty tough, even for Pearl Kravitz.

In the end, Anne and Ben made a home in West Philadelphia, near Anne's friend Belle Jacoby.

Anne later went on to represent the City of Brotherly Love at the Table Tennis State Championships and advanced into the finals. When she looked up into the stands, Ben and Matilda were there once again cheering her on. Anne and her opponent were closely matched and continued to rally back and forth; each player alternated in holding match point. Anne's opponent now held the lead: the audience was silent. A long volley ensued, and Anne tapped the ball, which

---

* By 1936, Milton Berle was already a radio star after appearing many times as a guest on the variety show *The Rudy Vallee Hour*.

† Milt was later a track star and a standout hurdler in the Penn Relays, a national collegiate event.

‡ The day that Anne and Ben returned from their honeymoon, Bea stopped by the house to see Pearl Kravitz. Milt and his sweetheart, Bea, had been seeing each other since grammar school; they had never dated anyone else. Milt worked long hours at the post office, even on holidays, in order to put himself through Temple University; he eyed a future for himself at University of Pennsylvania's Graduate School. He didn't want to put Bea's future on hold while he pursued an education, so he told her that she could date other men. Bea arrived at her future mother-in-law's house crying, "Milt doesn't love me anymore; he wants to drop me." Later on, when Milt returned home, Pearl Kravitz made her youngest son pick up the telephone and tell Bea that she wasn't being dropped. After that, they remained together forever.

touched lightly into her competitor's far corner. The referee, however, who was sitting on the opposite side, missed the call.

"Match!" he declared, and her opponent was crowned the Ladies State Champion of Pennsylvania. The girl who had made it all the way from the little town of Stavishche had to settle for second place.

CHAPTER TWENTY-FOUR

WHEN SUNNY MET HARRY

1937

Anne's younger siblings, Sunny and Beryl, sang beautiful operatic duets together. Sunny was blessed with a rare combination of beauty and talent that did not go unnoticed; a band from Philadelphia asked her to tour the country with them as their lead singer, but Sunny rejected their offer. She eyed other plans for her future.

She was head over heels in love and wanted to marry a young man who had just graduated from the Pennsylvania State College of Optometry. When his Russian Jewish parents saw that the relationship was getting serious, they paid a surprise visit to Rebecca and Isaac without their son's knowledge. "We have put our son through school at great financial sacrifice, and the parents of the girl that he marries will be responsible for setting him up in an office."*

"This is not Europe!" a furious Rebecca yelled. "I'm not selling my daughter! If they marry, there will be no conditions other than that they love each other!" She promptly showed the couple the door and slammed it behind them. Under her breath, an irate Rebecca spouted, "*Zol ze vaksen ze ve a tsibble mit de kopin dreid!*"†

Sunny was mortified.

---

* Much of the information in this chapter was extracted from an interview with Bobby Usatch Katz (see Notes).

† This is a Yiddish insult meaning, "You should grow like an onion with your head in the ground!"

Devastated over the breakup, there was nothing she could do. Over the next few months, Sunny showed little interest in dating or other social activities. One day, a girlfriend asked her to go to a dance held at a synagogue around the corner from the family's home on Mercy Street. She had no interest in attending the dance but went along to accompany her friend.

At this dance, she met Harry Usatch, a tall Jewish boy with thinning blond hair, a long face, and big blue eyes that shined. Harry was instantly drawn to Sunny. But her first impression of Harry wasn't quite as favorable. Thirty years later, their daughter stumbled upon Sunny's diary and read the following entry, written by her mother on the evening that her parents met: "Harry really isn't my kind of person. He is very generous and appears nice, but there is something about him that I don't like and I don't have any interest in seeing him again."

Harry's persistence, however, paid off with another meeting, and Anne and Ben double-dated with the couple. Harry picked them up, and the couple sat in the rumble seat in the back of his fancy new car. Still, Sunny's entries in her diary essentially remained unchanged; she still found Harry to be a little too rough around the edges.

"Now, I haven't changed my mind," she wrote. "He's really not the person for me."

Harry continued to ask Sunny out on dates, and she continued to say no.

Out of desperation, Harry asked Ben's advice on how to win his sister-in-law's affection. Ben took him aside and gave him a lesson on women. "Stop calling her," he advised. "Let her think about why you aren't interested in her anymore."

Ben, of course, was right. After two weeks of being ignored, Sunny began to wonder about him. She missed Harry's attention and finally agreed to date him. When Harry brought Sunny home to meet his mother, Anna, whom he adored, the two women took an instant liking to each other. Nervous but nurturing, it was Anna, not her own mother, who cared for Sunny after she had a tonsillectomy. Anna was warm and loving toward Sunny and wanted Anne's younger sister to marry her little "Hershela."

Years earlier, when Harry's father, David Usatch, left his wife, Anna, and infant son behind in Kiev when he immigrated to America, he did so with the hope of making a better life for his family in the New World. Rumors soon circulated that David took an instant liking to his new homeland; in particular, he enjoyed the company of American women and the bachelor life.

Subsequently, it was the Hebrew Immigrant Aid Society (HIAS), and not David, who brought his wife and child to Philadelphia. When they finally arrived in 1915, Anna Usatch was diagnosed with tuberculosis and was admitted for a long stay at a New Jersey hospital. Three-year-old Harry was sent to live with a foster family while his cigar-smoking father continued to enjoy the perks of single life. Harry was confused in his new environment at the foster home and missed his ailing mother terribly. He was once so desperate to escape that he climbed on a metal heater and out a window, sustaining serious burns.

When David Usatch refused to take back his ill wife and child, a group of local women from HIAS picketed his office and waved unflattering signs in an effort to embarrass him. Their public scheme to humiliate him worked. David took back his young son and European spouse, who had by then given up wearing her *sheitel* (a wig worn by married Orthodox women as a sign of modesty) while recovering at the hospital. Despite their new living arrangements, when twenty-eight-year-old David Usatch registered for the United States draft in June 1917, he signed the government document as a single man with no dependents.[*]

Eventually David and Anna reunited, and the couple had a second child together. David Usatch put his young son to work in his junk business in Philadelphia, having the grade school–age boy drive a truck during the middle of the night. Harry would fall asleep every morning in the classroom, and it was not long before he was asked by his teachers to leave school. He often sat solemnly on the stoop with his young and bright buddies Ike and Irv, who had their friend memorize pages from Webster's dictionary in order to improve his grasp of the English language.

March 13, 1938

On the day of Sunny and Harry's big formal wedding, the rain was relentless. The stress of planning a wedding, combined with poor weather conditions and a major glitch with the floral bouquets, was enough to tip a typically nervous woman like Anna Usatch over the edge. It didn't help matters that the wedding was held on the superstitious thirteenth day of the month. All these factors set

---

[*]   Source: WWI draft registration card of David Usatch, signed by him in Philadelphia on June 5, 1917 (roll 1907610, draft board 8).

Anna off; she disrupted the affair with her emotional outbursts over the flowers. Harry's mother managed to dampen what was already a very wet day. Despite the wedding fiasco, Sunny loved Anna, and was kind and forgiving of her new mother-in-law.

Sunny got pregnant almost immediately. As soon as the newlyweds returned from their two-day honeymoon, Harry's father decided that his junk business could not financially support two households. So he gave Harry a truck and three hundred dollars and sent him off to make a living on his own. Ultimately, Harry became more successful than his own father could ever have imagined. He worked as a metal and rags dealer and later exported used clothing to countries around the world.

Harry's childhood buddies, who sat by his side on the stoop, also became strikingly successful. In May 1963, paper manufacturer Irv Kosloff and attorney Ike Richman purchased a basketball team from Syracuse and relocated the club to Philadelphia; the franchise was renamed the Philadelphia Seventy-Sixers.

Anne looked back fondly on those early days when Sunny and Harry first met. She had no idea that those double dates when she and Ben sat in the rumble seat of Harry's car would mark the beginning of a loving friendship between two families that would span more than seven decades.

CHAPTER TWENTY-FIVE

BERYL

January 1940

Lebn is vi a blits.
Life is like lightning.

The pain and trauma Isaac and Rebecca suffered in Europe left them with scars and memories that would never disappear, but nothing could compare to the blackness that engulfed their small family in Philadelphia when their youngest child Beryl died.

Beryl, known to his friends and basketball teammates* at Southern High School as Benjamin Caprove, is generally remembered more for dying at the young age of seventeen than for how he lived and was loved. The following story is the family's last happy memory of Beryl.

On New Year's Day in 1940, the family gathered, as was their tradition, at Ben's Nickel Inn, the luncheonette that Anne and Ben owned across the street from the high school. They were fortunate to have the place to themselves and sat on the tall stools near the counter drinking hot chocolates and ice cream

---

* Some of Beryl's former classmates believe that he played high school basketball as an underclassman with Red Klotz, who later became, at five foot seven, one of the shortest players in the NBA. The endearing guard also became the coach with the most defeats in history, losing fifteen thousand games to the Harlem Globetrotters.

floats. Beryl showed off the class ring with the ruby-colored stone that Sunny had bought for him, and he talked animatedly about his upcoming winter graduation.

That year, the holiday was particularly special because both Anne and Sunny were new mothers. Sunny had her baby first—a boy named Jerry; Anne followed with a daughter named Marcy. Beryl was enjoying his new status as an uncle.

Once they finished their drinks at the luncheonette, the family headed over to the church next door. The priest gave them a key so that the families could sit in warmth with the babies while having a front-row seat, by a second-story window, to the city's most famous parade. Anne looked on at Beryl's wide grin, dimples, and twinkling brown eyes as he pointed to the flamboyantly dressed mummers marching by; he was apparently enjoying the parade as much as his infant niece and nephew.

Less than two weeks later, on January 13, Beryl's luck took a turn for the worse. While working at Harry's rag shop, Beryl caught two of Harry's employees stealing, and when he confronted them, they roughed him up, throwing him into a baler machine (a large hanger with wire that tied up bales of clothing). Beryl sustained a serious cut on his leg, and when Harry found him, he took him to the hospital, where Beryl received stitches and was then released.

On the evening of this incident, Beryl was scheduled to go on a date with a girl he adored. Despite his weakened condition, he insisted on going. While escorting the girl back and forth on a trolley, Beryl was caught outside during a major snowstorm. As a result of this exposure, he became sick with pneumonia.

When Anne went to visit Beryl at her parents' house the next day, on January 14, he was jaundiced, and she rushed him to Pennsylvania Hospital, across the street from her house on Spruce Street. Each evening after work, Anne rushed to the hospital to see how Beryl was doing, but on the fifth day she was stopped at the door. The building was quarantined because there was a case of scarlet fever, thus limiting entry into the hospital to members of the medical staff and the clergy.

Luckily, Anne happened to be friendly with a nurse at the hospital who took care of her when she gave birth to her daughter Marcy ten months earlier. After finishing her shift each evening, the nurse stopped by Anne's house for coffee and ice cream and gave the concerned sister updates on her brother's condition. To her relief, she was told that Beryl was improving and that the doctors were planning on releasing him soon.

However, Anne's relief turned out to be short-lived. After dinner on January 23, a local rabbi, who was permitted to enter the still-quarantined hospital, stopped by her brother's room and offered to play cards with him. When one of the cards fell to the floor, Beryl bent over to pick it up, resulting in blood rushing to his head, which the family initially believed caused his immediate death.

Beryl's death was sudden and shocking, and the family never really understood what happened to him. Years later, Anne read his death certificate, which stated that the principal cause of death was from a "pulmonary embolism" and the secondary factor was "lobar pneumonia." A blood clot, probably resulting from the injury to his leg, must have traveled to his lungs, which were already in a weakened state due to the pneumonia.

Beryl was the baby of the family, the only child left at home. His death shattered everyone close to him into a million pieces. Each one suffered their own breakdown. Sunny, who was the closest to him, was so devastated that her parents feared that during the funeral she would try to throw herself into Beryl's grave. Their fears were unfounded, but she suffered miserably for an entire year from gastrointestinal problems.

After the funeral, Ben took Anne away to Atlantic City, where the couple started a new business that was already in the works before Beryl was hospitalized. He hoped that the move away from Philadelphia would help his wife heal, but it was difficult being so far from her grieving family.

Her mama and papa stopped functioning and could no longer care for themselves, so Harry moved them into his and Sunny's home and tried to look after them. After Beryl's funeral, Rebecca became so emotionally ill and confused that at times she often forgot where she was. While still struggling during her early days of mourning, she once walked down the street and heard a group of people say, "Oh, here comes a crazy lady."

Isaac became so depressed that he stopped eating and lost a tremendous amount of weight. He didn't know what to do with himself. Harry took Isaac to work with him at the rag shop every day to get his father-in-law out of the house. When Isaac commented one day on the inviting aroma of one of the worker's ham sandwiches, Harry was not about to pass up an opportunity to feed his wife's undernourished father, so he gave him a ham sandwich without ever telling Isaac, the grandson of a rabbi, that he was eating pork. Isaac loved it, and Harry continued to give him a ham sandwich every day.

It wasn't just Beryl's family who grieved over his death. A week after his funeral, Beryl's classmates graduated, but instead of celebrations, an overwhelming feeling of sadness hovered over the commencement exercises at South Philadelphia High School. Even sixty years later, Beryl's classmates recalled how shaken they were by the youngster's sudden death.[*]

Somehow, the family managed to survive 1940. A year later, they found themselves gathered with all of Rebecca's family from New York at Mount Lebanon Cemetery in Philadelphia, this time for Beryl's gravestone unveiling. An unusual eight-foot-tall gray headstone, carved in the shape of a tree with its limbs cut short, was erected at his grave. It symbolized a young life cut down in its prime without ever having the chance to grow.

As Anne stood there, she could not help but think back to that happy day eighteen years earlier, when everyone celebrated her brother's brit milah in the yard in Kishinev. Her papa held Beryl proudly before the crowd, overjoyed that he finally had a son, a Kaddish. Now underweight and frail, her father stood by his beloved son's graveside; he put on his pair of round spectacles as he opened to the last page of his prayer book. With all his loved ones by his side, Isaac slowly began to recite the words of the Kaddish, in memory of his only Kaddish.

---

[*]   Life continued for these boys, and many of Beryl's friends were soon drafted and fought overseas during World War II. Even many of the physicians and nurses from Pennsylvania Hospital served in the war. The young doctor who signed Beryl's death certificate, Garfield G. Duncan, served as a lieutenant colonel and advised General Douglas MacArthur on malaria suppressive therapy. After the war, he became a leading expert and author on the treatment of diabetes mellitus.

PART V

RABBIS AND REUNIONS
1941–1950

RAINBOWS
1925 AND 2003

CHAPTER TWENTY-SIX

RABBI PITSIE AVRAM IN THE BRONX

While a child is still in the womb a light burns above its head. The fetus is able to see from one end of the world to the other. It learns the entire Torah. But as it enters into the air of the world, an angel comes and strikes it directly above the mouth and makes it forget the entire Torah.

—Babylonian Talmud, *Niddah* 30B

1941–1942

The old rabbis of Stavishche relied on this ancient story to persuade their restless young grandsons to study Torah instead of frolicking in the fields on hot summer days.

In all probability, Rabbi Yitzhak Avraham Gaisinsky, known to everyone as Rabbi Pitsie Avram, must have shared a similar tale with his own son and grandsons.

A brilliant scholar of Gemara (part of the Talmud) and Shulhan Arukh (Code of Laws), Yitzhak Avraham was the fourth generation of his family to represent Stavishche as its spiritual leader and decision maker. His warm and friendly demeanor, combined with his self-assurance and determined strength, won the hearts of all those who knew him. Rabbi Pitsie Avram firmly believed that God looked after him, and in return for this divine protection, he felt a keen sense of responsibility to represent his people and to look after them. In this respect, he was remarkably successful.*

After narrowly escaping the fires in Stavishche in June 1920, Rabbi Pitsie Avram and his wife, Sara, fled the shtetl with another grandson in tow, eight-year-old Laizer Spector. The child had become separated from his widowed mother, Libby, and younger sister, Nina, during an earlier pogrom when the family fled into a forest. Pitsie Avram and Sara brought the boy to England, where they lovingly cared for him.†

Soon after Pitsie Avram's arrival in England, he secured a position as a rabbi at the prestigious Philpot Street Synagogue in East London. He is pictured in a poignant photograph taken there during the Yom Kippur holiday of 1922.‡

Laizer grew up in England under Pitsie Avram's care and close tutelage and decided from a young age that he wanted to follow in his grandfather's footsteps and become a rabbi. He did not stray from what was to become his genealogical destiny: not only was his maternal grandfather descended from a long line of Jewish spiritual leaders, but his late father was Rabbi Aryeh Judah Spector and his paternal grandfather was the respected Rabbi Israel Nissan Spector of Zhivotov.

On July 28, 1925, the eve of his bar mitzvah, Laizer wrote a story in a careful Hebrew script describing his grandfather's powerful religious influence on him. Although the child did not provide a source for the story on his paper, the tale can be summed up as follows: There were three merchants who were in the

---

* Pitsie Avram's only son among six children was a rabbi and an honored merchant in a nearby shtetl. Pitsie Avram's oldest grandson, Moise Haissinsky, was born in 1898, nearly forty years before the birth of his youngest grandson, who was also named Moshe. Pitsie Avram had brought the elder Moise to Stavishche as a boy from his home in Tarashcha to become a rabbi, but instead he became a brilliant scientist. The elder Moise earned a PhD in chemistry and was a well-known physicist and radiochemist. According to *Rossiyskaya Evreiskaya Entsiclopediya*, he eventually settled in Paris, working at the Curie Laboratory. He later became the director of France's National Center for Scientific Research.

† The reason why Pitsie Avram chose England is unknown. Most likely, it was easier to gain entrance into England than America at that time. Pitsie Avram and his wife were among many Stavishchers who fled to Great Britain.

‡ Very little else is known about Pitsie Avram's impressions of, and adjustment to, life in England.

woods upon the entrance of the Sabbath. Two of them decided to go on with their journey and they came to a bad end; the one who remained in the woods was protected by a bear because he observed the Sabbath.

The proud grandfather marked the child's paper with his personal seal of approval—a stamp bearing his name as rabbi of the Philpot Shul.

As the years passed, Laizer thought often about the fate of his young mother, Libby. Unknown to Laizer, after Libby lost sight of her son, she and her daughter (Laizer's sister), Nina, traveled from one location to another in Ukraine, desperately seeking refuge. Finally, in June 1923, the resilient thirty-seven-year-old and her young daughter showed up in Kharkov, probably on the doorstep of one of her sisters, Golda or Fruma.*

Libby tried applying for an international passport, which would enable her to leave for America, but she was unable to obtain a visa to enter the United States, probably due to the same heavy quota restrictions to which the Caprove family had been subjected.

So was it fate, destiny, or just a dose of old-fashioned luck that instead sent Libby and Nina in the direction of England? A bureau in Moscow granted permission for mother and daughter, easing their way to immigrate to Great Britain.† On November 21, 1923, they left from the port of Libau, Latvia, and landed on the shores of Southampton, England, on December 3, 1923. Later, other Stavishchers would sail from this Latvian port to Argentina, seeking freedom and a better life in Buenos Aires.

A little divine help from the rabbis above may have guided an unknowing Libby toward her son, who was waiting for her in London. Years later, her granddaughter Shirley recounted that "the family had lost contact for many years and according to Laizer, they met by an amazing coincidence, neither party having any knowledge of the others' whereabouts."‡

---

* Tucked inside of a small pocketbook that Libby had filled with her personal letters, documents, photos, and mementos, her granddaughter Patricia Ricardo Bezalel found her Russian passport. This enabled the author to retrace Libby's journey from Russia (Ukraine) to England.

† Although this cannot be confirmed, there was probably an official reason why Libby (or any other passport holder) had to communicate with a bureau in Moscow in order to obtain permission to leave for England.

‡ The author was unable to uncover any more information regarding the incredible circumstances of the reunion between mother and son.

The Goldene Medina

After being reassured that his grandson was safely reunited with his mother and sister, and knowing that the child was well on his way to becoming a rabbi in London, Pitsie Avram and Sara made the long pilgrimage to America, sailing from England to New York, where they landed on June 19, 1928. The rabbi longed to live closer to his only son, Nissan,* and youngest daughter, Havah (Eva), in America. The couple boarded the SS *Majestic*, carrying with them the precious Sefer Torah from Stavishche, along with its breastplate and two priceless antique silver Torah crowns, transported in oddly shaped cases.

After a brief visit with Nissan in Philadelphia, Pitsie Avram faced the untimely death of his wife. Not long after her passing, the elderly rabbi moved in permanently with Havah in New York, and became the spiritual leader of Agudat Achim Anshei Stavishche in the Bronx.

It was in this reconverted storefront that the resettled landslayt of Stavishche worshipped with the elderly Pitsie Avram at its helm. The precious items that he heroically saved in 1920 from the burning synagogue in Stavishche found their new home in the ark of this synagogue, which stood among several other Jewish houses of worship on 167th Street, just a few short blocks from the family's apartment on Fox Street. The old rabbi conducted services in Hebrew but conversed with his Orthodox congregation in their native Yiddish. Havah, and her husband, David Zaslawsky, were among the regular group of worshippers who sat in the sections segregated by gender, according to tradition.

As in most Orthodox synagogues in its day, the men's section had a superior view of the *bimah* and the ark, with a large window nearby to catch a much-needed breeze. The women's section, on the other hand, was rather stifling; it was located to the side of the building, with no view or window, and was cordoned off from the men's quarter by a drape.

The rabbi reveled in the fact that in his advancing years, he was blessed with one more grandson, a little boy named Moshe.† Pitsie Avram favored his grandson over his lovely granddaughters, for this was a child whom he believed

---

* Shortly after the rabbi's son, Nissan (Nathan or Nicholas), arrived in America in December 1927, it is believed that he had close ties to Congregation Keilas Adas Israel in Philadelphia.

† The boy's mother, Havah (Eva), her husband, and oldest daughter sailed to America on September 1, 1923, the same day that the Caprove family did, but on a different ship. Havah gave birth to Moshe in America in 1937.

would become a rabbi like himself. He took great pleasure in sitting the child on his lap, patiently answering questions from the bright and curious toddler who asked about the *tefillin* on his grandfather's head. The old rabbi envisioned that the boy would become his spiritual heir and welcomed his curiosity. On *Sukkot*, after services, he enjoyed having little Moshe sit next to him every year in the *sukkah*, where they ate herring and walnut bread together. As the revered rabbi's grandson, Moshe had complete run of the synagogue and his grandfather's apartment. As far as the lively four-year-old was concerned, the synagogue was his playground to enjoy.

When the High Holy Days came around in 1941, Isaac and Rebecca decided to return to New York City for the first time since their departure in 1925. Their reasons were twofold: Rebecca wished to visit her ailing brother, Yunkel, in Brooklyn, and Isaac yearned to attend Rabbi Pitsie Avram's Rosh Hashanah services at Agudat Achim Anshei Stavishche in the Bronx.

Rabbi Pitsie Avram, who at eighty-two had been too old to make the long journey to Philadelphia to attend Beryl's funeral, welcomed Isaac to his shul. He sat Isaac in a place of honor, next to his son-in-law, David. During the service, the young shoemaker observed Moshe's antics. Like most children, Moshe became restless in the heat, and started climbing in and out of the window. Nobody dared to stop the boy, for as Rabbi Pitsie Avram's youngest grandson, Moshe was beyond reproach.

It was apparent to all that little Moshe exuded the same confidence as his powerful zeyde. Soon bored of climbing through the window, the four-year-old put on a short *tallis*, covering his head just like the rabbi. He walked up to the bimah behind his old grandfather, who was praying while facing the ark. Little Moshe began praying, too, mimicking Rabbi Pitsie Avram's every move. The rabbi, deep in concentration, did not notice his grandson standing behind him, and only looked up when he heard the laughter of his congregants.

Looking at them curiously, the congregants signaled to the rabbi to turn around, and he caught sight of his young grandson imitating him. The rabbi never stopped praying and neither did Moshe. He smiled warmly at the child and turned the other way, signaling for someone to get his daughter Havah to come and take the child away while he himself continued to *daven*. It took a few minutes for the man to reach the boy's mother, who was sitting in the women's section. By the time Havah arrived to scoop Moshe into her arms, laughter had spread across the entire congregation.

When Havah asked her father's assistant, "Why didn't you stop my son?" he simply shrugged and answered, "He is the rabbi's grandson; he can do whatever he wants." Little Moshe was not reprimanded by his parents, and the old Stavishche rabbi was secretly delighted by the fact that his grandson davened and prayed in his image.

The rabbi's enjoyment of his grandson, though, would be short-lived. On a sunny afternoon in March 1942, Rabbi Yitzhak Avraham Gaisinsky, while walking home from Agudat Achim Anshei Stavishche, was crossing the busy intersection at West Avenue and Fox Street when a taxicab turned the corner and fatally struck him. The eighty-four-year-old rabbi, who two decades earlier earned the respect of the murderous hetmans Zhelezniak, Zeleny, and Denikin while successfully negotiating with them for the lives of Stavishche's four thousand Jews, died from massive injuries on a crosswalk in the Bronx. He rarely looked while crossing a street, believing that God was always with him.

The day that he died, his daughter, Havah, went into hysterics. Later, when she was sitting shiva for the father that she idolized, her three daughters Frannie, Ruthie, and Sylvia "staged a revolution."* Worrying that their young brother Moshe was not receiving an adequate education in English while attending the local yeshiva, they burned his Hebrew school clothes and took him to a barber.

With their larger-than-life grandfather now gone, the girls wasted no time in putting an end to little Moshe's future as an orthodox rabbi. His *payas* was cut, and his sister Sylvia, who was the closest in age to him, lovingly picked up and pocketed her baby brother's curls from the barbershop floor. A child without payas and yeshiva clothing would have to attend a public school; when the children returned home, their grieving mother did not even recognize her own son.

Little Moshe grew up to be a scientist, like his cousin. Showing great promise as a young scholar, his older cousin, the first Moise, met with him once in New York in the summer of 1954 when he was visiting from Paris, where he was soon to become the director of France's National Center of Scientific Research in 1955. The rabbi's oldest grandson wanted to bring his young cousin to study alongside him at the Sorbonne.

Little Moshe, who did not speak French, chose to remain in the United States, where he became a respected nuclear engineer. He worked at Livermore, Los Alamos, the Fermi Lab, the Savannah River Lab, and in Washington, DC, on

---

* The late Max Zaslawsky, the esteemed rabbi's youngest grandson, who is referred to here as "Little Moshe," was a friend of the author who told her about his sisters' rebellion.

a number of programs. At one time he directed a US Israeli Technical Assistance program for the US State Department where he was a guest lecturer at the Technion* on seismic issues and structural engineering. As part of the Technical Assistance Project, he led a group of engineers at both the Technion and Livermore. He was the youngest among a select group of elite scientists representing the United States; many of his elders in this group had worked on the Manhattan Project back in the 1930s. One colleague was a much older Hungarian-born scientist, Edward Teller, known today as "the Father of the Hydrogen Bomb."

The older Moise became one of France's top scientists, and the younger Moshe was a noted scientist in the United States; they were first cousins with deep roots in Stavishche. In Russian, the letter *H* is often replaced with the letter *G*. Related surnames that begin with these letters, such as Gaisinsky and Haissinsky, are often spelled in different ways. It was not widely known to the outside world that the two men were related, since they were decades apart in age and the spellings of the surnames differed within their families.

Neither of the Moshes became a rabbi as their strong-willed grandfather desired, nor did the oldest and youngest grandson of Yitzhak Avraham Gaisinsky ever meet or communicate again as each pursued landmark careers on different sides of the ocean. Instead, the two progenies of the brilliant Stavishche rabbi became leading scientists of their day, each representing countries on opposite corners of the world.

Rabbi Pitsie Avram's magnificent headstone,[†] erected in the First Stavishter Benevolent Association section of the Old Montefiore Cemetery, is befitting a rabbi[‡]; his epitaph is befitting the man. Brushing aside the now overgrown ivy, one can read the Hebrew which states across the top:

---

* This is a science and technology research university in Israel.

† The rabbi's headstone was beautifully photographed for the author by Dr. Ira Leviton of New York City. It was translated from Hebrew into English by Zev Meisels. The rabbi's grave is located at the Old Montefiore Cemetery in Queens, New York. His name was misspelled in English as: I. Goisinsky; he was buried on March 20, 1942, in the First Stavishter Benevolent Association section.

‡ Engraved on the headstone is an eternal flame, a Jewish star/shield of David, and the Luchos, a tablet symbolic of the Ten Commandments.

Man is established from dust
And his end is to dust.

Here lies
The rabbi, the righteous, our teacher
Rabbi Yitzhak Avraham son of Rabbi Yisrael
Gaisinsky

Straight and righteous his path*
The holy flock he led
Loving-kindness and mercy on his tongue
Unyielding as the pit (she'ol) his fear (of God)

Our brothers from death he rescued
Blessed is his memory forever
Chariot of Israel and its rider
He saved Israel from affliction
His rest is in Eden.†

Our beloved father
Died on the 1st day of Nissan
In the year 5702
May his soul be bound in the bonds of everlasting life.
March 19, 1942

To those once led by the great rabbi of Stavishche, the powerful words of the acrostic poem etched across his remarkable headstone rang true. Twenty-three years later, they could not forget the vision of their courageous leader as he calmly gathered his shaken community that was seeking refuge in nearby Vinograd after a brutal pogrom in Stavishche. Pitsie Avram led the long walk in front of his people as they trekked on foot all night through miles of fields. Along the way,

---

*   This stanza is an acrostic poem made from the Hebrew letters of his name.

†   An engraving of two lions, facing one another, follows.

refugees from Belaya Tserkov, Tarashcha, and Lukashifka ran out and followed him and his flock as they headed back home.*

In America, on March 18, 1941, one year before his untimely death, Rabbi Pitsie Avram petitioned for naturalization to become an American citizen. An affidavit of witnesses was completed, and the petition was signed and stamped by both the rabbi and the deputy clerk of the Southern District of New York. Rabbi Yitzhak Avraham Gaisinsky was killed before swearing the oath of allegiance, the final step before obtaining citizenship. On January 3, 1946, nearly four years after the heroic rabbi's death, his petition to become a United States citizen was formally denied.

---

* This was an early pogrom in Stavishche, around April 1919. A group of farmers from Vinograd threatened to exile the Jews who lived in their village if the Stavishche Jews who were seeking refuge in Vinograd did not leave. Pitsie Avram then led the pilgrimage home.

CHAPTER TWENTY-SEVEN

THE EVENTS THAT DEFINED
THEIR LIVES IN THE NEW WORLD

1941–1950

The year 1941 didn't prove to be much happier than the year that preceded it. Ben, after enduring a relentless headache for more than a day, was walking up a flight of stairs to an appointment with his cousin George Shucker, a medical practitioner in Philadelphia, when he was struck by severe pain that paralyzed most of his body.

Conscious, but weak and unable to walk, Ben was athletically fit at thirty-three years old. He used his astounding upper body strength, which he had relied on years earlier to pitch fastballs, to save his life. Using his arms, he crawled up dozens of steps and managed to get to the office. Dr. Shucker and his secretary took one look at Ben and immediately phoned for an ambulance.

Ben's condition baffled his team of doctors. Eventually, they diagnosed him with polio, a disease common in those days that was often associated with sudden paralysis in young, otherwise healthy, patients. On the upside, Ben was sidelined from serving in the war; on the downside, he was confined to bed for more than a year, weak and unable to walk. Anne suddenly found herself with the sole responsibility of caring for an ailing husband, an active toddler, and a hands-on business, which was their only means of financial support.

As the strength in Ben's legs and body slowly improved, doctors wisely suggested that he spend time in the fresh air of the mountains, where work involving physical labor would be therapeutic in his recovery. The couple, with their baby Marcy, took a long drive up to the heart of the Adirondacks and stopped to look around in Lake George, New York, a spectacular resort town famous for its panoramic views, boating, and fishing.

While stopping at a motel in Lake George, his pretty wife went ahead of Ben to inquire about a room for the evening and was told that there was a vacancy; she signaled for her husband and baby to get out of the car and come inside. When Ben approached the office to check-in and pay the bill, the desk clerk took a look at him. Suddenly, the room became unavailable to Jews. This was the first time that Anne ever felt the sting of blatant anti-Semitism in her adopted homeland.

Upset and shaken, the couple got back into their car and kept driving farther north, stopping next in Schroon Lake, a quaint upstate town frozen in time. The town was situated next to a nine-mile body of water with mini beachfronts framed by mountain peaks and tall evergreens. An entire rainbow of colors splashed across the top of the water; the young couple followed its sparkling trail to a little lakefront property where cottages were rented. There they met an elderly white-haired couple, Dr. Ernest Pratt and his wife, Emma, who were relaxing on wooden Adirondack rockers while enjoying the evening's breathtaking view of the lake.* Within days, the Pratts sold Anne and Ben their summer business, which they renamed Marcy's Beachfront Cottages. The fresh air and the tranquility of the mountains helped Ben to rebuild his strength and recuperate from his illness.†

A few years later, Ben received an unexpected phone call from his first love, Bebe, who had broken his heart by choosing another man for his money during the onset of the Depression. This man, who became her husband, had become abusive toward her, and she turned to Ben to come and help her. Anne was shocked but was understanding when Ben dropped the receiver and rushed to his former flame's side. Anne knew that he was simply checking on Bebe's safety and had every intention of returning to his life with her and Marcy, which he did. Anne and Ben remained together for sixty-six years.

---

* Over the years, Ben built many structures on this peaceful property that included a long strip motel, a handful of rustic cabins, and a dock used by fishermen that extended out many feet over the lake. For nearly thirty summers, their customers enjoyed nightly campfires, shuffleboard, table tennis, canoeing, and row boating.

† Years later, after Ben suffered a massive stroke during old age, he insisted that this medical scare in his young adulthood was the result of an aneurysm and not polio as the doctors had suspected.

❖

Weighing heavily on the minds of almost every Jewish family in America during this decade was the lack of information about, and communication from, their loved ones, who remained in the Old Country during the Holocaust years. Isaac and Rebecca had not heard a word from their families in Europe in almost a decade and just prayed that they had survived the war. During her lifetime, Rebecca never heard again from her brother Shalum or her sister Hiya.* She never knew if they had survived or perished during the Holocaust, or if it was simply that they could not trace each other's whereabouts.

Isaac, however, was unyielding in his search for his two sisters, Shifka and Piya (Pollya), who'd remained in Stavishche after he fled Ukraine. During the late 1940s, he had Russian-speaking interpreters from Jewish agencies send out letters to different cities inquiring about their whereabouts. Finally, a glimmer of hope brightened the end of a trying decade.

At Last—Isaac Receives a Letter from Europe!

After an exhaustive search for his sisters, Isaac, at last, heard some news of his long-lost family from Stavishche. In response to his letter sent with the assistance of a Jewish agency worker, Mrs. Esther Friedman, Isaac's niece, the daughter of his younger sister Piya, responded from Simferapool, the Crimea, to Philadelphia, Pennsylvania:

> *January 31, 1948*
> *Dear Uncle, Aunt, and Cousins!*
> *This letter is being written by your niece and cousin whom you do not know, the daughter of your sister Pollya T.—Sophia.*
> *I have no words to express our great joy at receiving a letter from you Esther Friedman. Mama actually cried from joy that she could hardly be calmed down. It's already ten years that we have not corresponded,*

---

* In 2007, four years after Anne's death, her granddaughter Lisa, the author, discovered a page of testimony at Yad Vashem's Hall of Names on Leib Cutler (Kotlyar), a son of Anne's uncle Shalum Cutler. Leib was thirty-seven years old when he was murdered during the Holocaust in Darnitsa, Ukraine, while in the Soviet army in 1941. The testimony was written by Leib's child Kira, who was no longer living at the Kiev address that was given when she had submitted the form ten years earlier. Lisa was unable to locate her.

during which time there have been so many changes, and you most
probably thought that we were no longer alive. But we did not know
anything about your life. Mama often cried as she thought about her only
brother and his family, for whom we have been separated for so long. She
said, "I would be so happy if I only could get a letter from my brother!"
And now this joy has smiled at us. However, when we received your
letter and photographs our joy was doubled. Dear Uncle, you are most
certainly already a grandfather, and Auntie a grandmother.

Sophia updated her family in the United States on their lives in the Crimea.
She wrote about her father's death before the war and the hardships that her
mother faced, having to work to support the two of them despite having a heart
condition. She, herself, signed up for a degree at the Crimean Teacher's Institute
in the Faculty of Foreign Languages in the English Department. She hoped
that after she finished her first year, she would be able to correspond in English.

Sophia wanted Isaac's entire family to know how much her mother wishes she
could see them and asked about the details of their lives in America. In addition,
she wrote Isaac that his sister Shifka, her husband, and their children were living
in Central Asia. Shifka was already a grandmother. Sophia promised to send
her aunt Isaac's letter along with his address in America.

She lives far from us, but of course is closer than you are.

Sophia included Shifka's address in the city of Chardzhou, TSSR (Turkmen
Soviet Socialist Republic).

Dear Uncle, Mama is interested in how Malya, Bassya, and Abram *
are, and where they live. Be well, dears. Mama and I kiss you and all
the children a million times.
Your sister Pollya and niece Sophia, who wish you much happiness,
life, and health; we impatiently await your letter.
"Good bay"†

---

* Sophia is referring to Rebecca's siblings, Molly, Bessie, and Avrum. Pollya was friends with them
in Stavishche.

† These short excerpts of Sophia's letter were translated from Russian into English by David Goldman,
MA. In an attempt to use her newly learned English, Sophia herself misspelled the word "goodbye" in
her letter.

Correspondence continued between the two families; both sides were overjoyed to be reunited, if only by mail. An old black-and-white photo of an attractive young woman was tucked away and saved with this letter. It was a photograph of Sophia, who wrote a sentimental inscription in Russian on the back: "As an eternal and fine memento to my dear uncle, aunt, and cousins. Please keep the photo and please do not forget me or my mother. From your cousin and niece, Sophia." It was dated five months later, on June 7, 1948, an indication that other letters were exchanged after the initial one.

Isaac greatly cherished these letters and photos from his lost family in Stavishche. Unfortunately, the treasured notes and keepsakes that traveled across the ocean would long outlive their recipient. Shortly after experiencing the thrill of finding his sisters, Isaac died of heart failure. During the early-morning hours of October 21, 1950, he suffered his fourth and final heart attack and died peacefully in his sleep.

Anne's eleven-year-old daughter, Marcy, hesitated to answer her grandmother Rebecca's early-morning phone call, as she knew in her heart that her grandfather was gone. Anne then telephoned Sunny and told her to meet her at their parents' home on North Warnick Street. She said, "Come over quickly; Papa is ill."

Sunny rushed over in a taxicab from her home on Oxford Circle. Her teeth were chattering during the entire ride as she relived in her mind the events of the preceding day, when she had taken her father to a top cardiologist in Philadelphia, who had given him a clean bill of health. Sunny told her eight-year-old daughter, Bobby, riding beside her in the taxi, that she knew it was much more serious than her sister had let on over the telephone. "I know he's dead. I know that Anne wasn't telling me the entire truth. I can feel it; I can feel that he's no longer alive."

When Sunny arrived at eight thirty in the morning, Anne could see by the expression on her sister's face that she already knew. Anne had covered her papa's body by pulling a bedspread over his face, but Sunny insisted on seeing him one last time. She gently placed her cheek next to his and cried, "Oh, Pop, Oh, Pop . . ." Her father had truly loved her unconditionally.

With their father's passing, much of the sweetness in their lives disappeared.

On a table beside Isaac's body sat an old prayer book that he'd cherished since his arrival in America twenty-eight years earlier. Before the final passage, which the grandson of Rabbi Meir Caprove had no doubt read hundreds of times, clear instructions for the Kaddish were written in English: "Kaddish to be repeated by sons during the eleven months after the death of their parents, also on *Jahrzeit*, i.e., the anniversary of such death."

Isaac's only son, his beloved Kaddish, had predeceased him, leaving only close adult female relatives, a wife, two daughters, and two sisters, in North America, Europe, and Asia, to recite the mourner's prayer in his beloved memory.*

---

* Years later, Rebecca shocked her children by marrying a man she hardly knew. She went on a vacation to Florida and instead of bringing back a souvenir, she returned with a man who would soon become her second husband. When Rebecca first introduced her new flame to her children, they instantly understood her attraction to him—he looked just like their father. Unfortunately, the honeymoon was short-lived; while he resembled Isaac in looks, his personality was totally different, and she tired of him. Shortly after their marriage, he suffered a minor stroke. Rebecca nursed him back to health—a full recovery—but decided he wasn't for her and had the marriage annulled.

CHAPTER TWENTY-EIGHT

RAINBOWS

1925 and 2003

R ainbows: As a child, Anne loved them. The great rabbis believed that "the rainbow is a sign of peace because it shows a weapon, the bow, in a harmless state pointing away from the earth with no bowstring."* Anne experienced the beauty of these arched wonders while living in Europe, but it wasn't until she set foot on American soil that she actually began to believe in them.

From her hospital bed on a snowy morning in late February 2003, with her daughter, Marcy, and granddaughters, Lisa and Mindi, by her side,† Anne sorted through old family photographs. She pulled out an 8 x 10 sepia image taken in 1925 for Lisa to use in the family's memoir. For Anne, the portrait brought back happy thoughts of rainbows—as one had miraculously appeared on the day of her aunt Bessie's wedding in New York City. While other guests freely strolled outside to admire the colored archway that emerged just before sundown, Bessie insisted that her family remain indoors. She wanted everyone together, dressed in their new fashionable American attire, to pose for a formal family portrait.

Bessie deeply loved and valued her family: it meant the world to her to have them together in America at her wedding. Anne smiled at the photograph that was of such importance to her aunt. Twenty-three family members posed for

---

* Genesis 9:12

† Anne's beloved husband, Ben, had died the previous year, in March 2002.

the snapshot, and it was Bessie, standing in the back row next to her handsome bridegroom, Ben Baker, who smiled the widest.

A casual observer examining the portrait would never be able to guess, from the bright smiles on everyone's faces, the horrors that they had endured just five years earlier during the pogroms. Bessie, in particular, suffered immensely. She overcame horrific tragedies, and was now embarking upon a new chapter of her life.

History books rarely depict or explore the horrendous suffering caused by the pogroms in Ukraine. Jewish immigrants who lived and survived such misery in Kiev Guberniya usually chose not to speak of it. Most considered their lives to have begun the moment that they stepped off the boat in America. However, their lives in the old country were always colorful. For if there was no adversity, pain, or suffering, or a story to tell, it is doubtful that anyone would venture across an ocean and leave their world, with everything and everyone they love in it, behind.

They survived, and for at least a brief moment in time at Bessie's wedding, were all together again. Anne continued to study the portrait of those dear to her, putting names to the important faces that her granddaughter was writing about.

Standing in the back row on the left was Uncle Avrum Cutler, who came to the celebration with his wife, Slova Ova Denka, and oldest daughter, Fay, who were standing in front of him. Their infant son, born in Romania, was not in attendance. Their youngest son, Charles, who was born in New York the following year, was given the Jewish name Kalman, after his grandfather. Their family had left Jaffa, Palestine, in 1923 after Avrum suffered serious eye problems resulting from the dry climate. At the time of the wedding, they were staying with Avrum's siblings in New York.*

---

* Years later, Avrum and Slova Cutler moved from Philadelphia and settled in California. Jonathan Cutler shared with the author memories of his grandparents' final years: "When my father [Charles Cutler] took us [Jonathan and siblings] to see them on the occasional Saturday morning, we'd allow them to pinch our cheeks and say over and over . . . 'Bubbela! Bubbela!' I recall that usually she'd cry . . . and we cried too because she pinched our cheeks so hard. Once past the greeting ritual, we'd be offered ginger ale and Hershey bars, then sent to the backyard to play while they and my father babbled in Yiddish for an hour or so; then it was time to go. I never knew them as people at all. Their house seemed dark and foreboding, with a musty smell and the drapes always pulled shut. I don't think she left the house much if at all . . . they seemed fearful to me . . . always locking doors and peering out from the corner of the window. . . . At age sixty-six, Pop [Avrum] survived a heart attack but shortly after, to prove he was strong and fit . . . he attempted to mow the lawn and place fertilizer down on a sizzling hot summer day using the old push-mower. He died in the sun on a half-finished lawn."

At the far right were Aunt Molly and Uncle Itzie Stumacher, who brought with them a brood that had by then grown to include four children. In addition to Ruby, Moe, and Fay, little Kolman, also named for Zeyde Kalman, was born in America. Their fifth and youngest child, Abe, would be born a few years later.

Uncle Yunkel and Aunt Esther Cutler sat in the center with three of their children standing behind them, including Anne's favorite cousin, Daniel, who courageously warded off the bandits when he was a young boy in Stavishche. Their youngest daughter, Sheva, also known as Bessie in America, stood next to both her new American fiancé, Max, and her older sister, Sarah. Their son Paul sat in the front row. Although Yunkel looked robust in this portrait, he later found himself wheelchair-bound after being stricken with terminal cancer. On December 15, 1944, the extended family heard that while trying to escape the excruciating pain of his illness, he'd jumped to his death* from a rooftop of a building in Brooklyn, New York. Esther lived many years afterward as a young widow without her beloved Yunkel; she remarried later in life.

Anne's eyes then trailed to the left of the photograph, where her own mother and father sat with their three beloved children. Her little sister, Sunny, was almost nine, and her baby brother, Beryl, three, sported a pageboy haircut. Anne stood just behind Beryl, who was propped up high on a chair by the photographer, at the end of the second row. Anne was thirteen years old. Thankfully, her hair had finally grown in over her ears since suffering from the humiliating lice incident aboard the *Braga*, allowing her to wear it in a short, fashionable bob.

Anne finally came to appreciate this special gathering in her past. She remembered how tedious it was back on that sweltering August day for the photographer to capture his twenty-three subjects with such perfection. By the time he had finished, that enchanting rainbow had disappeared. The group picture, however, that Bessie had insisted on taking, remained for eternity.

Seventy-seven years later, Anne felt nostalgic when looking at everyone together in that photograph. The feeling was bittersweet. She realized that she and Sunny, along with a younger cousin Fay, were the last three living family members who attended the gathering. For her, the photograph embodied happy memories, frozen in time, which could never be relived.

Through Anne's hospital window, Lisa saw the snowfall accumulating quickly. She had just one last photograph to show her grandmother—her favorite

---

* In addition to family stories, this was sadly confirmed by his City of New York death certificate #24428.

sepia-toned portrait of her great-grandmother and young grandmother taken in Stavishche. "That was on my mother's shelf in Atlantic City," Anne recalled, her voice weakened from pneumonia. "You used to stare at it and ask so many questions. That's Mom holding me up on a stand, sometime before the First World War. I hadn't met my father yet."

It was this image, taken in Russia and now gracing the cover of *Tears Over Russia*, that ignited in Lisa a lifetime desire and an unwavering quest to unlock the secrets of her family's past.*

---

* If studied closely, one can see the water damage to the photo sustained when it fell overboard into the Dniester River with the family and their belongings during their daring escape in November 1920.

APPENDICES

THE COLORFUL HISTORY OF BRANICKI PALACE AND THE SECRET IDENTITY OF ITS FIRST COUNTESS

The Branicki estate, which distinguished Stavishche from other villages and hamlets, was, prior to the revolt, a great source of pride to many of the town's Jews, who had settled in the town long before the arrival of the first Count Branicki and remained well after the last one. The 143 years of the peaceful coexistence between the Jews of the town and the Branicki heirs were marked by an intriguing history little-known to those living beyond the gates of the city.

The charming village of gentle hills, green meadows, and bountiful rivers and lakes dates back officially in the record books four centuries to 1622, when the chief of the Bialacerkiew district, Stanislaw Lubomirski, established a new settlement there.* Originally, he named the new settlement Lubomir, after himself. It is first mentioned in a census that year stating that "the settlement of Lubomir and Pasieczna has started; the serfs have just begun building houses."† Tartars would soon destroy the land, which years later would be renamed Stavishche (Stawiszcze). Two hundred ninety-five years later, peasants were responsible for

---

* Some sources suggest a possible ownership and settlement of the land prior to 1622, but many sources recognize the census of that year to be the first written confirmation.

† Source: The 19th-century gazetteer *Slownik Geograficzny*.

another major destruction that befell the most beautiful corner of the Russian village.

In 1774, Poland's last king, Stanislaus Augustus, gifted the estate, along with the vast properties of the Bialacerkiew district, to the Polish magnate Franciszek Ksawery Branicki and his descendants.* Count Branicki seemed to own every village in the area: the deed listed 134 villages, including the tiny dorf of Skibin,† where Rebecca Caprove's oldest daughter Channa was born, and the nearby towns of Stavishche and Belaya Tserkov, where both would later reside.

Franciszek Ksawery Branicki's beautiful young wife, Aleksandra Engelhardt, was known to the world as a favorite niece of Prince Grigory Potemkin and a distinguished member of the Russian court. She was also instrumental in helping her husband increase his considerable fortune, much of which was spent on renovations in Stavishche. One of history's best-kept secrets, however, might be her true identity: the first countess of Stavishche, who resided in Branicki Palace, was rumored to have been the biological daughter of the world's most famous empress, Catherine the Great of Russia.

Aleksandra Engelhardt has been historically portrayed as a trusted friend of Catherine the Great of Russia. She remained under the monarch's protection during her entire lifetime, and at the time of her marriage in 1781, the empress provided a large dowry.

It was during the lifetime of Aleksandra Engelhardt‡ when people began to question whether she was truly the daughter of Wasil Engelhardt and his wife, Marfa Elena Potemkin, who was Grigory Potemkin's sister. French writers were the first to circulate unsubstantiated rumors that she was the biological daughter of Catherine the Great of Russia and her lover, Prince Grigory Potemkin.

It is generally accepted by historians that one of Catherine's lovers, Sergei Saltykov (not her husband, the Grand Duke Peter of Holstein-Gottorp§), had fathered her son, Tsarevich Paul (later Tsar Paul I), who was born in 1754, the same year that Aleksandra was born. Surprisingly, the boy grew up to be ugly

---

* Source: *Slownik Geograficzny*.

† Skibin was a small dorf located six miles southwest of Stavishche; Belaya Tserkov was the largest town on the way to Kiev, located almost thirty miles north of Stavishche.

‡ She was also known as Aleksandra Von Engelhardt and Countess Branicka (1754–1838).

§ The Grand Duke Peter of Holstein-Gottorp was a grandson of Peter the Great of Russia and the son of Empress Elizabeth's sister, Anna, who died when the child was three months old. Elizabeth had him proclaimed her heir in 1742.

and did not resemble the beautiful Catherine or any of her dashing lovers. Most of Catherine the Great's early biographers attribute his appearance to an illness that may have disfigured the child.

At least two Polish sources have suggested that neither Catherine nor her lover were the tsarevich's true parents. Rumors, passed down through generations of the Branicki family, suggest that a switch may have been made at birth to appease Catherine's predecessor, Empress Elizabeth, who wished to have a second male heir in line for the throne of Russia.

A bold entry in *Polski Slownik Biograficzny*, a large Polish biographical dictionary with many volumes, named Aleksandra as the first biological child of Grand Duchess Catherine, later Catherine the Great, and her lover Sergei Saltykov.* It was believed that immediately following her birth, Empress Elizabeth's aide switched her with a newborn baby boy named Pavel (Paul).

The scandalous yet intriguing entry in *Polski Slownik Biograficzny* continued to describe a young Aleksandra as completely enamored with Grigory Potemkin, her uncle and a favorite of the empress. Catherine bestowed upon the young woman, her close confidante, several titles in her court. The empress even insisted that Gavrila Romanovitch Derzhavin, one of the most highly esteemed Russian poets before Pushkin, write verses honoring the young Aleksandra.

In *Arystokracja*, a 1998 work on Polish aristocracy, Marek Miller interviewed Anna Wolska, the daughter of Count Adam Branicki. In Polish, Mrs. Wolska openly addressed rumors pertaining to her great-grandmother Aleksandra Engelhardt Branicka's parentage. Her father had told her a similar tale reported in *Polski Slownik Biograficzny*. When Catherine gave birth to a daughter, a switch was made after one of her ladies-in-waiting bore a son. Catherine's daughter was then raised by the Engelhardt family.

With this stunning revelation of a possible mother-daughter connection, historians should take a closer look at Catherine's masterful manipulations. King Stanislaus Augustus, possibly once a lover of Catherine the Great who ascended to the Polish throne with her assistance, awarded Franciszek Ksawery Branicki a vast estate in 1774. A few years later, the recipient of the king's generosity married Aleksandra Engelhardt, who was possibly the secret daughter of Catherine. It may be no coincidence that Aleksandra ended up the wife of a man who was awarded an estate the size of a small country.

---

* Other rumors, also unconfirmed, said that she was the daughter of Catherine and Grigory Potemkin.

Many now believe that the Branicki family, landowners of Stavishche for nearly 145 years, could be descendants of the most brilliant, if not the most manipulative, female sovereigns in all of history. This news, if proven true, might question the true lineage of those who sat on the throne of the Russian Empire following the death of Catherine II.

APPENDIX B

FUNERAL SPEECH FOR COUNT WLADYSLAW M. BRANICKI, LAST NOBLEMAN OF STAVISHCHE

SUCHA, POLAND, SEPTEMBER 21, 1922

I n 1914, shortly after the passing of Wladyslaw Branicki in the city of Nice, France, a twenty-year-old poet named Jaroslaw Iwaszkiewicz visited the count's estate in Stavishche. Soon to become a significant novelist of classics in Poland, the young author, whose own mother was baptized in the church next to the palace, was hired as a tutor for the son of Mr. Hanicki, who oversaw the administration of the count's estates. The poet eulogized the beloved nobleman, remarking that he was the subject of many legends, resembling a prince from the 15th or 16th century. Above all, his family, friends, and employees would remember him as a man of exceptional and great goodness.

In 1922, the remains of Count Wladyslaw Branicki and his wife, Countess Julia (née Potocka), were brought back to Poland long after their deaths in France in 1914 and 1921, respectively.* They were buried in Sucha, where a memorial was held at a lovely castle and substantial estate originally purchased in 1846

---

* The couple were survived by four daughters: Maria, Anna, Julia, and Rosa. Their only son died during childhood.

by Wladyslaw's father, Count Alexander Branicki. Wladyslaw later gifted the estate to his daughter, Countess Anna Tarnowska.*

The following eulogy for the count and countess was presented at that memorial in Sucha, Poland, by a former key employee of the Branicki estate in Stavishche in the fall of 1922. This stirring tribute, beautifully written and delivered in Polish before a large crowd by Mr. M. Mazaraki, a well-educated, highly literate, and devoted employee of the Branicki family, gives us a small glimpse into the noble character of the Polish magnate and last male Branicki heir to own the land called Stavishche.

Credit: Special thanks to Countess Stanislas Rey (Countess M. Rey) of Montresor and Count Paul Potocki of Paris for helping the author to obtain a copy of this speech.

Translation credit: Special thanks to Mrs. Monika Hendry for her stunning translation of the original Polish into English.

The Funeral of Wladyslaw Branicki "Adzio"†

We are here standing at the grave in which, for eternal rest, lies Count Wladyslaw Branicki with his beloved wife and devoted life companion, Julia.

We are standing at the grave of one of the last members of Polish border gentry who with his great political wisdom and attributes of his soul was throughout his life a great builder of a mighty Poland, which was strengthening its influence in the border areas, not through brutal violence and sword but through great Christian love, spiritual culture, and relentless work.

Apart from a great number of people who came here because they are connected to the count and his wife by links of blood and

---

* Count Wladyslaw Branicki willed his vast and beloved estate in Stavishche to his third-born daughter, Countess Julia Potocka. In 1917, long before bands of murderous hooligans raided the town with the intent of murdering its Jewish population, Countess Potocka became an early victim of unrest in Stavishche when unruly peasants robbed and destroyed the estate. Luckily, the countess and her family were not in Stavishche at the time.

† This is a pet name, short for the diminutive of Wladyslaw—Wladzio.

friendship, we, the former employees of their previous estate,* came to give our tribute and pay homage. There are not many of us here because only a few of our vast numbers were allowed to return to our homelands. Many are still in foreign lands, and many gave their lives when protecting their masters' property and the Polish culture in the border areas till the very end.

We have come back to the country that is very tired morally and physically, but with the remnants of our strength we started our work again in our resurrected and free Motherland, and with pride we can state that we are not parasites on her body. As this is the case, we owe this to the school of work and the traditions created and installed in us by you, the honorable count, as you were not only an employer to us but also a father, a guardian, and a teacher.

You did good deeds, without seeking glory; you had your heart, eye, and your hand open. You sympathized with our sadness and rejoiced at our successes, and you showed understanding at our failures.

Keeping in mind your philosophy, we are silent about your achievements and we will also be silent about those plans that you did not manage to turn into reality, there are many. . . .

The grateful memory of you is kept by many a youth that you helped to receive education, hundreds of widows and orphans that you supported. "Let not know the right hand what the left is doing" was your motto, and we respect it in this painful moment when we say our farewells to you for eternity.

The whole population would cry at your grave—Ukrainian locals of Stawiszcze, Polesie, and Szarogrod, if their perception was not blinded by the memories of others' faults rather than remembering the great benefaction that they experienced from you, the count . . .†

More eloquent live word or pen will keep for posterity your deeds, Count, as a citizen, social contributor; [we will] remember your Christian principles, which you cherished, your love of the

---

* The Branicki estate in Stavishche was destroyed by peasants during the Russian Revolution of 1917.

† He is referring to some unnamed discord among the peasants, probably the Revolution of 1917 in which the local peasants in Stavishche revolted, pillaged, and destroyed the Branicki estate. He feels that the locals should remember the good things that the count did for them.

motherland and your honest Polish soul, the nobility of your actions, understanding of fellow beings, empathy, love, and many other attributes. Let the soil be light on you[*] and God repay you for what you contributed to mankind.

By paying tribute to your memory, we also lower our heads for your wife who endured seven years of widowhood, which was for her a time of remembrance of her departed spouse. With her whole heart and soul she followed in the footsteps of her husband, following his wishes and his deeds. We are witnesses to attest to that.

You followed him too soon—but it has happened!

The last service which we give to our employers, overcome in grief and sadness after their loss, is to pledge to cherish their memory and pass that onto our children.

So rest with God, along with your honorable mother, who will also be remembered for eternity.[†]

These are the words of farewell from us, the employees, but let me add a few words from myself.

For many years I not only carried out your count and your countesses's orders, but I was also your respected confidante. I always strived to be worthy of the position you gave me. This period of my life of direct contact with you is too dear for me to not have it all alive in front of my eyes at the moment.

Rest peacefully with God. Your memory will be cherished by your family, compatriots, and us, your employees.

September 21, 1922, Sucha

M. Mazaraki

---

[*]   This is a Polish idiom.

[†]   M. Mazaraki alludes that he also served as an employee for the count's mother, Anna Nina Holynska, wife of Count Alexander Branicki and daughter of Elizabeth, born Countess Tolstoy. She died in 1907.

APPENDIX C

THE STAVISHCHE POGROM TOMBSTONE LIST (PARTIAL)

1918–1920

Source: YIVO Institute for Jewish Research, New York; Tcherikover Archive, file 21642
Special thanks to Leo Greenbaum of YIVO
Translation from Yiddish by David Goldman, MA

THE LIST OF FIRST AND LAST NAMES AND AGES OF
THE RESIDENTS OF STAVISHCHE FROM 1918–1920

Number & Name

1. Berkun, Mordechai, age 55
2. Berkun, Buzo/Buzy, age 23
3. Berkun, Meir, age 18
4. Shtatsky, Shmuel, age 46
5. Tovrovsky, Benny, age 47
6. Maltsavansky, Benny, age 54
7. Levin/Levine, Avraham Eli, age 50
8. Platinsky, Feivish, age 55
9. Zhivotovsky, Lipa, age 56

10. Stefansky, Elek, age 30

11. Mannis, Yitzchak, age 50

12. Stefansky, Mendel, age 21

13. Sochy/Tochy, Yitzchak, age 70

14. Shvitska, Shalom, age 48

15. Lantsman, Shalom, age 45

16. Glisinska, Batya, age unknown

17. Valoshik, Avraham, age 53

18. Valoshin, Feiga, age 47

19. Kortchevsky, Chana, age unknown

20. Shub, Yaakov, age 62

21. Rosenblit, Sarah, age unknown

22. Rosenblit (Sarah's daughter), age 17

23. Rosenblit (Sarah's daughter), age 18

24. Wilfand, Menashe, age 65

25. Wilfand, Batsheva, age 52[*]

26. Wexler, Beila, age 47

27. Besidsky/Besitsky, Mony, age 68

28. Shechzal, husband, age 60, burned

29. And his wife, age 60, burned

30. Shadchan, Yitzchak, age 24

31. Shubinsky, Avraham Abba, age 50

32. Yaralinsky, Moshe, age 24

33. Altman, age unknown

34. Modorevitch, age 10

35. Kaplivotsky, Sarah, age 80

36. Spira, Sarah, age 75

37. Zhivotovsky, Yaakov-Ber, age 70

38. Alper, Sarah, age unknown

39. Dvorah, [illegible],[†] age 77

40. Nechama, (the hairdresser), age unknown

41. Shostock, Yaakov, age 20

---

* There is a word over the two Wilfand names that appears to be "farbrent" (burned).

† Looks like Srbebn.

42. Avraham Appel (Kerziner*), age unknown

43. Reuven (religious teacher), age 45

44. Yonah (wagon driver), age unknown

45. Levi (wagon driver), age unknown

46. Nachum Velvel (wagon driver), age unknown

47. Platoshnik, Avraham, age unknown

48. Guthartz, Mordechai, age 37

49. Dolganas, Avraham, age 23

50. Desyotnik, Mechel, age unknown

51. Kadosh, age unknown

52. Frantsman, age unknown

53. Boyarsky, Simcha, age unknown

54. Charnitsky, Nachum, age unknown

55. Charnitsky, Kalman, age unknown

56. Kalman Charnitsky's fiancée, age unknown

57–64. Eight old Jews from a Home for the Aged—Bikkur Holim (Medical Aid Society)

Told by: Nachum Kaplotsky and Avraham Solganik. Recorded by the Administration of the All-Ukrainian Jewish Central Committee, CUPE. H. Hoffman (date looks like April 6, 1921)

---

* May refer to the term used for a government-appointed rabbi, but may be a name.

APPENDIX D

PARTIAL LIST OF STAVISHCHE RESIDENTS MURDERED BY GRIGORIEV'S BAND, HEADED BY ZHELEZNIAK

JUNE 1919

Source: Megilat Ha-tevah, *page 2 (Stavishche).*
Compiled by: Eliezer David Rosenthal
Translated from Hebrew to English by: Dr. Ida Selavan Schwarcz. *List courtesy of*
GNAZIM ARCHIVE

1. Peysi Kartshevski, 52, horse trader
2. His sister-in-law Haya, 40
3. Batya Gusinski, 40
4. Berish Platenski, [illegible], 55, shop of iron objects
5. Avraham Kurznir, [illegible], 37
6. Itsik Shadken, 21
7. Shalom Shvidki, 42, sugar merchant
8. Beni Voldavanski, 42, horse trader
9–11. The wife of Eliezer Klezmer, 43, and her two daughters, 15 and 11
12. Avraham Abba (wagoner), 52
13. [illegible] Melamed, 52

14.   Elik Kovel, 26
15.   Ya'akov Shohet, 40
16.   Levi (wagoner), 40
17.   Motel Tsirelnik
18.   Hirsh Zagatovchik
19.   The Wilfond girl, 13

A total of nineteen murdered. (Author note: This is believed to be a partial list.)

APPENDIX E

A PARTIAL POGROM MEMORIAL LIST
1920

Source: The Forward (Forverts), December 30, 1920, page 1
Credit: The Forward Association
Translation from Yiddish to English by Dr. Ida Selavan Schwarcz
Translation used with the permission of Dr. Robert Barnes

Names of One Hundred Murdered Jews in Stavishche, Province of Kiev

Special cable to the Forward from N. Shifrin, Berlin, December 29:

"I have received the names of over one hundred murdered Jews in Stavishche, Kiev Province."

The following have left behind a wife and four children:
1. Avraham'l Litvak, 40 years old
2. Ben-Tsiyon Maladavski, 46 years old
3. His son, Reuven
4. Meir the teacher, 38 years old
5. Mikhl Papirovitsh, 55 years old
6. Yaakov the ritual slaughterer, 40 years old
7. Nahum the carpenter, 55 years old

The following have left behind a wife and five children:

    8. Binyamin Natavski, from Yanashivke, 35 years old

    9. Shmulik Stavski, 45 years old

  10. His wife, 38 years old

  11. Mordekhai Leyb Frenkel, 45 years old

  12. Avraham the ritual slaughterer, 55 years old

  13. His wife, 50 years old

The following have left behind a wife and six children:

  14. Tsevi Grabman, 44 years old

  15. Shalom Shvetkay, 38 years old

The following left behind a wife (or spouse) with one or two children:

  16. Tsevi Lazanski, 40 years old

  17. Avraham Dvinski, 35 years old

  18. Gitl Senderovski, 35 years old

  19. Esther, Kalman the hatter's daughter, 60 years old

  20. Mordshe Berkum, 48 years old

  21. Bayets Berkum, 22 years old

  22. Meir, 16 years old

  23. Ele Stepanski, 35 years old

  24. His brother, Mendl, 23 years old

  25. Yitshak Kagan, 35 years old

  26. Motl Fishman, 28 years old

  27. Avraham Meir Fishman, 38 years old

  28. Nahum Frants, 33 years old

  29. Fayvish Platinski, 55 years old

  30. Tittsek the miller, 55 years old

  31. Khvelye Dartshevski, 40 years old

  32. Motl Gutharts, 35 years old

  33. Volke (Zeev) Vaynshteyn, 45 years old

  34. Fayvl the blacksmith, 45 years old

  35. His son, David, 28 years old

  36. Veksler the dentist, 40 years old

  37. His wife, Belah

  38. Hershl the cobbler (Zagatavshtik[?]), 35 years old

39. Ayzik Kanski, 58 years old
40. Shalom Denest, 55 years old
41. Avraham'l the (shinder/shingler) 50 years old
42. Asher the water-carrier's stepson, 30 years old
43. His wife
44. David Itsik's, 32 years old
45. Shalom Salganik, 55 years old
46. Jacob Grinshpan, 35 years old
47. Stapla, wife of Ben-Tsiyon the teacher, 35 years old
48. Hayke, 15 years old
49. Zelde, 5 years old
50. Rahel, 9 years old, wounded
51. Feyge, 4 years old
52. Baby, 2 years old
53. Nahum Velvel Bershadski, 60 years old
54. His brother Yonah, 50 years old
55. Meir Miratshnik, 55 years old
56. Hanah Meszibovskaya, 50 years old
57. Yaakov David Zshivatavski, 60 years old
58. Levi the waggoner, 30 years old
59. Mosheh Shelomah Kushnier, 25 years old
60. Unknown young man
61. Mahlah Kaptshevskaya, 70 years old
62. Avraham, son of David the [platatshnik], 12 years old
63. Ayzik Rizanski, 55 years old
64. Avraham Sukanik, 75 years old
65. Yankel Shumski's mother, 70 years old
66. Gitl Rive Krasilavskaya, 75 years old
67. Yosl Zshabtshinksi, 75 years old
68. His wife, 70 years old
69. Zeydl Volodarski, 25 years old
70. Avraham Abba (Efrayim Tshudinski's son[?]), 30 years old
71. Beni, son of Aharon the tailor, 22 years old
72. Pine, son of Yeruham, 8 years old
73. An old lame woman, "Di Litvatshke," 75 years old
74. Daughter of Avraham the ritual slaughterer, 20 years old

75. Itsik Tori, 40 years old
76. David, son of the shingler, 25 years old
77. Tsevi Pisnay, from Stanislantshik, 16 years old
78. Gessl son of Yisrael Yonah, 22 years old
79. Yankl Grafman, 25 years old
80. Avraham Shestak, 23 years old
81. Tsevi Zagatavshtshik, from Rakitina, 45 years old
82. Yitshak Shatshan, 23 years old
83. Pesye Kartshevskaia, 55 years old
84. Sarah Rosenberg (Rosenblit[?]), 45 years old
85. Her daughter, Hanah, 22 years old
86. Her daughter, 18 years old
87. Shime Boyarski, 35 years old
88. Shelomoh Zalman the galoshes maker, 75 years old
89. Mosheh Nesyer (the bander; coopersmith), 20 years old
90. Sarah Shapira, 55 years old
91. Ittse Mazeraki, 50 years old
92. Golde Dikstevitsh, 50 years old
93. Mother (Sarah[?]) of Pittse Kaplavitsh, 70 years old
94. Lipe Stepanski, 60 years old
95. Avraham son of Mosheh Tankel, 20 years old
96. Kalman Nahum the carpenter, 25 years old
97. His bride, 20 years old
98. Berl Yaladarski, blind, 80 years old
99. Sarah the brunette, a disabled woman, 80 years old
100. Sarah the waitress, 80 years old
101. Alte the weaver's daughter, 30 years old
102. Her husband, 32 years old

The *Stavishche Yizkor Book* lists two others left off the list:
103. Yosef Rubtshinski, the butcher, 87 years old
104. His wife, Batyah, 84 years old

"These are the last martyrs who were murdered by Zhelezniak's band in the big bet hamidrash, possibly the last Jews in town." (Note from both the translator and the author: this is inconsistent with the dates. Zhelezniak's attack was certainly not the last.)

Source: *Stavishche Yizkor Book,* 1961

1. Levin, Avraham-Eli, murdered in August 1918
2. Kohen, David, 20, murdered in 1919
3. Svirski, unknown, 18, murdered in 1919
4. Fishlin, Reuven, murdered in 1920
5. Landsman, Shalom, murdered in 1920
6. Frenkel, Shelomoh Zalman, murdered in 1920

7–8. Smaliar and his wife, burned alive in their home[*]

---

[*] Author's note: Moshe Smaliar and his wife were a young Jewish couple in town.

APPENDIX F

DEATH LIST (PARTIAL): STAVISHCHE

(TRANSLATED FROM YIDDISH INTO ENGLISH)*

1. Moldovansky, Benzi, 45 years old
2. Shachan, Itzhak, 25 years old
3. Yosef Stepansky, 38 years old
4. His brother, 22 years old
5. Herschel the Zagatovshik, 40 years old
6. Gusinskaya, age 50
7. Kartshevsky, 80 years old
8. Shostok, age 25
9. Stepansky, Herschel, 40 years old
10. Kerziner, Avram Isaac, 40 years old
11. Weiner from (illegible)
12. Dalgonas (Solganis) 35 years old
13. Mordechai, the house sweeper, 45 years old
14. Sarah Rosenblatt
15–16. her two daughters
17. Zhavatovske, Jacob Ber, age 60
18. Wexler, Baila, the female dentist, 40 years old

* Source: Kiev Reginal Commission of the Jewish Public Committee for the Assistance to Victims of Pogroms. List of victims of pogroms in Tarashcha Uyzed, Kiev Guberniya, written between February 6, 1920 and September 23, 1921. State Archive of Kyiv Oblast., Fond P-3050 inventory 1 case 43. There are 199 sheets in this document; this is one page with a handwritten number of 196. See Notes.

19.   Herschel Zagatovshik's wife, 40 years old
20.   Makarevich, 10 years old
21.   Avraham Voloshin, the shokhet
22.   His wife, Feiga
23.   Jacob the shockhet
24.   Kalman Charnitsky
25.   His bride
26.   Ozarovsky
27.   A young boy from Zhaskov
28.   Nahum Velvel the wagon driver
29.   Yonah the wagon driver

APPENDIX G

THE POGROM SURVIVORS: STAVISHCHE
1923

The 1917–1921 pogroms were the worst and most violent acts against the Jews in the 20th century except for the Holocaust. If not overshadowed by the brutality of the Nazis two decades later, this infamous episode in history would not have been nearly forgotten today . . ."*

Although the Jewish population of Stavishche suffered many casualties, a large majority survived the pogroms by fleeing the country. The estimates of this great Jewish exodus from Stavishche range between 3,500 and 4,000; the majority made their way to the United States, Canada, England, Israel, and Argentina.

It is ironic that the pogroms and the ensuing horror inflicted upon the Jews of the town may have ultimately saved the lives of thousands (including Channa's family); for if the pogroms didn't force the people to flee, most would have been murdered during the Holocaust.

On June 29, 1923, while the Caprove and Cutler families were still living in Kishinev, a report on Stavishche† was sent to the American Jewish Joint Distribution Committee in New York, to the attention of the Landsmanschaften Bureau, from its Moscow headquarters. What remained of its Jewish population and their depraved living conditions was reported in the two letters below,

---

* Source: David A. Chapin and Ben Weinstock. *The Road From Letichev, Volume 2: The History and Culture of a Forgotten Jewish Community in Eastern Europe.* Writer's Showcase Press, 2000.

† In the English translation of the report and letter, the town was spelled Stavische and Stavishe.

discovered in the American Jewish Joint Distribution Committee Archives, collection # 21/32, file # 504.

Special thanks to Misha Mitsel, JDC (NY) Archives

June 1923 Report on Stavishche, Belaya Tzerkov Ouzarav, Kiev Guberniya

The population of Stavishche before the war was 9,500 persons, of whom 1,245 families were Jews. Now the population is 3,600 persons with 600 Jews. Jewish houses have decreased from 550 to 73 and shops from 200 to 2 and 20 stalls. Of the 73 houses sold to peasants, 12 were returned to Jews and 61 are still occupied by peasants. The remaining Jewish houses were burned down during the pogroms.

The number of pogroms in the town was 10. The results of them are as follows: 160 persons killed and 40 wounded.

In June, July, and August 1919 the town was repeatedly attacked by various bands, and the Jews left it three times for other cities.

In 1922, the refugees began gradually to return to their town and by about October 1922, there were already fifty Jewish families in Stavishche.

The refugees from Stavishche inhabit neighboring places and Kiev, but the majority of them are in Belaya Tserkov.

Only twelve houses are at present occupied by Jews; the latter live in unsanitary conditions, crowded in small rooms.

The three remaining synagogues (there were six formerly) are occupied by returned refugees. Each returning family appropriated a part of the synagogue making partitions and adapting it for living. The remaining population is living in Jewish houses and peasant cottages, paying rent (see attached photographs).* Of the returned refugees only one is constructing a house for himself. In order to improve the living conditions thirty houses must be redeemed.

Children's institutions: There are in the town one children's home and one public school. There are, however, no Jewish children in them.

Medical institutions: There exists one district hospital with surgical and therapeutic wards and a dispensary, extending possible relief to the population.

---

* In the cover letter to the committee, it is indicated that there were additional materials included that the author was not able to locate. These included three photographs, a list of names of orphans in Stavishche, a list of names of half orphans, a list of names of widows, and a list of names of artisans.

Medicaments are furnished by the Belaya Tzerkov Ouzarav and by the ARA. The hospital also has a dental dispensary.

The bathhouse is destroyed.

The population of Stavishche received from the JDC in March 1923, eight food packages that were distributed among seventy-eight families.

BUDGETARY REQUIREMENTS

1. School asylum for one hundred children: one-time repairs, equipment, and clothing $500. Monthly maintenance $150.
2. Subvention to the hospital $50 (monthly).
3. Repairs to the bath $200 (one time).
4. Redemption of thirty houses for returning refugees $2,000 (one time). Total (one time) $2,700. Monthly: $200.

Letter of thanks for help rendered: JDC Kiev Division

Herewith, deep gratitude is expressed by the Stavische (Stavishche) population to the Kiev Office of JDC for help rendered; eight food parcels were sent for distribution among the poorest population. This aid could not cover the requirements of the poorest population in Stavishche; the distressing situation of many families now returning to Stavishche is still critical. Living quarters are needed very badly. The greater part of the population lives in anti-sanitary conditions.

There is an acute need for a bathhouse that should be built. We enter a request for improvement of living-quarter conditions since ten people live in one room. Houses of worship have been taken up by the Stavishche inhabitants. Each house shelters from ten to twelve families.

As there are orphans and half orphans it is necessary to organize a children's sheltering home. We, who have returned to Stavishche, worn out by hunger, cold, and various epidemic diseases that we had gone through in strange parts, can do nothing to contribute to the prosperity of the town. We need outside help. Many refugee families lack the opportunity to return to Stavishche since there are no living accommodations there.

We hope that JDC will take cognizance of the distressing situation of our town, which is on the road of reestablishment, and will render the necessary help. We appeal to you and to our brothers in America for urgent help.

Citizens of the Town Stavishche

APPENDIX H

FATES OF THE VILLAGERS

1920s

E ach of the Stavishche villagers described in these pages experienced his or her own miraculous tale of exodus from the shtetl. They are fascinating stories of survival, relocation, and, for many, just plain luck.

For those fortunate enough to have close relatives in the United States, letters of unimaginable hardships were sent along with desperate pleas for help. Just as Barney Stumacher had received such a letter from his elderly father in Belaya Tserkov begging for help, others from Stavishche pleaded with their family members to come to Europe and save them.

Philip Postrel*

Philip Postrel, whose father was Yehuda Leib (Leb),† once the keeper of the bathhouse in Stavishche, received a letter that was sent to him in New York City in February 1921 from his recently widowed relative, who had lost both her husband and son to pogrom violence. Stranded in Bessarabia with no hope, she begged her American relative to come to her rescue. Postrel wrote and signed the following affidavit in the state of New York that accompanied his emergency

---

* The applicant's first name is spelled two different ways throughout the passport application: Philip and Phillip.

† Yehuda Leib was also known as Pitsie Postrel.

passport. Many Americans who faced a similar situation were frantically scrambling to obtain passports in order to return to Europe to save, as their desperate relatives aptly reminded them, "their flesh and blood."

Phillip Postrel, being duly sworn, deposes and says:

> I am twenty-six years of age, a naturalized citizen of the United States, residing at 222 St. Nicholas Avenue, New York City.
>
> I am an ex–service man, having had active service abroad, fought in various battles in the recent war, wounded, having performed my duties of a citizen loyale and faithfully to the best of my abilities and received an Honorable Discharge, as can be verified by the records in the War Department.
>
> At present I am in business in the stationery and cigar business for myself in the city of New York, but the needs of my immediate relatives, such as my sister and her family and cousins are so great that I must give up my business temporarily and render them such relief as there may be in my readiness and ability to do so.
>
> They are at present stranded on the Russian Romanian border, as I am informed and believe, and are actually starving, having no means whatsoever and nobody to take care of them or in any way help to assist them in their dire wants of the most elementary necessities of life. If I do not go up quickly with my aid and assistance, I fear, I have ground to believe that they will all perish and not survive.
>
> I therefore make this affidavit with the purpose of inducing the State Department to grant me a passport immediately for the purpose above set forth, so that I might save yet that which was left from the ruin caused by the last few years of war and European disturbances, and I respectfully request that a passport be granted at once.
>
> Sworn before me this day of [illegible] 1921:
>
> Signed by the Notary Public of New York County.
>
> (Signature) Philip Postrel*

---

* Source: Philip Postrel's application for an American passport dated Feb. 10, 1921, National Archives microfilm publication, M1490. It was issued on February 15, 1921. Although Philip was also a nephew of Chiah Sura Spivack, it is believed that he was not involved with her departure from Europe.

❖

Other villagers, who did not have the luxury of calling upon relatives to save them, found other ways to escape the hardships and cruelty of their lives in Stavishche.

Shika de Potch (Yehoshua Golditch the Postmaster)

Shika de Potch held an important position as the Jewish postmaster of Stav-ishche. When government officials traveled through the poor village,* he supplied them with fresh horses and carriages, which were kept in two large stables on his property. His dwelling was such an important fixture that the first floor housed a bank and the only telephone office in town. His daughter Fania was one of the first telephone operators in Stavishche.

Shika de Potch, later known in America as Sam Gold, fled with his younger daughter, Dvora, to Boston, Massachusetts. After borrowing money from his wealthy landslayt who were already established in the New World, Shika de Potch was finally able to bring over the remainder of his family. On July 8, 1923, less than two months before the Caprove family set foot on Ellis Island, the SS *Carmania* docked at Boston Harbor carrying his wife, Esther, and their two sons.† It was at the immigration center that the postmaster's wife first realized that their eighteen-year-old handicapped son, Hymie, might be denied entrance into the country. Hymie was a deaf-mute.

Esther and her older son, Bennie, who as a boy spotted Count Branicki riding in the first automobile in town, devised a plan. They would not, under any cir-cumstance, leave Hymie behind and were determined to get him through the crucial first round of examinations. Esther stood closely in front of Hymie in line, and Bennie stood right behind him. When the official assigned to their section asked Hymie questions, he moved his lips as Bennie shouted out the answers.

---

* Some important early visitors who arrived in Stavishche on horseback (well before Shika de Potch's day) included Stanislaw Koniecpolski (1641), Chief Jurko Chmielnicki, and Crimean chief Mechmet Girej (1661). Stefan Czarniecki and future king Jan Sobieski also visited in the early 1660s.

† Pearl, the new bride of Shika de Potch's son Bennie, also accompanied the family on their journey. A daughter, Fania, immigrated with her husband on another ship.

The obviously distracted official was fooled, and everyone made it through the first round of examinations, enabling the family to eventually reunite on the Boston pier.[*]

In America, Sam Gold struggled to earn a living and was demoralized when he experienced difficulty finding a job. He eventually secured a position as a rag and burlap bag sorter. He was probably among the hundreds of other Jewish immigrants who flooded the Boston area in the early 1920s and found work in the prosperous rag businesses owned by the Cutler and Wise families of Chelsea.

Sol Moser

Sol arrived in America in 1921, wearing his older brother Schmuelik's[†] Russian leather boots. His cousin Harry Goldberg was conscripted into the Russian army and did not return in time to leave with his parents to America. Harry's sister died of typhus while waiting for her passport. So Sol's aunt, Mima Motley Goldberg, plucked the resilient orphan and his older sister, Goldie, off of the streets of Belaya Tserkov[‡] and brought them to America in her children's place.

Once in New York, however, Mima Motley, who was kind enough to bring the children to America, was unable to support the two waifs. Sadly, the children once again found themselves in a familiar situation—bounced around from relative to relative. Eleven-year-old Sol found himself selling newspapers on the subway in New York City. He often slept there, too, falling asleep to the alluring smell of ham sandwiches that the Gentile riders munched on as late-night snacks.

While dozing off on the subway to the forbidden yet delicious aroma of pork, Sol was occasionally haunted by memories of screeching pigs in Stavishche. During the First World War, when German soldiers invaded the village, Sol would watch as they threw live pigs into boiling water so that the animals' hairs

---

[*] Boston passenger records suggest that authorities eventually discovered that Hymie was a deaf-mute. A bond was posted, and he was allowed to remain in Chelsea with his family. However, it is believed that had Hymie not successfully passed through the early medical rounds, he probably would have been sent back to Europe.

[†] In the 1960s, Sol returned to Stavishche to visit his older brother, Schmuelik, who had been imprisoned for six years for selling chickens and eggs on the black market. His Soviet jailers allowed the two brothers, who had been separated for more than forty years, to wave to each other from a prison window.

[‡] The children had wandered into Belaya Tserkov after escaping a violent pogrom in Stavishche.

would fall out before they ate it. The Ukrainians, at least, would slit the pigs' throats first, but German soldiers left the pigs to squeal in pain.

Sol could not doze off in any location without remembering some horror that he had endured in the Old Country.

In New York, his fifteen-year-old sister, Goldie, agreed to marry a bank teller named Dave and was finally able to provide her younger brother with the first home that he had known since their parents, Haika Stepansky and Itzie Moser, died. Goldie and her new husband opened a bakery in New York, similar to the one that the Moser family ran in Stavishche. Sol and his cousin Daniel Cutler, idealists who believed in the trade union movement, organized a strike on Goldie and Dave's new establishment. Chased by the police, the two teenagers separated in an alleyway and escaped capture. The incident did not, however, go over well with Sol's furious sister; the duo failed to escape her wrath.

Goldie eventually forgave the boys. The mischievous pair later ran a business together in Brooklyn called Sol and Dan's Produce. They were wholesalers who bought produce directly from farmers and filled up their trucks, delivering fresh fruits and vegetables each morning to retail establishments.

Just a few years later, Sol, an idealist who believed in Tikkun Olam (repairing the world), joined the Young Communist League (YCL). It was an era when idealist young people in America, who believed in fighting for the rights of immigrant sweatshop workers, flirted with Communism. It was at one of those YCL meetings that Sol met his future wife, Dorothy.*

Chiah Sura Spivack

Chiah Sura, known for her skills in cupping, an old healing technique similar to acupressure, and her husband, Dovid Spivack, finally received news, a few years after they last saw him, on the whereabouts of their handsome son, Leib. He was drafted into the tsar's army during WWI and was immediately mobilized to the German front.

After the Treaty of Brest Litovsk finally ended the war between Germany and Russia in 1918, a Jewish prisoner of war who returned to Kiev Guberniya

---

* The couple later (in the late 1940s) sent their two children to the first integrated children's summer camp—Camp Wo-Chi-Ca (Workers' Children's Camps). Entertainer Paul Robeson used to go there to sing to the children.

stopped in Stavishche hoping to give the couple news; it is believed that he may have later found and told them while in Romania.* He had spoken with Leib in a POW camp located in Austria called Kleinmunchen ("Little Munich"),† and their son wanted to send them his regards.

His parents and younger siblings blindly hoped that Leib would soon return home, but he never did. Between 1919 and 1920, the family fled with most of the Jews from the village, as violent pogroms broke out, one after another. After each attack, they returned home to their shattered town in hopes of receiving word of their son.

Eventually, it was no longer safe for Jews to remain in Stavishche. Chiah Sura, Dovid, and their two youngest children, Mendel and Nechama, made their way to Bucharest, Romania. In June 1922, Dovid bought steamship tickets to take the family to America but decided that he could not leave without conducting one last search for his son. It is believed that Dovid went to Kleinmunchen on a mission to find his beloved Leib. However, he had no success. There were never any letters or news of his whereabouts; Leib had disappeared into thin air.

With heavy hearts, the family eventually set sail for America and were reunited with their oldest daughter, Minnie, who had immigrated in 1908. Many of Chiah Sura and Dovid's relatives owned candy stores in New York City and the surrounding area. Chiah Sura continued to perform her Old World cupping techniques on her loved ones in the United States.

At the same time that they departed for America, many of their Spivack (Spivak in Israel) family members immigrated to the Holy Land. Chiah Sura's nephew Avram Postrelka,‡ who was already known in Eretz Yisrael as Avraham Harzfeld, was a pioneer in the Labor Zionist movement and helped many Stavishchers in need.§ During the 1920s, the police chief of Tel Aviv was also

---

* It is unconfirmed where and when the soldier told the family about Leib. The author originally believed that the most likely scenario is that he knew Leib was from Stavishche and went there in search of his family. It is possible that the soldier told the family after running into them in Romania, which may have explained Dovid's sudden trip across Europe in search for his lost son before he sailed to America.

† The WWI POW camp Kleinmunchen is believed to have been located in Austria near Linz. Some family members believed it was in Germany, or that Dovid went to Germany. It is unclear whether at that time Dovid knew to search in Kleinmunchen, and or whether his search brought him to Germany or Austria. The author believed Leib had been in Kleinmunchen.

‡ The name was also spelled Postrelke and Postrelko. In America, it was shortened to Postrel.

§ Harzfeld was also a key figure in early Israel's agricultural and kibbutz movements. He later served in the Knesset.

a former Stavishcher; when his many landslayt arrived in Palestine, jobless, he took them into the police force.

Chiah Sura and Dovid Spivack died heartbroken in their adopted country, having never learned the fate of their son.

Sarah Cutler

Sarah was delirious. Childbirth in the New Country was surely safer than when she was born to her parents, Esther Moser and Yunkel Cutler, back in Stavishche in 1904.* In her delirium, the new Mrs. Herman Antanir flashed back to one of her earliest memories of her childhood in Russia. A cute toddler with curly blond hair, Sarah wandered into the nearby wooden home of an elderly Jew. A Russian bandit was pointing a gun at the head of the old, bearded man, who wore long payas and a yarmulke.

"Say your last prayer, Jew!" the bandit barked at him.

"*Neyet!*" the young girl screamed at the bandit, and she wrapped herself around the leg of the elderly victim.

The bandit was unable to pry the clinging child loose. Instead of shooting the old man, he left the shack in frustration. Even the vicious thug could not bring himself to injure or murder a child as beautiful as Sarah Cutler.

Sarah, still delirious, then dreamed of the time, a few years later, when she sat with her mother by the bedside of Esther's dying 103-year-old great-aunt, Rochel. Rochel, possibly Stavishche's oldest resident and the aunt of Esther's father, the respected cantor David-Yosel Moser, held Esther's hand tightly.

"Your next child will be a daughter," she told her devoted grand-niece, "and you will name her for me."

Rochel's deathbed prediction came true. However, Esther, who tended to her four other children while they suffered from the measles, became ill during her fifth and final pregnancy. A baby girl, whom she named Rochel, was born to her, but the baby did not survive the day. The old woman's dying wish to have a living namesake was not to be—at least, not yet.

Fifteen years later, Esther's oldest daughter, Sarah, who was in labor with her first child in a New York City hospital, had a vision: old Aunt Rochel appeared

---

* The metric book in Stavishche recorded Sarah's birth on November 8, 1904. American records have her born in 1905. She was probably named for her father's sister who died during childhood.

before her and bowed down to her. Sarah interpreted this spiritual visit from her elderly aunt to mean that she would soon give birth to a daughter. Her child, born in 1929, bore the Jewish name Rochel. Sarah believed that it was good luck to name her child after a woman who had lived such a long life. And so this child, Rochel, was one of the first of the new generation of Stavishchers born in the Golden Land.

FAMINE, FASCISTS, AND THE HOLOCAUST: STAVISHCHE

1931–1945

In the early 1930s, during the interwar period, collectivization under Stalin triggered a Soviet man-made famine in Ukraine, often referred to as "Holodomor." Since the Ukrainian opposition to collectivization was viewed by the Kremlin as a threat against Communism and a fight for independence, the powers-that-be retaliated by starving the population to death.

In a 1988 report by the US Commission on the Ukraine Famine, case history SW34, an unnamed person who lived in Stavishche as a child in the 1930s explained the effects on the population who were forced onto collective farms and deliberately left without animals, tools, and farming implements, rendering them incapable of toiling the land and feeding themselves.

"At the time I lived close to the [Stavishche] hospital," the witness reported. "People were being driven in from villages near and far, as well as from Stavishche, my native village. People were even bringing in their own children, who were already swollen . . ."

The interviewee then spoke about a large park beside the hospital where the cemetery was located. "Enormous open pits were dug and doctors carried on stretchers the bodies of those who had died [from starvation] and tossed them into the pits. The process would be repeated each day until the open pit was filled and covered over with dirt shoveled over it. . . . Later they didn't bother with the morgue anymore, but took the corpses straight to the open pits on stretchers. Often nurses carried as many as ten children on stretchers and tossed them into the pit."

The collectivization process that caused the deadly famine did not distinguish between its victims. Both the Jewish and Christian populations of Stavishche starved to death. Less than a decade later, the Jews of Stavishche were once again singled out, much like they were twenty years earlier during the pogroms. Arial photographs that gave the Nazis a bird's-eye-view guided their entrance into the town. Jewish eyewitness accounts of the few survivors who were in Stavishche after the Nazis' raid state that some of the local Ukrainians also collaborated with these evil killers by pointing out where the Jewish families lived, thus signing their death warrants.

On July 17, 1941, as loudspeakers and sirens went off in town centers in nearby Belaya Tserkov warning its residents of the impending attack by the Germans, the Jews who were isolated in the small shtetl of Stavishche were caught by surprise. Men of age were away in the army, but within two weeks, the young boys and elderly males were rounded up in front of the women and girls and were shot in the forest.

Two sisters from Belaya Tserkov, thirteen-year-old Raisa Bershadskaya and her seventeen-year-old sister, Ida, were spending the summer of 1941 in Stavishche visiting their paternal grandparents, Basya and Zelig, when Nazis invaded the town. After witnessing the murder of her grandfather, Raisa was able to escape by running for her life while both her grandmother and sister were captured, along with the remaining 150 Jewish women and children in the town.

Very little information has been documented about the genocide that occurred in Stavishche during the Holocaust, but a small handwritten entry found in Yad Vashem, the Holocaust Martyrs' and Heroes Remembrance Authority, citing signature member in the Yad Vashem Archives, YVA M.52/235, frame 2045–2051, stated in Ukrainian:

> Then the Gestapo came to the village. The population was deeply distressed by their savage treatment of the Jewish residents. Everybody from small children to old people were taken to the forest and shot near the hole that was made beforehand. Young people who were braver watched the bloody terror over the poor people. They were going along the road followed by (Fascist) policemen with guns. Women

were carrying small children. In the forest, the executioners with machine guns were waiting for them already. The policemen took the victims to the hole and the executioners shot them with machine guns. Four Jewish families from our village were killed in such a way.

The same document gave a glimpse of what happened to some of Stavishche's non-Jewish residents. "Three-hundred forty-four people from Stavishche were sent to Germany for hard labor."*

Oppression of the Christian residents, although not as devastating as the mass murders that were committed against the Jewish ones, haunted those remaining in Stavishche. "Every week many people were caught and sent to hard labor. All of them were gathered in the town of Stavishche in a two-storied building. Very often young people jumped from the second floor and hurt themselves and became invalids just in order to stay in their native place. They also jumped out of carriages when the train was on its way. Fascists shot and often killed them. And only after some time relatives got to know the sad news about their children."

After the war ended in 1945, ten Jewish families, all with loved ones living in Stavishche during the war, gathered in Belaya Tserkov. Together, they made the decision to return to Stavishche to discover the fate of their loved ones. A few older men led the group, which included Raisa Bershadskaya, her parents, and her younger sister, who were searching for Raisa's older sister and grandmother, who were still alive when she fled from the town. They returned to the spot in the forest, located close to the Jewish cemetery, where Raisa had witnessed the shotgun murders of her grandfather and the other boys and men of the town.

To the group's surprise, their loved ones' bodies were easily found. The scene of death, one of savage murder, remained strangely intact and untouched four years later. While the corpses had rotted and decomposed, the pits that they were thrown into were never covered, and the remains of the bodies were exposed. The skeletons of about two hundred Jewish men, women, and children, who had been heartlessly massacred, were now in the process of being claimed by

---

* The daughter of Raisa Bershadskaya believes that her mother may have been the only Jewish survivor of the Holocaust in Stavishche who was sent with this group of young Christians from her town to Germany for hard labor.

surviving family members and friends who tried desperately to identify them by their clothing, hairpieces, shoes, and eyeglasses.

In an ironic twist of fate, these Jewish families were forced to pay the local Ukrainians—some who may have even helped to send their loved ones to their death—with money and liquor for their assistance in exhuming the bodies. The corpses were removed from the open holes and were brought to the nearby Jewish cemetery for a proper burial. Two mass graves, separating the bodies by gender, were used for their group burial. The Jewish people of Stavishche, who had died together at the ruthless hands of the Nazis in 1941, were finally laid to rest together four years later with a religious ceremony.

Today the mass graves, which are surrounded by chains,* each have an attractive memorial stone made of brown marble tablets engraved in both Russian and Hebrew with beautiful etchings, including one of an elderly grieving Jew wearing a tallis. In the 1970s, a Jewish man who was living in Belaya Tserkov named Michael Malin (Mikhail, son of Yosef) was instrumental in getting permission from the Soviet authorities to have the monuments erected in the Jewish cemetery in Stavishche. He also donated a large sum of money, along with other Stavishche families who had immigrated to America, toward the headstones that memorialize the local Jewish victims of the Holocaust.

It is unclear when the murders actually occurred as eyewitness, published, and archival accounts, as well as the dates on the actual memorial headstones, differ. A small entry in the Encyclopedia of Jewish Life Before and After the Holocaust reveals that in 1939, the Jewish population in the town was 319 under the Soviets. Stavishche was occupied in July 1941, and within a couple of weeks, most of the Jewish men were murdered. Three months later, the Jewish women and children followed a similar fate.

The number of Jews remaining in Stavishche by 1941 decreased significantly from the 1939 population figures because many of the young men were away in the army. All that is truly known is that the executions occurred between July

---

* Forty years later, grass covered the raised mounds, as described in an article that appeared on September 22, 1988, in the Jewish Journal North of Boston, page 9. It details Dr. Murry Rich's visit to the Holocaust Memorial tablets and graves at the Jewish cemetery in Stavishche. (Rich is the grandson of Shika de Potch, the postmaster, and the son of Dvora Golditch, a classmate of Daniel Cutler's at the Russian school.) Twenty years later, in May 2008, the grandson of another Stavishcher visited the same memorials. He reported that the mounds have since weathered and flattened out.

and December of 1941 and that the old men and boys were killed before the women and girls.

Here is the inscription written on a plaque in Hebrew on both stones:

> A memorial stone
> To honor
> The holy martyrs
> Who were murdered by
> The Fascist murderers
> For the sanctification of God's name
> In the month of Tishrei
> The year 5701
> In the town of Stavishche
> May God remember them in favor
> And may He avenge the spilled blood of His servants.
> The date is October 1941.

> Written in Russian on the women's mass grave:
> Ponder, O Man!
> These unfortunate people did not live to see victory.
> German-Fascist executioners and their police
> Viciously destroyed the life, breath, voice,
> thoughts of 150 Soviet citizens—Jews
> old, young, women and children.
> These are your mothers, your sisters, daughters, and grandchildren.
> [Pay] attention to the spiritual and physical sufferings
> of these dead and you will know all the depth
> and magnitude of their struggle
> for your bright and happy life.

> On the bottom plaque, written in Russian:
> [Do] not suffer but penetrate [into] hatred
> And suspicion toward Fascism and understand
> That [you] never will allow
> Repetition [of] such victims.

Maintain the memory of the martyrs
alive in your children.

Written in Russian on the men's memorial gravestone:
Here rests the dust
Of fifty old men and children
Soviet citizens and Jews
Beastly slain by German
Fascists and their police
In September 1941 from the village of Stavishche

On the bottom plaque, written in Russian:
People be aware!
This should not happen again.
Let's not forget nor forgive
The fascist murderers and their
policemen.

APPENDIX J

SEARCHING FOR A HISTORICAL TREASURE: THE *MEGILAT HA-TEVAH*, TEL AVIV, 2003

In December 2002, a quick email tip that the author of *Tears Over Russia* received from an Israeli genealogist/writer eventually led to the rediscovery of the original copy of what might be one of the most significant pogrom manuscripts ever compiled. The genealogist heard that a few years earlier researcher Michael Ben-Gershon, who followed a lead in an Encyclopedia of Hebrew Authors that he believes he probably looked at in Israel's National Library, saw, with his own eyes, the historical treasure in a Tel Aviv archive.

The location of Eliezer David Rosenthal's (1856–1932) original copy of the *Megilat Ha-tevah* (Scroll of the Slaughter) may have eluded many Jewish historians. Rosenthal, a writer living in Odessa, felt compelled to leave a written testimony of what happened to the Jews of Russia (and Ukraine) during the pogroms of 1917–1921.

Rosenthal, who was seriously ill while struggling to complete his work, traveled from town to town across Ukraine, collecting eyewitness accounts and evidence of the pogrom massacres. He penned his masterpiece in a beautiful Hebrew script and organized it in alphabetical order by the names of the afflicted towns.

Emma Goldman, the Jewish political activist, anarchist, and writer who was deported by the United States to Russia in December 1919, wrote of an interesting chance encounter that she had with the poet Chaim Nahman Bialik in Odessa.[*] Bialik, who later became one of Israel's most famous writers, was accompanied by a man whom Goldman referred to as a "literary investigator."[†] While she did not name this "investigator," she reported that he had visited seventy-two cities, collecting the richest materials on the pogroms. It's possible that Goldman may have met with Rosenthal.

In the mid-1920s, it is rumored that Rosenthal may have smuggled the manuscript out of Ukraine in pieces to his son who lived in Israel.[‡] Possibly with the help of Chaim Nahman Bialik, who also hailed from Odessa, the first half of the manuscript was published in three volumes in Jerusalem and Tel Aviv during the years 1926–1930.[§] The publishers of these volumes included a brief introduction, written by Bialik, providing details of Rosenthal's struggles to compile his historical masterpiece.[¶]

After the deaths of both Rosenthal (1932) and Bialik (1934), the second half of this rare historical find, which contained the pages on Stavishche, was never published. The original handwritten work, which also included many pogrom memorial lists naming the victims from various towns, was believed to be eventually donated by Rosenthal's survivors to Gnazim National Institute, known to Israeli researchers as the Archive of the Hebrew Writers Association.

The original manuscript appeared to have been sitting untouched in Gnazim for many decades until Ben-Gershon took it out of its old brown envelope. The librarian who assisted Ben-Gershon said that in the many years she had been working there, she had not seen anyone else looking at the document. Ben-Gershon, however, spent three hours that day looking through Rosenthal's masterful compilation in amazement. It would be a few more years before the author would learn of his discovery.

From her computer in the United States, the author, after receiving a tip from and communicating extensively with Ben-Gershon, began a search for the Israeli archive, which, at that time, had no online presence or email. She contacted and

---

[*] Certain historical timelines place Goldman in Odessa in September 1920.

[†] Source: Goldman, Emma. *My Further Disillusionment in Russia*. Garden City, New York: Doubleday, Page, 1924, page 10.

[‡] Some referred to Israel at that time as Eretz Yisrael. Prior to its independence in 1948, Israel was a British Mandate of Palestine.

[§] Some of Rosenthal's entries also appeared many decades ago in the Hebrew journal *Reshumot*.

[¶] Some of the information in this appendix regarding Rosenthal's early struggles to write and publish his masterpiece was based on the aforementioned introduction. (See Notes for more details.)

was assisted by Benjamin Haspel of the University of Tel Aviv Archive, who then communicated back and forth for months with the staff at Gnazim on her behalf.

In June 2003, Mr. Haspel wrote to the author that he was informed by Gnazim that they did not have the materials she had requested. However, since Ben-Gershon had seen the document just a few years earlier among their holdings, an exhaustive search soon followed that was conducted over the summer. On August 27, 2003, the institute's general manager was kind enough to email the author from her own computer to tell her that the *Megilat Ha-tevah* had at last been located. She then advised the author that, unfortunately, the document was found in very bad condition and could disintegrate upon handling. The manuscript could only be handled by a paper preservation specialist, which would mean that the pages of interest could not be sent to her at that time.

The historical importance of the *Megilat Ha-tevah* prompted a restoration project that soon followed. It was done in the restoration department in the National Library of Israel, headed by Tova Szeintuch, and generously funded by the Vivienne and Sam Cohen Charitable Trust.

Finally, in March 2004, sixteen months after her search first began, the author was able to experience the thrill of holding a few coveted pages of eyewitness testimony on Stavishche!* Never before published, they confirmed the horrors that her grandmother Anne described long ago in her bedtime stories. A chilling 1919 tombstone list with the names of Zhelezniak's victims, depicted in the eighth chapter of this book and translated in Appendix D, was found among the pages on Stavishche. A small pinhole at the top of the page resembling a tack mark indicates that the list was likely posted somewhere in the shtetl following the massacre.

Officially titled (in an English translation) *Scroll of the Slaughter: Material about the Days of Pogroms and the Slaughter of the Jews in the Ukraine, in Greater Russia, and in White Russia*, it is item number 341 at the Gnazim National Institute.† The author believes it to be one of the most significant sources regarding this often-forgotten time period of Jewish history, rivaled in importance by the distinguished files in YIVO's Tcherikower Archive.

---

* The institute's then general manager assisted the author in retrieving the pages on Stavishche.

† This item number was current at the time when the author was first in contact with the archive. The archive has since moved to Beit Ariela.

THE STUNNING DISCOVERY
OF THE STAVISHCHE TORAH CROWN

2005

For more than fifty years, a quaint synagogue that sits on the top of a hill in a northern New Jersey town has housed a treasure within the walls of its sacred ark. An exquisite antique silver Torah crown (keter) has enjoyed anonymity among the sacred scrolls, breastplates, and rimonim.

It has been a safe refuge for the keter that once belonged to the Jewish community of Stavishche, Ukraine. Its original home, where it adorned the top of a sacred Torah in the Old Country, was burned to the ground by hateful bandits more than a century ago. Rabbi Yitzhak Avraham Gaisinsky (Rabbi Pitsie Avram) was responsible for its miraculous rescue from the flames. He understood how beloved and special the crown was to the Jews of his shtetl. Fleeing first to England and later to America from his native country, the rabbi carried with him what we would later learn was in all likelihood the last Jewish artifact to survive from Stavishche.*

In 1954, twelve years after the rabbi's tragic death, his newly married granddaughter, Sylvia, donated the precious crown, which sat in her younger brother Max's bedroom for more than a decade, to a growing young congregation.†

---

* The Stavishche Torah Scroll itself survived, but the rabbi's grandchildren could not remember where it had been donated fifty years earlier, so it was not located.

† For privacy reasons, the author has chosen not to name the synagogue or its location.

Another fifty-one years would pass before Rabbi Pitsie Avram's youngest grandson, Max, and the author, who is Channa Caprove's oldest granddaughter and Isaac the shoemaker's great-granddaughter, would together bring the priceless crown back to center stage. In 2005, they met with the rabbi of the temple: inside the ark they spotted the precious relic. Jews around the world with roots in Stavishche would now be in awe of this precious item, which is rich in history and almost vanished into obscurity.

Their eyes lit up as they held a piece of their families' history in their hands. The Hebrew inscription, which was on a plate affixed to the front of the Torah crown, read as follows: "This keter was a gift to Agudat Achim Anshei Stavishche given by the hand of Rabbi Yitzhak Avraham Gaisinsky, son of Rabbi Israel Gaisinsky."

The plaque is believed to have been affixed to the crown after the rabbi came to America and donated the item in 1929 to his new synagogue in the Bronx.

The following transliterations and translations from the Stavishche Torah crown are credited to Dr. Ida Selavan Schwarcz, the daughter of Esther Malka Spector of Stavishche. Also in attendance was her husband, Dr. Joseph M. Schwarcz. The couple met with the author at the synagogue in 2006, a year after the rabbi's grandson led her to this historical find.

On the plate affixed to the back of the crown, in Yiddish:

Z"N [unknown meaning]
Leydis akzileri Benot Sarah Agudat Ahim Anshe Stavishche
Tsherni bat Yisrael Hofman prezidentin
Dov ben R' Aahron Valis, sekretar
Zeh haketer Torah natnnu bematanah le–Vet Keneset
Agudat Ahim Anshe Stavishche
Asher nityasda al yede Harav R' Titshak Avraham ben
Harav R' Yisrael Gaisinsky

Ladies Auxiliary Daughters of Sarah, Agudat Ahim (organization of brothers)
Anshe Stavishche (Men or People of Stavishche)
Cherni daughter of Israel Hofman, President
Dov son of Aharon Valis, Secretary
Which was founded by Rabbi Isaac Abraham, son of Rabbi Israel Gaisinsky
Names of the Ladies on the Bells

Below is a translation of the women's names that are engraved in Yiddish on the many tiny bells that hang from the Torah crown.

Top row:
Meni bat Mordekhai Grinshpan
Lea bat Avraham Grisin

Meni, daughter of Mordekhai Greenspan
Leah, daughter of Abraham Grisin

Second row:
Feyge bat Yisrael Faynberg
Menuha Maykelson bat R'Eliyahu
Brakha bat Harav David Ludmiri
Freyde bat Eliyahu Hofman

Feyge, daughter of Israel Feinberg
Menuha Michaelson, daughter of Eliyahu
Brakha, daughter of Rabbi David Ludmiri
Freyde, daughter of Eliyahu Hofman

Third row:
Brakha bat Yeshayahu Rabinovits
Rivka bat Yeshoshua Hastrov
Rivka bat Eliyahu Kesavitsh
Sara Rahel bat Simha Klaiman
Rahel bat Avraham Gaisinsky
Haya Rahel bat Eliyahu Spektor

Brakha, daughter of Isaiah Rabinowitz
Rivka, daughter of Joshua Hastrov (Gastrow?)
Rivka, daughter of Eliyahu Kesavich
Sara Rahel, daughter of Simha Kleiman
Rahel, daughter of Avraham Gaisinsky (translator's note: may not be referring to the rabbi)
Haya Rahel, daughter of Eliyahu Spector

Fourth row:

Havah bat Yoar Dadyak

Rahel bat R'Ya'akov Shakerman

Havah bat R' David Gaisinsky

Havah bat Harav Yitshak Avraham Zaslawsky

Havah, daughter of Yoar (Joel?) Dadyak

Rahel, daughter of Jacob Shakerman

Havah, daughter of David Gaisinsky

Havah, daughter of Rabbi Isaac Abraham Zaslawsky

Author's Notes Regarding the Stavishche Torah Crown

- Interpreting the combination of the names appearing on the bells: When the father's personal name follows their daughter's personal name (ex: Havah, daughter of Rabbi Isaac Abraham), it is then followed by the woman's married name rather than her maiden name. Therefore, it is important *not* to combine the first name of her father with the last name of her husband outside of this list's context. Example: On the very last bell, Havah, who we know was the daughter of Rabbi Isaac Abraham Gaisinsky and the wife of David Zaslawsky, is listed as Havah, daughter of Rabbi Isaac Abraham Zaslawsky.

- Some of the engravings on the bells were not legible due to its advanced age; some were worn over time. A few of the bells were missing or replaced with newer bells that had no names engraved on them.

- While it is reasonable to assume that the plates were probably affixed to both the front and the back of the Torah crown after the crown was donated by Rabbi Gaisinsky to his congregation in the Bronx, it has not been definitively established in what year or in which country the names on the bells were engraved. It is possible that they were engraved by former Stavishchers who were members of the Bronx congregation as a fundraiser in honor of the rabbi, but it is also possible that they were engraved while the crown was still in Stavishche. The former is more probable.

- Three additional Torah items that Rabbi Gaisinsky brought to America from Stavishche have not been located. One of those items, a Torah scroll that was housed in New York at Agudat Achim Anshei Stavishche between the

years 1928 and 1942, was donated after Pitsie's Avram's death to a Jewish
group in the Bronx, where the esteemed rabbi once served as a scribe.
A silver breastplate that once hung on that Torah, as well as a matching
Torah crown, possibly slightly larger in size and most likely containing
the names of men on the bells, could not be found. The grandchildren
of Rabbi Pitsie Avram state that three items, two Torah crowns and a
breastplate, were all donated together in 1954 to the same synagogue,
but two of the items were not present when the Torah Crown was redis-
covered in their ark in 2005.

The story of the rediscovery of the Stavishche Torah crown was depicted in a
newspaper article that was written by Channa's granddaughter, the author of this
book. Below is a copy of the article that appeared many years ago in the *New
Jersey Jewish News*. Channa's tales spotlighted the rabbi who saved the Stavishche
treasure from the Old Country.

It began with my grandmother Anne's famous bedtime stories.
Faced with the dilemma of entertaining an eight-year-old insomniac, she could only hold my attention by drawing on stories from
her own youth.

Hers was a childhood in Stavishche, Ukraine, mixed with
memories of picking flowers in Count Branicki's botanical gardens
and running from the pogroms that ravaged the town following the
Russian Revolution.

Stavishche, a small shtetl located twenty-seven miles south of
the larger Belaya Tserkov, was a community of 8,500 before the
Revolution; half of the population was Jewish. What made Stavishche stand out from other shtetls was the mysterious but kindly
Count Wladyslaw Branicki, a Polish magnate who owned the land
and presided over an estate of astonishing beauty adorned with
Arabian horses.

Many years after conducting interviews with the last generation
of Jews who lived in the town, I have resumed writing my grandmother's memoir with renewed vigor. With doors now opened

by the popularity of the Internet, families with ties to Stavishche living in seven countries around the world have shared personal stories with me. They are the anecdotes not only of the shoemaker (my great-grandfather), but also of the blacksmith, the butcher, the baker, the candlestick maker, the rabbi, the cantor, and of course, the count.

What I did not expect during this journey was the colorful side story that would emerge of the brilliant Stavishche rabbi Yitzhak Avraham Gaisinsky, who was affectionately known as Rabbi Pitsie Avram.

Pitsie Avram felt that it was his duty to protect his people, which was quite a task during the pogroms of 1918–1920. When the murderous Russian bandit Zeleny raided Stavishche in the summer of 1919, Pitsie Avram put himself in harm's way by demanding a face-to-face meeting with him. The rabbi's brave spirit and negotiating skills (which no doubt included a payoff) impressed the pogrom leader, who restrained his soldiers from killing the town's Jews.

A search for Rabbi Gaisinsky's descendants led me to Paris, New York, and finally California, where I found his youngest grandson, Max Zaslawsky. With the help of Max and my own mother, Marcy Brahin, we went on a quest to find the Torah items that Pitsie Avram had saved from the ark of the Stavishche synagogue in the spring of 1920 when it was torched by pogrom bandits; the old white-bearded rabbi emerged from the burning building cradling the Torah, its breastplate, and a pair of Torah "crowns" (keters). A second Torah had already been burned by local bandits, causing the cantor of Stavishche to collapse and die of a heart attack.

On a Shabbat morning in March 1942, Rabbi Pitsie Avram, who had sailed to America in 1928 with the Stavishche Torah items, was struck and killed by a taxi as he crossed the street near the Bronx synagogue that he led. After his death, the Torah was donated to a local Jewish group; the pair of crowns and the breastplate was retained by the rabbi's family. The pieces remained in the custody of his young grandson, Max, until his sister donated them to a New Jersey synagogue in 1954.

It was now a must that we go see these Torah items that Pitsie Avram held so dear.

On a beautiful and memorable morning in 2005, the rabbi of the temple opened the ark, and before the eyes of the Stavishche rabbi's grandson, my mother, and myself, sat one of Pitsie Avram's precious Torah crowns. In Hebrew, I could not believe what I read; engraved on an identification plate was the name of the town—Stavishche!

It was a magnificent antique three-tiered crown made of filigreed silver on the top and bottom, with brass in its center. Its delicate craftsmanship boasted many tiny bells hanging in layers on the crown, once used to adorn the top of the Stavishche Torah; a closer look at the engravings on the bells revealed the names of the women who once lived in the shtetl.

It was a magical discovery—probably the only Jewish artifact to survive from my grandmother's shtetl. It was here in New Jersey, and I was holding it. Never in my late grandmother Anne's wildest dreams would she ever have imagined that her bedtime stories would yield such a prize.

ACKNOWLEDGMENTS

W here do I even begin in thanking all of those who have assisted me on a lifetime quest? Unfortunately, many of you, like my grandmother, did not live to see this day, but I hope that in your hearts you believed that this book would someday come to fruition.

To avoid being repetitive, I have already acknowledged a great many of you in my bibliography and notes, and next to various sources and footnotes that appear in *Tears Over Russia*.

To my husband, Michael, and to our family—mine, his, and ours—as well as my close friends: thank you for your endless support. A special shout-out to my mother, Marcy Brahin, Channa's daughter, and to my sister, Mindi Beaver, who have always believed that I could achieve this dream. I think that my dad would have been proud, too.

Thank you to the many archivists, librarians, genealogical researchers, volunteers, and curators located in several countries around the world, and to the many important institutions who hold such prized historical documents. Special thanks to all the linguists who shared their amazing talents, especially Ida Selavan Schwarcz and Monika Hendry, who generously volunteered their time over the years.

To the many family historians and extended family members and friends with ties to Stavishche who shared their stories with me, and to those whom I interviewed in my youth who once lived in the town, I thank you.

To my fabulous agent, Kathryn Willms of the Rights Factory, thank you for your wisdom and your invaluable help; to Sam Hiyate, president of the Rights Factory, thank you for your assistance. To Jessica Case and Claiborne Hancock and the staff of Pegasus Books, thank you for recognizing the importance of this lost history and for giving me this precious opportunity to share it with the world.

I'd also like to thank three men, none of whom lived long enough to see this publication but who wanted their heroic family members to be remembered in my book. To my friend, Max Zaslawsky, the grandson of Rabbi Pitsie Avram, thank you for helping and encouraging me throughout the years. To Norman Stumacher and Phillip Silverman, the son and son-in-law of Barney Stumacher, thank you for your generosity in supporting me to tell Barney's story. I promised that I would acknowledge you all, and I'm keeping true to my word!

Finally, to all of our ancestors who endured hardships and made daring voyages like my grandmother and her family, thank you for ensuring that your children and their children would enjoy the freedoms afforded to all of us in the Golden Land.

GLOSSARY

ataman: a Cossack chief, synonymous with hetman; leader of an armed band; both words are used here referring to pogrom leaders

bar mitzvah: ceremony marking a youngster's reaching the age of religious majority, usually thirteen

bet din/beit din: court of law

bet hamidrash/beit hamidrash: house of study or learning

bimah: platform, high place where the Torah is read

bris/brit malah: circumcision ceremony

bubbe: grandmother

challah: braided white bread often used for the Sabbath and holidays

chazzan: cantor

chuppah: wedding canopy

datcha: country house; a camp-like setting

daven: to recite Jewish prayers

dorf: a village that is smaller than a shtetl

get: a divorce

Goldene Medina: Golden Land (reference to the United States)

graf: a count or nobleman

guberniya: county or province

gymnasium: school

Haftorah: selection from one of the biblical books of the Prophets read on Shabbat or on holidays after the Torah reading

hetman: leader, synonymous with ataman

intergesl: side street, backstreet, or alley

Kaddish: Jewish prayer recited during the three daily synagogue services and by those who are mourning the death of a relative

kapchonka: smoked and salted whitefish

kest: boarding provided by the parents of newlyweds through the early period of marriage; this is written in the marriage contract

keter: crown

kibitz: to chat or converse

kloyz: small synagogue or house of study

kreplach: small noodles or dumplings that are often filled with meat; they can also be filled with cheese, potato, or fruit

kugel: savory or sweet pudding with noodles

landsman (plural: landslayt/landsleit): a person from one's hometown or shtetl

melamed: teacher of young children in a Jewish school

minyan: quorum of ten adult Jews necessary for public prayer

mohel: ritual circumciser; one who performs the ritual of brit malah

pitseleh: little one

pogrom/pogromit: an organized, often officially encouraged massacre or persecution of a minority group, especially one conducted against Jews; to outrage or to wreak havoc

poritz/porets: nobleman, lord, or landowner

portyanki: foot cloths worn under Russian boots

preetza: noblewoman, usually the wife of a poritz

rugelach: Jewish pastry/dessert with a filling rolled up inside. In Yiddish, it translates to "little twists" and is of Jewish Ashkenazi Polish origin.

Shavuot: Jewish holiday, the Day of Pentecost, receiving of the Torah. It is also the beginning of the wheat harvest.

sheitel/sheytel: traditional wig worn by Orthodox Jewish women

shidduch: an arranged marriage

shtetl (plural: shtetlach): a small town or village with a large Jewish population

shul: synagogue

tallis: prayer shawl

tante: aunt

Tenaim: engagement contract

uyezd: district

vants (plural: vanzen/vantsn): bedbug

varenikes: Ukrainian word for "kreplach" or "pierogi"; dumplings that are filled with meat, cheese, potato, or fruit

viorst: a Russian measure of distance equal to about 3,500 feet (about .662 mile/ 1 kilometer)

yarid: marketplace

Yizkor Book: any Holocaust memorial book

zaftig: juicy, succulent; often used to describe an overweight person

zeyde: grandfather

NOTES

ABBREVIATIONS
DUPIY1919: *Di Ukrainer Pogromen in Yor 1919*
MH: *Megilat Ha-tevah*
NYT: *New York Times*
PYB: *Pochayev Yizkor Book/Pitchayever Yizkor Bukh*
SYB: *Stavishche Yizkor Book*

NOTES
Please note that in many instances, the dates and exact details of events differ slightly in certain sources. Family histories, compositions, stories, reports given to committees and archives, reports used in previously published materials, and those being interviewed are often recalling events that happened months, years, and, in many instances, decades earlier. Therefore, the exact details are dependent upon the accuracy of the memories of those reporting the events. In addition, the Jewish and Gregorian calendars can often become confusing; events are sometimes referred to as having happened "around" the time of a certain Jewish holiday, the dates of which may differ from year to year. After carefully reviewing all the sources, the author has tried to the best of her ability to acknowledge these possible differences in her notes and to make the best determination of the details and time of events portrayed in the book.

Please also note that the general overall story is based on the oral interviews, recordings, and letters of the author's grandmother Channa Caprove, so it is impossible to include her name everywhere in the notes. However, at times she is mentioned when it's in combination with others who are also being credited.

Much of the dialogue in the book is re-created from interviews that the author conducted as well as from other family history stories.

Please note that at the time of the birth of the author's grandmother Channa, the town of Stavishche was located in Russia. During her lifetime the borders changed: today Stavishche is located in Ukraine. However, many who were interviewed who lived in the region at the time often interchanged the names of the countries, as the borders changed often. The author also refers to the capital city of Ukraine by its old spelling, Kiev. Today, the city is referred to as Kyiv.

PREFACE

p. xi   Cabinet Portrait: Many old Russian photos (such as this one, taken
               before the Revolution) were mounted on thick backboards and displayed
               in cabinets. According to historian Deborah G. Glassman's article
               "Learning Your Lyakhovichi History from Family Pictures," which first
               appeared on Jewishgen's website in 2005, English paper suppliers were
               the backbone of Russia's photography supply market. At the bottom of
               these card stocks, underneath the photos, the words "Cabinet Portrait"
               often appeared in English, sometimes accompanied by scrollwork. This
               explains the unexpected appearance of English words on many old Russian
               photographs.

CHAPTER ONE: FAMILY FOLKLORE

p. 3   According to Jewish law, there was a "special rule regarding the *get*": Freeze,
               Jewish Marriage and Divorce in Imperial Russia, page 144.

p. 3   Since the marriage could only be dissolved: According to Freeze, *Jewish
               Marriage and Divorce in Imperial Russia*, page 144.

p. 3   "Behold, this is your get . . . permitted to marry any man": Freeze, *Jewish
               Marriage and Divorce in Imperial Russia*, page 144.

p. 4   Less than five hundred divorces were reported: Freeze actually states 461 in
               Jewish Marriage and Divorce in Imperial Russia, page 302.

p. 4   obligation known as *kest*: Zunser, *Yesterday*, page 272.

p. 5   Estimates ranging from over one hundred thousand: Researchers
               disagree on the numbers, so a range was placed here. Gannes, *Childhood
               in a Shtetl*, page 121, places the numbers in the higher end of the range
               given.

p. 5   "Kill the Jews and Save Russia!" During various interviews, this slogan was
               mentioned by a few of those, including Channa, who lived in the town.
               Gannes, *Childhood in a Shtetl*, page 119, confirms the slogan in this way: "Kill
               the Jews, Save Russia." Heifetz, *The Slaughter of the Jews in the Ukraine in 1919*,
               page 275, used the variation: "Kill the Jews" and "Save Russia."

p. 6   During warm summer evenings: Barbara Stumacher, in a composition written
               about her grandmother Molly Cutler, read by her father, Abe, on audiotape.

p. 8   khapn a keek": Rita L. Antanir Posin, in an interview with the author.

p. 8   "You SHOULD marry her!": Rita L. Antanir Posin, in an interview with the
               author.

p. 8   called the river "Lazy Tikatch": Kushnir, *The Village Builder*, page 19.

CHAPTER ONE FOOTNOTES

p. 4   The general Jewish population: Freeze, *Jewish Marriage and Divorce in
               Imperial Russia*, page 302.

p. 4   The term *feldsher*: Rousselot et al., "The Evolution of the Physician's
               Assistant," page 1479.

p. 4   Peter the Great of Russia: Rousselot et al, "The Evolution of the Physician's
               Assistant," page 1479.

CHAPTER TWO: A TOTAL ECLIPSE

p. 12   He slept in a bunk by an ongoing fire: Bobby Usatch Katz, in an interview with the author.

p. 14   "looking through a piece of smoked glass" and "an evil event": Lessure Mayers, "My Family History," page 1.

p. 15   benches that were shaded by very old pine: Moshe Galant in SYB, pages 77–84.

p. 15   a stunning view of a huge pond: Aftanazy, *Dzieje Rezydencji Na Dawnych Kresach Rzeczypospolitej*, page 328.

p. 16   windmill . . . Micinski, who set his novel *Wita*: Iwaszkiewicz, *Ksiazka Moich Wspomnien*, pages 134–35.

p. 17   "Oyfn Pripetshik": Mark Warshawsky (1848–1907); this is a well-known Yiddish lullaby.

p. 17   After peasant boys threw pebbles: Dr. Murry Rich, in a letter to the author.

CHAPTER FOUR: DAYS OF INNOCENCE

p. 22   By 1763, the Jewish population: Rulikowski, *Slownik Geograficzny: Stawiszcze*, page 299.

p. 22   half of the 8,500 residents: Yaroshevich, ed., *All South-Western Region Information and Address Book of Kiev, Podolia and Volyn Districts*, pages 601–02, gives a total over slightly over 8,500 residents of Stavishche. This was a 1913 figure. Channa and many others interviewed, as well as many sources, place the Jewish population at about half that number.

p. 24   Leaper managed to avoid the mud: Sol Moser, in an interview with the author.

p. 24   "Haika de Zhitomir": Sol Moser, in an interview with the author.

p. 24   "Lepe the egg merchant": Kaminsky, "The Stepansky Family Story," page 1.

p. 24   "There was a pogrom": Sol Moser, in an interview with the author.

p. 24   Jewish babies were murdered: Vivian Moser Flamm, in an interview with the author.

p. 25   Chiah Sura Spivack . . . "cupping": Emily Bayard, in a letter to the author.

p. 25   "escaped exile in near Yakutsk": The place of exile was also confirmed in Vladimirsky, "Jewish Settlement in Siberia," page 6.

p. 25   "He now calls himself": Daniel Cutler, in an interview with the author.

p. 25   Pitsie Sheynes, the husband of Shika de Potch's sister Pearl: Dr. Murry Rich, in an interview with the author.

p. 25   "Pitsie Postrel, the overseer of the forest": Sanders, "A Brief Memoir," page 1. The different Pitsies in town were recounted by several children who lived in Stavishche, in interviews by the author. Sanders's brief memoir confirmed the occupations of his Pitsie, or Pitzie.

p. 25   "Zionist from Zhashkov": Discussed by Daniel Cutler, in an interview with the author, with the dialogue re-created from that interview. However, it was Pitsie Avram's grandson, Max Zaslawsky, who confirmed a cousin relationship with the Dayan family, in an interview with the author.

p. 25   The names of Eliyahu and Shmuel Dayan are confirmed by the Rabbi M. Halevi in SYB, pages 41–45.

p. 26   Shika never charged a sick person: Dr. Murry Rich, in an interview with the author.

pp. 26–27   Christian peasants walked out on the frozen river. . . . During the ceremony: Bayard, "Yasha Kainer's Stories About Russia," page 4. This was recounted to Ms. Bayard by another child witness, Yasha Kainer. Yasha described in beautiful detail but did not name the event that the author believes was Epiphany, or Kreshchenie.

p. 27   "When the fair came, everyone was busy": Yosl Golub in SYB, pages 95–118.

p. 28   Sholem Alecheim: Draznin, *It Began with Zade Usher,* pages 122–23. Aleichem's marriage and his connection to the Loyev and Mazur families are mentioned in Draznin's book, as well as that Olga was born in nearby Shubovka (see footnote).

CHAPTER FOUR FOOTNOTE

p. 26   Eliyahu and Shmuel Dayan: The brothers were mentioned by Halevi and others in the SYB; Eliyahu, their father, and their famous ancestor the Shpole Zeide were mentioned by Y. Dayan, "Bayit Be-Yisreal:Eliyahu ve-Batya Dayan," chapter 1.

CHAPTER FIVE: AVRUM CUTLER'S BRIEF BETROTHALS

p. 29   His nieces . . . could not help but laugh: Rita L. Antanir Posin, in an interview with the author.

p. 31   Myer Ova Denka: Early US records list his name as Averdenko and then Over; the transliteration of Russian records has the name listed as Ovadenko and Ovadenka. Channa stated it was Ova Denka.

p. 31   once made a pair of leather boots: Anne Caprove Kravitz, in oral stories, tapes, and in a 1990 letter to the author, page 5.

CHAPTER FIVE FOOTNOTE

p. 32   Channa's aunts used a similar Yiddish saying regarding *zaftig* women as did Zunser, *Yesterday,* page 208.

CHAPTER SIX: COUNT WLADYSLAW BRANICKI AND THE NOBLE FAMILY OF STAVISHCHE

p. 34   It was on a market day: Some former residents of Stavishche, who were children during this time period, believed the violence at the count's estate was on a market day and took place at the beginning on the Revolution, possibly the fall of 1917. One Polish source had the estate destroyed by 1918.

p. 35   dragging a very large mirror: Lessure Mayers, "My Family History," page 1.

p. 35   castle that was inherited by: O. Polozova, in a letter to the author regarding the Kiev Guberniya Notebook.

p. 35   "with a shattered mirror and a bleeding cow!" Lessure Mayers, "My Family History," page 1.

p. 36   commissioned back in 1857: Rulikowski, *Slownik Geograficzny: Stawiszcze*, page 299.

p. 37   peculiar-looking water pump: Aftanazy, *Dzieje Rezydencji Na Dawnych Kresach Rzeczypospolitej*, page 328.

p. 37   described as shy and unassuming: Tarnowski, "Stawiszcze and the Branicki Family," page 2.

p. 37   concerned about the welfare of widows and orphans: M. Mazaraki (see Appendix B).

p. 38   including the Jews of his village: Kushnir, *The Village Builder*, page 34.

p. 38   in the court of the tsar: Kushnir, *The Village Builder*, page 34.

p. 38   In the winter of 1887, a Hebrew language newspaper *Hazefirah* and "May he be rewarded in full.": "Hachovesh" (believed to be a pseudonym of an unknown writer). *Hazefirah* (Newspaper). Warsaw, Russian Poland. February 9, 1887, page 2.

p. 38   wrote that like Casimir the Great: Iwaszkiewicz, *Ksiazka Moich Wspomnien*, pages 134–35.

p. 38   he purchased a drilling machine: Kushnir, *The Village Builder*, page 34. Note: Kushnir's translation uooo the name Count Berntizky, but the proper spelling is Branicki.

p. 39   Count Branicki's dense pine forest: The location of Count Branicki's forest was mentioned by Meyer Spector in SYB, pages 85–94, but was also recounted by Channa and many other villagers interviewed by the author.

p. 39   Stavishche, though, was famous for its horses: Rulikowski, *Slownik Geograficzny: Stawiszcze*, page 299.

p. 39   who set up stables: Aftanazy, *Dzieje Rezydencji Na Dawnych Kresach Rzeczypospolitej*, page 328.

p. 39   morning horseback rides: Iwaszkiewicz, *Ksiazka Moich Wspomnien*, pages 134–35.

p. 39   the noble's much-talked-about purchase: A. Ben-Hayim in SYB, pages 179–82. This story was also recounted by others, such as Channa's mother, Rebecca, who told her a story that the Arabian was purchased in Cairo, while her father, Isaac, disagreed with his wife and told a story that that the horse that collapsed was purchased in Damascus.

p. 39   took out their brooms and swept the streets: Elise Moser, in a letter to the author, where she recounts a story told to her by her grandfather Sol Moser.

p. 40   the noble's priceless Arabian, with Count Branicki proudly saddled: A. Ben-Hayim in SYB, pages 179–82. Again, Isaac also told this story to Channa.

p. 40   "Look at that—no horses, nothing!": Dr. Murry Rich, from his interview with family members.

p. 40   the nobleman owned: Mrs. O. Polozova, in a letter to the author regarding the Kiev Guberniya Notebook. In 2004, she wrote from the Central State Historical Archives of Ukraine in Kiev that Count Branicki's name was found listed in a chapter called "List of Landowners of Tarashcha district that owned above 1,000 desyatins of land." She also wrote that Branicki was the owner of 1,835 desyatins of the land in the town of Stavishche from 1910 to

1913, and by 1914 he was the owner of 2,623 desyatins (about 7,087 acres). From this letter, the author interpreted it to mean that the desyatins were all in Stavishche, but without further investigation, the author couldn't confirm that this didn't include acreage of any surrounding lands within the district.

p. 40   Many of his grandchildren later told their children: Count Paul Potocki, in a letter to the author.

CHAPTER SIX FOOTNOTES

p. 35   During a tour of the estate: Aftanazy, *Dzieje Rezydencji Na Dawnych Kresach Rzeczypospolitej*, page 325. Aftanazy mentions Chlopicki's 1881 description of the interior of the estate.

p. 35   Julia . . . inherited the estate: Mrs. O. Polozova from the Ukraine Government Archives (Kiev) wrote the author a letter about an entry in the Kiev Guberniya Notebook, in a chapter titled "List of Landowners of Tarashcha district that owned more than 1000 desyatins" of land. It stated that, by 1914, Wladyslaw owned 2,623 desyatins of land in Stavishche. From the succession of the deed and knowing the date of the Count's death, the author deduced that Julia inherited the land. Also, Count Ladislas Tarnowski wrote in his family history that Julia inherited Stavishche, owning it until the Treaty of Riga.

p. 36   managed by the great botanic scholar: Aftanazy, *Dzieje Rezydencji Na Dawnych Kresach Rzeczypospolitej*, page 328, and Rulikowski, *Slownik Geograficzny: Stawiszcze*, page 299.

p. 36   Andrzejowski also wrote: Aftanazy, *Dzieje Rezydencji Na Dawnych Kresach Rzeczypospolitej*, page 328.

CHAPTER SEVEN: STAVISHCHE UNDER SIEGE

p. 44   an urgent telegram: Committee of Jewish Delegations, "The Pogroms in the Ukraine Under the Ukrainian Governments 1917–1920," page 7.

p. 44   In August 1918: Klavana Kohen in SYB document, pages 221–34.

p. 44   "To His Honor, the Honored and Learned Rabbi": Rabbi Yitzhak Avraham Gaisinsky et al in SYB, translated by Dr. Ida Selavan Schwarcz, pages 235–238.

CHAPTER SEVEN FOOTNOTE

p. 44   included a bloody riot: Committee of Jewish Delegations "The Pogroms in the Ukraine Under the Ukrainian Governments 1917–1920," page 7.

CHAPTER EIGHT: GRIGORIEV'S BANDITS

The backdrop of this story was provided by Channa Caprove, with facts of the attacks (and sometimes names) confirmed by various sources.

p. 48   the second day of Shavuot: K. Kohen in (SYB Document) pages 221–34. Several sources cite Grigoriev as the ataman, while others indicate that his underlings Zhelezniak, Yatsenko, and Voytsekhovsky were doing his local bidding. Khlavna Kohen in SYB document, pages 221–34, places Zhelezniak and Yatsenko as the leaders and states that they are from Grigoriev's unit; Rosenthal in MH (unpublished manuscript), pages 1, 34–35, places Zhelezniak at the scene. On page 1, he pairs Zhelezniak with the infamous bandit Tutilnik (Tutunik). Heifetz, *The Slaughter of the Jews in the Ukraine in 1919*, pages 287–88, mentions Grigoriev's band. On page 179, Heifetz places Yatzenko and Golub together. Yosl Golub (no relation to the former Golub) in SYB, pages 95–118, and his brother Isaac Golub in SYB, pages 119-29, both place Zhelezniak and Voytsekhovsky together. Israel Senderowitz in SYB, pages 155–57, mentions Zhelezniak in the Shavuot attack. On page 266 of "The Pogroms in the Ukraine Under the Ukrainian Governments 1917–1920," the Committee of Jewish Delegations places Grigoriev's band in Stavishche on June 15, 1919.

p. 48   "White Guards": Heifetz, *The Slaughter of the Jews in the Ukraine in 1919*, page 287.

p. 49   *sikrikim* or *sikriks*: Zhelezniak, Yatsenko, and Voytsekovsky: E. D. Rosenthal in MH, pages 34–35, also confirms the usage of the words *sikriks* and *Sicarii* under the section on Stavishche and *sikrkim* under the section of Tetiev.

p. 50   group of peasants from the nearby village of Pshienka: E. D. Rosenthal in MH, pages 34–35.

p. 50   collect a contribution of 400,000 rubles: E. D. Rosenthal in MH, pages 34–35, and Heifetz, *The Slaughter of the Jews in the Ukraine in 1919*, page 287.

p. 50   along with eight hundred measures of cloth and six hundred sets of underwear: E. D. Rosenthal in MH, pages 34–35.

p. 50   He, along with other witnesses, recognized among the bandits: Heifetz, *The Slaughter of the Jews in the Ukraine in 1919*, page 287.

p. 50   take it upon himself the "good deed" of revenge on the Jews: E. D. Rosenthal in MH, page 35.

p. 50   With the assistance of several well-respected men from Stavishche: Isaac Golub in SYB, pages 119–29.

p. 50   357,000 rubles and "showed mercy and handed back seven-thousand": Heifetz, *The Slaughter of the Jews in the Ukraine in 1919*, page 287.

p. 51   Phillip "Yitzhak" Kohen, had been killed: Israel Senderowitz in SYB, pages 155–57. Phillip's name, which appears as Yitzhak Kagan, is on the Forvets' tombstone list in Appendix E.

p. 51   several thousand rubles to be given to Israel's newly widowed sister: Israel Senderowitz in SYB, pages 155–57.

p. 51   sister, Chaika, and baby daughter, Bella: Harry Senders, in a correspondence with the author.

p. 51   They tortured and raped many women: E. D. Rosenthal in MH, pages 34–35, and Khlavna Kohen in SYB document, pages 221–234.

p. 51   loaded 180 wagons with all kinds of goods: E. D. Rosenthal in MH, pages 34–35.

p. 51   two and a half dozen heads of cattle: Khlavna Kohen in SYB document, pages 221–34.

p. 51   Three old women told of the unthinkable torture: E. D. Rosenthal in MH, pages 1, 34–35. Wilfond's murder is described in MH. Channa remembered hearing her mother in conversation with neighbors describing what they had heard was the rape of a young girl; this description was compatible to the entry on Stavishche in MH naming Wilfond as the victim.

p. 52   Bandits burst into Hirsh Zagatovtchik's home: E. D. Rosenthal in MH, pages 34–35. Hirsh's murder is detailed in MH. Zagatovtchik's name appears on the tombstone lists in Appendices D, E, and F. The death list in Appendix F also states that Hirsh's forty-year-old wife was a murder victim. An early story of Channa's places her father conversing with the rabbi about the murders in town of two men, thus making the author conclude, from the description, that Isaac was told about Hirsh's murder.

p. 52   a Christian neighbor of Motel's: E. D. Rosenthal in MH, pages 34–35. Motel's murder is described in MH. See above explanation of how the author concluded that Isaac heard about this murder as well.

p. 52   bandits printed large anti-Semitic posters: E. D. Rosenthal in MH, pages 34–35. Rosenthal does not name Zaslawsky as the owner of the shop, but the author knew from his grandson that he was.

p. 52   Their most lethal raid of June 15–16 is recorded in Khlavna Kohen's SYB document, pages 221–34, and Heifetz, *The Slaughter of the Jews in the Ukraine in 1919*, page 287. Heifetz, page 287, placed the death toll at twenty-two on the night of the June 15–16 raid, with a total of forty for the week; Channa stated about thirty in all.

p. 53   Outside on the street, in front of his shoe factory: This scene and its dialogue were re-created from interviews and stories, both oral and written, not only from Channa but also from others who lived in the town.

p. 53   "Itsie Shadken was shot": Yosl Golub in SYB, pages 95–118, confirms this fact that was re-created in dialogue.

p. 53   He bled to death before reaching the hospital: Berl Rubin in SYB, pages 159–161, confirms this fact that was used in dialogue. Golub and Rubin both confirm Channa's account of others talking about his death. Itsie was also remembered on the Tcherikover, *Megilat Ha-tevah*, Forverts' death lists as well as the Death List that appears in Appendix F.

p. 54   Mordechai Gutharts's death is recorded in Khlavna Kohen's document in SYB, pages 221–34. Kohen confirms Channa's account that the young man was killed sometime during Zhelezniak's weeklong raid. Channa believed it was on the night of June 15–16. Gutharts's name appears on the Tcherikover and the Forverts' death lists.

p. 54   "They killed Chaim Mayer's stepson, Asher!": Channa places Asher's murder during Zhelezniak's June 15–16 raid; Isaac Golub in SYB, pages 119–29, confirms that it happened sometime during the week of Zhelezniak's raid. Asher's name appears on the Forverts' death lists.

p. 55   Nearly eight hundred Jews: Heifetz, *The Slaughter of the Jews in the Ukraine in 1919*, page 288, in a reference to the mass evacuation to Belaya Tserkov.

p. 56   northwest toward Volodarka: Heifetz, *The Slaughter of the Jews in the Ukraine in 1919*, page 288; Khlavna Kohen in SYB document, pages 221–34; Isaac Golub in SYB, pages 119–29; and E. D. Rosenthal in MH, pages 34–35.

p. 56   set fire to the old, wooden bridge: Khlavna Kohen in SYB document, pages 221–34 (he named it the Rasi River) and E. D. Rosenthal in MH, pages 34–35.

p. 56   "Bring out boards for a makeshift bridge!": Khlavna Kohen in SYB document, pages 221–34, and E. D. Rosenthal in MH pages 34–35, confirmed this, as well as Havah (Eva) Goldman in SYB, pages 55–59. (Note: Havah, when recalling the exodus that her own grandfather Pitsie Avram led to Volodarka, most likely confused the names of the bandits Zhelezniak and Zeleny in her story, which was written forty years after the events unfolded. Several other written sources confirm that it was Zhelezniak's attack that she was describing.)

p. 56   to give the small group of frazzled Jews bread: Khlavna Kohen in SYB document, pages 221–34. In a small footnote by the editor of *Reshumot*, volume 3, 1923, pages 380–82, under Vinograd, there is a mention, but not a confirmation, that Zhelezniak gave the Jews of Stavishche a loaf of bread as he ordered them home from Volodarka. Others confirmed that it was the rabbi who persuaded the hetman to do so.

p. 57   selected a day to fast as a remembrance: Rabbi Laizer Spector, "The Adventures of My Life," page 1. Note: Laizer specifically names Zhelezniak, but the date he reported was contrary to some other reports. He was a child of only seven years old during the incident.

CHAPTER EIGHT FOOTNOTE

p. 57   Jewish folklore quietly refers to Belaya Tserkov as "Shvartse Tume." This nickname, along with the meaning of "Black Abomination," is confirmed in an *Encyclopedia Judaica* entry of Belaya Tserkov, volume 4, pages 278–79.

CHAPTER NINE: FROM VILLAGE TO VILLAGE

p. 61   Myer's daughter, Slova, Avrum's feisty wife, looked through a window: Charles "Chuck" Cutler, in an interview with the author.

p. 62   A Jewish committee of aid set up in Belaya Tserkov to assist the refugees: Heifetz, *The Slaughter of the Jews in the Ukraine in 1919*, page 288.

p. 62   At ten o'clock: Rochela Feinzilberg (Ruth Feinsilver), "An Adventure," page 1.

p. 62   Rochela couldn't imagine her life ending that evening: Rochela Feinzilberg (Ruth Feinsilver), "An Adventure," pages 1–2. Channa also told a similar story when she hid in the bet hamidrash.

p. 62   God finally heard their prayers: Rochela Feinzilberg (Ruth Feinsilver), "An Adventure," page 2.

p. 64   Jewish children grew up fearing the Church: Gannes, *Childhood in a Shtetl*, page 151, see footnote quote for details.

p. 64   Published testimony suggests that even some of the priests: Heifetz, *The Slaughter of the Jews in the Ukraine in 1919*, page 287.

p. 64   The son of a poor peasant: DUPIY1919, chapter 11.

p. 64   "the prototypical representative of the rebel movement": DUPIY1919, chapter 11.

CHAPTER NINE FOOTNOTES

p. 58   whenever the tsar's mother: Rita L. Antanir Posin, in an interview with the
          author.

p. 60   Gittel died of an infection: Ruby Stumacher, in an interview with Abe
          Stumacher.

p. 64   "In Jewish history, generally, the Church was the millennial symbol": Gannes,
          Childhood in a Shtetl, page 151.

p. 64   like the one in nearby Winograd, who risked his life: Gannes, *Childhood in a
          Shtetl*, page 153.

p. 64   Then there was the Peshinke priest, Leyavitch: Isaac Golub in SYB, pages
          119–29.

CHAPTER TEN: ATAMAN ZELENY MEETS RABBI PITSIE AVRAM

p. 66   "*Kol Yisrael Arevim Ze ba Ze*": Talmud (Shavuot 39a).

p. 66   "Take me to your ataman!": In a story recounted by the rabbi's granddaughter,
          Havah (Eva) Goldman in SYB, pages 55–59.

p. 67   "provide you with boots, sugar, salt, and money": Havah (Eva) Goldman in
          SYB, pages 55–59.

p. 67   agreed to send two of his soldiers to accompany: Havah (Eva) Goldman in
          SYB, pages 55–59.

p. 67   Six hundred thousand rubles were collected: Tcherikower Archive, files
          21641–21643, page 2.

p. 67   a group of nearly thirty men: Khlavna Kohen in SYB document, pages
          221–34.

p. 67   Only two or three murders: Tcherikower Archive, files 21641–21643, page 2.

p. 67   prevented his henchmen from committing: Tcherikower Archive, files
          21641–21643.

p. 67   "I am neither a Jew-lover, nor a Jew hater": DUPIY1919, chapter 11.

p. 68   Pitsie Abram's birth date of June 5, 1857, is found in the New York City death
          record of the rabbi.

p. 68   He was ordained by Rabbi Michel: Gottlieb, ed., *Ohole-Schem, Biografien und
          Adressen d. Rabbiners*, pages 361–62.

p. 68   in 1883, Pitsie Avram succeeded: Gottlieb, ed., *Ohole-Schem, Biografien und
          Adressen d. Rabbiners*, pages 361–62.

p. 68   "honored merchant in the town": Gottlieb, ed., *Ohole-Schem, Biografien und
          Adressen d. Rabbiners*, pages 361–62.

p. 68   married Rabbi Zelig Tanicki: Gottlieb, ed., *Ohole-Schem, Biografien und
          Adressen d. Rabbiners*, pages 361–62.

p. 69   one of the founders of radiochemistry: *Rossiyskaya Evreiskaya Entsiclopediya*,
          entry 1354.

p. 69   all important life-altering discussions: Havah (Eva) Goldman in SYB, pages
          55–59.

p. 69   he had made his decision: Havah (Eva) Goldman in SYB, pages 55–59.

p. 70   "Besides being a pious scholar": Havah (Eva) Zaslawsky in SYB, pages 189–94.

p. 70   Jewish eyewitnesses described seeing: DUPIY1919, chapter 11.

CHAPTER ELEVEN: THE MURDER OF BESSIE CUTLER'S HUSBAND

p. 71   two or three miles north: Gillman, *The B'Nai Khaim in America*, page 3.

p. 71   Alexander Kraidin: Sheila Lidz, in an interview with the author.

p. 71   August 2, 1919: Miller and Miller, eds., *Sokolievka/Justingrad*, page 54; DUPIY1919, chapter 11. Committee of Jewish Delegations, "The Pogroms in the Ukraine Under the Ukrainian Governments 1917–1920," page 111: The date August 2, 1919, of the pogrom committed by Zeleny is confirmed on that page, along with 146 as the number murdered.

p. 72   "as long as I live, no blood will be spilled in my town": Channa "Anne" Caprove Kravitz, in an interview with the author in the late 1970s. Channa remembered the story of the famous words of her aunt's rabbi and his tragic fate. This clue, coupled with Channa's mention on page 17 in her letter to the author where she states that Bessie was living in Konela, (a dorf of Sokolovka Justingrad), and her husband being the victim of a winter pogrom where two hundred men were murdered, is what led the author on a quest to research Sokolovka Justingrad. The famous words of the rabbi were later recorded by Rosenthal in MH, according to Sima Lisnovsky, pages 8–11, and Miller and Miller, eds., *Sokolievka/Justingrad*, page 54. Children of Kibbutz Mashabei-Sadeh, "Ustingrad-Sokoliveka: A Town That Was Destroyed," rough draft, page 29.

p. 72   began to believe the rabbi's promise: Miller and Miller, eds., *Sokolievka/Justingrad*, page 54. Children of Kibbutz Mashabei-Sadeh, "Ustingrad-Sokoliveka: A Town That Was Destroyed," rough draft, page 29.

p. 72   "light in his eyes": Rosenthal in MH, according to Sima Lisnovsky, pages 8–11. Sima used the phrase "light in his eyes" to mean that as long as the rabbi lived, he wouldn't allow Jewish blood to be spilled.

p. 72   made their way to the house of the beloved Reb Pinchas'l: Miller and Miller, eds., *Sokolievka/Justingrad*, page 54.

p. 72   the rabbi's large courtyard, brandishing a gun: Children of Kibbutz Mashabei-Sadeh, "Ustingrad-Sokoliveka: A Town That Was Destroyed," rough draft, page 29.

p. 72   seventy-six-year-old Torah chanting rabbi: Children of Kibbutz Mashabei-Sadeh, "Ustingrad-Sokoliveka: A Town That Was Destroyed," rough draft, page 29. (Note: Gillman, *The B'Nai Khaim in America*, page 33, states that the esteemed rabbi was eighty-eight years old at the time of his death.)

p. 72   approximately 150 were shot by a hidden machine gun: Rosenthal in MH, who wrote the testimony of Yosef Zilberg, pages 8–11. (As per the translation, Zilberg indicates that the date of the attack was July 9, 1919.) DUPIY1919, chapter 11, indicates the number of victims to be approximately 152, and the date as a few days before Tisha B'av 1919, the holiday that fell on August 5. This would support Miller's date of August 2, 1919, and follows Zeleny's trail as attacking the town right after Stavishche. Miller and Miller, eds., *Sokolievka/Justingrad*, pages 55–56, mention 150 murdered after the initial rounds of ten and ten. Gillman, *The B'Nai Khaim in America*, page 33, mentions approximately 138 victims, but lists the date as August 1918. However, all other sources that the author found confirm that the year was 1919. The Committee of Jewish Delegations, "The Pogroms in the Ukraine Under the Ukrainian Governments 1917–1920," page 111, confirms the date of August 2, 1919, with 146 killed. Four eyewitnesses from Sokolovka Justingrad reported this to the Committee.

p. 73   Kebe was born and raised in the nearby village: Rosenthal in MH, according to testimony of Hayke Levik, pages 38–39.

p. 73   second killing spree, which took place right after Zeleny's summer massacre: Rosenthal in MH, according to Sima Lisnovsky, pages 8–11.

p. 73   murdered thirty-six of his prey: Rosenthal in MH, according to testimony of Hayke Levik, pages 38–39.

p. 74   Denikin's army, retreating from a loss in Belaya Tserkov: Rosenthal in MH, according to Yosef Zilberg, pages 8–11, and Miller and Miller, eds., *Sokolievka/Justingrad,* page 57.

p. 74   Two hundred bloodied bodies: Rosenthal in MH, according to Yosef Zilberg, pages 8–11; Miller and Miller, eds., *Sokolievka/Justingrad,* page 57; and Children of Kibbutz Mashabei-Sadeh, "Ustingrad-Sokoliveka: A Town That Was Destroyed," rough draft, page 32.

p. 75   The men had been stripped naked: Rosenthal in MH, according to Yosef Zilberg, pages 8–11, Miller and Miller, eds., *Sokolievka/Justingrad,* page 57.

p. 75   who then tied the hands of their victims and bound them together: Rosenthal in MH, according to Yosef Zilberg, pages 8–11.

CHAPTER ELEVEN FOOTNOTES

p. 72   local Christians rescued their Jewish neighbors: Children of Kibbutz Mashabei-Sadeh, "Ustingrad-Sokoliveka: A Town That Was Destroyed," rough draft, page 28.

p. 72   The rabbi may have been survived by a son-in-law: Children of Kibbutz Mashabei-Sadeh, "Ustingrad-Sokoliveka: A Town That Was Destroyed," rough draft, page 29.

p. 72   The rabbi's twenty-two-year-old grandson, Gedalya Mandel: This information appears on Sokolovka Justingrad's memorial lists, found in the Millers's book and in the composition by Children of Kibbutz Mashabei-Sadeh. His name also appears on the memorial tablet.

p. 73   Popivka was a village two miles southwest: Gillman, *The B'Nai Khaim in America,* page 3.

CHAPTER TWELVE: GENERAL DENIKIN'S MILITIA

p. 76   The use of the words "feeling revived" were used by both Anne Caprove Kravitz, in an interview with the author, as well as Yosl Golub in SYB, pages 95–118. It is unclear if groups of boys and girls were separated in the shul during this celebration.

p. 76   carrying little blue-and-white flags: Channa "Anne" Caprove Kravitz, in an interview with the author. Yosl Golub, Channa's childhood friend, also remembered the holiday, in SYB, pages 95–118.

p. 77   Yunkel Cutler, experienced firsthand: One of the sources of this story was Daniel Cutler, who confirmed this in an interview with the author.

p. 78   Without their parents' knowledge: Both Sol Moser and Daniel Cutler confirmed this story in an interview with the author.

p. 78   As if the young widow hadn't already suffered enough: Elba Muler de Fidel, in a letter to the author.

p. 79   As he walked over to a gate: One of the sources of this story was Daniel Cutler, in an interview with the author.

p. 80   Chaos continued: One of the sources of this story was Sol Moser, in an interview with the author.

p. 81   registered as high as 107.6: Betty Einbinder, "The Sudden Call," who actually states her mother had a high fever of 41 degrees C, which translates to 107.6 degrees F. Her statement of a deadly high fever confirms Channa's story of a high fever in town during the Denikin raids.

p. 82   in the tsar's 31st Aleksopol Infantry: Identified by Mark Conrad, a Russian uniform military expert, in an email to the author, who studied a few photos of Moishe in his military uniform.

p. 84   they forced everyone to strip off their clothing: Khlavna Kohen in SYB document, pages 221–34. Z. Greenberg, Tcherikower Archive, files 21641–21643, page 3. Greenberg mentions the same details with a slightly earlier approximate date, but Khlavna Kohen gives similiar details associated with Denikin's raid.

p. 84   became so afraid during the hostage crisis: Sanders, "A Brief Memoir," page 4. Sanders does not specify a date, but the general time period he mentions, (sometime after the Jewish holidays, in the fall/winter 1919) along with details of a roundup and hostage crisis in the synagogue, led the author to the reasonable conclusion that she died during Denikin's raid on Stavishche.

p. 84   he distracted the bandits by conversing with them: Havah (Eva) Zaslawsky in SYB, pages 189–94.

p. 84   the rabbi instructed: Havah (Eva) Zaslawsky in SYB, pages 189–94. Havah does not give a date, but Khlavna Kohen's document confirms it was during the Denikin raids.

p. 84   they threatened to cut off the rabbi's right hand: Khlavna Kohen in SYB document, pages 221–34.

p. 84   He stopped the execution: Havah (Eva) Zaslawsky in SYB, pages 189–94.

p. 84   feasted on food and liquor that they had ordered be brought: Khlavna Kohen (Cohen) in SYB document, pages 221–34.

p. 84   Christians should live a long life: Khlavna Kohen (Cohen) in SYB document, pages 189–94.

CHAPTER TWELVE FOOTNOTES

p. 79   whose own brother, Lepe, the egg merchant: "The Stepansky Family Story," page 3.

p. 79   arranged for Sheindel and her two remaining children: Elba Muler de Fidel, in a letter to the author.

CHAPTER THIRTEEN: REFUGE IN BELAYA TSERKOV

p. 85   Found nine-year-old Sol on her doorstep: Sol Moser, in an interview with the
         author. Sol told the author that he thought that the white things creeping up
         his pant legs were lice that arose from the horse manure he slept on the night
         before to keep warm.

p. 86   "staved off the worst hunger": Elise Moser, in a letter to the author.

p. 86   When he collected enough: Sol Moser, in an interview with the author. His
         granddaughter Elise Moser also mentions this in a letter to the author.

p. 89   first of Elul. . . . Three hundred and fifty Jews lost their lives: Rosenthal in
         MH, according to Avraham Dolgenes (translated by Tzippi Zach and Henry
         Tobias), pages 5–7, 9–12, reported that the number of deaths (350) from
         Denikin's raid in Belaya Tserkov is confirmed in the Kehillah's records (the
         records of the Jewish community of the town).

p. 89   families managed to enjoy some happy days: Channa "Anne" Caprove Kravitz,
         in an interview with the author, and Ruby Stumacher and Daniel Cutler, in
         an interview with the Abe Stumacher.

p. 89   a carpenter's tool with a blade, called a plane: Bayard, "Yasha Kainer's
         Stories About Russia," page 10. Ruby Stumacher, in an interview with Abe
         Stumacher, also described making homemade matches that he sold to the
         soldiers in Belaya Tserkov.

p. 90   Jews were burned alive in the synagogue in the nearby city of Tetiev:
         Rosenthal in MH, pages 78–79, states the number as about 1,500; in Tetiever
         Khurbn, Part I #16, Rosenthal again states the number as about 1,500. On
         page 240 of Annex 49, the Committee of Jewish Delegations, "The Pogroms
         in the Ukraine Under the Ukrainian Governments 1917–1920," states the
         number of victims in the synagogue as 2,000. In the actual text on page 112,
         it states "over 1,000 Jews" (were inside the synagogue). On page 11, Saul S.
         Friedman also states the number of synagogue victims as 2,000.

         Please note: Various sources seem to interchange the bet hamidrash
         and the synagogue in Tetiev, as if they were one and the same. The author
         presumed they were one building.

p. 90   Ataman A. Kurovsky: The Committee of Jewish Delegations, "The Pogroms
         in the Ukraine Under the Ukrainian Governments 1917–1920," page 111,
         gives the initial A for the first name of Ataman Kurovsky.

p. 91   were the sick, disabled, and elderly: Khlavna Kohen in SYB document, pages 221–34.

p. 91   At the Jewish Bikur Holim: Khlavna Kohen in SYB document, pages 221–34.
         H. Hoffman, who also reported this incident found on a memorial list in the
         Tcherikower Archive, file 21642, reported eight Jews (whose sexes were not
         identified) murdered at the Bikur Holim.

p. 91   In the home of Shlomo Zalman Frankel: Khlavna Kohen in SYB document,
         pages 221–34.

p. 91   tore the screaming, bedridden, and elderly from their beds: Stavishcha Relief
         Organization in Kishinev, "The Destroyed City of Stavishcha."

p. 92   the old chazzan's heart gave out: Rita L. Antanir Posin, in an interview with
         the author.

CHAPTER THIRTEEN FOOTNOTES

p. 88   forty thousand Jews: Rosenthal in MH, pages 5–7.

p. 89   General Anton Denikin: New York Passenger Records, 1820–1957, Ellis Island Website.

p. 89   A smaller pogrom: Rosenthal in MH, pages 9–12.

p. 91   Frankel's murder: Khlavna Kohen in SYB document, pages 221-34.

p. 91   were arrested some time later for the murders: Stavishcha Relief Organization in Kishinev, "The Destroyed City of Stavishcha."

CHAPTER FOURTEEN: THERE WAS A PLACE NEARBY, WHERE THEY MADE THE LITTLE COFFINS

p. 95   heard a rumor that young children were being kidnapped and murdered: According to Yasha Kainer, reported in a story by Bayard, "Yasha Kainer's Stories About Russia," page 10.

CHAPTER FIFTEEN: THE UNLIKELY ARRIVAL OF BARNEY STUMACHER, AN AMERICAN HERO

Most of the quotes in this chapter and much of the storyline about Barney's miraculous trip and entrance into Ukraine are attributed to Barney Stumacher, who spoke about his adventures on a 1963 audio tape recorded by his son-in-law, Phil Silverman. Special thanks to and courtesy of Phillip Silverman and Norman Stumacher.

p. 98   cloaks salesman: 1920 US census.

p. 99   the SS *Franconia*: Ellis Island passenger records.

p. 99   All three of the letters in this chapter, including a copy of the letter that Barney received from his father in Belaya Tserkov, are an official part of his passport application originally dated July 24, 1920 (Source: General records of the Department of State/US Government Record Group 59), and is on record at the National Archives, NARA microfilm publication M1490. It appears under US Passport Applications from 1/2/06–3/31/25. It is certificate number 78037 issued on August 4, 1920.

p. 112   The Caprove family ran outside: Channa "Anne" Caprove Kravitz, in an interview with the author. Ruby Stumacher, in an interview with Abe Stumacher, also spoke about witnessing Barney's arrival.

p. 113   business had been torched: Letter from Nechame Stumacher to Barney Stumacher, explaining the fate of Nissel's dry goods store.

p. 113   was no longer permitted to go to school, Nissel decided it was time to leave: Holtzman, *Who Said It Would Be Easy?*, page 5.

p. 114   Itzie Stumacher added an additional twenty people: Channa "Anne" Caprove Kravitz, who was a part of that number, in an interview with the author.

p. 115   to the shop of the tombstone-maker: Channa "Anne" Caprove Kravitz, in an interview with the author.

CHAPTER SIXTEEN: THE GREAT ESCAPE: THE WAGON TRAINS

p. 117   Seeing his little brother standing before him in his pitiful stocking feet: Viviam Flamm, in an interview with the author.

p. 118   She was harboring a well-guarded secret: Rita L. Antanir Posin, in an interview with the author.

p. 119   Blind in both eyes: Barney Stumacher, on an audio tape.

p. 120   During the course of their journey, the wagon group stopped in Tetiev: Channa "Anne" Caprove Kravitz, in an oral story that she told the author, described a town, whose name she did not recall, that the group passed through while traveling from Belaya Tserkov to Romania. She said the group was searching for a synagogue to spend the night. In this town, the group learned of a massive pogrom that months earlier had massacred the Jewish population. The synagogue was deliberately burned, killing many Jews who were hiding and trapped inside. The author, using that information as a lead, thoroughly researched the region. She concluded that the massacred town her grandmother described passing through as a child must have been Tetiev; she then set out to share what she researched to be the absolutely devastating fate of the Jews of Tetiev.

p. 120   where the old, somewhat oriental-looking wooden synagogue: Friedman, *Pogromchik*, page 11.

pp. 120–21   where between 1,500 to 2,000 Jews had sought safety: Rosenthal in MH, pages 78–79, mentions the number 1,500. Rosenthal in Tetiever Khurbn, Part I, #16, also states 1,500. On page 240 of Annex 49, in "The Pogroms in the Ukraine Under the Ukrainian Governments 1917–1920" by the Committee of Jewish Delegations, the number of victims in the synagogue as 2,000. The text on page 112 states that "over 1,000 Jews" were inside the synagogue. On page 11 of *Pogromchik*, Friedman states that the number of victims at the synagogue was 2,000.

p. 121   Ataman Kurovsky: The Committee of Jewish Delegations, "The Pogroms in the Ukraine Under the Ukrainian Governments 1917–1920," page 111.

p. 121   Ostrovsky as he incited hate in a speech: The Committee of Jewish Delegations, "The Pogroms in the Ukraine Under the Ukrainian Governments 1917–1920", page 112.

p. 121   men, women, and children: Rosenthal in MH, pages 78–79.

p. 121   Young children were snatched from their parents and thrown violently: The Committee of Jewish Delegations, "The Pogroms in the Ukraine Under The Ukrainian Governments 1917–1920," page 112.

p. 121   A woman in labor: Spevack, in his family story, "Recalling My Youth [in Tetiev]."

p. 121   Bandits . . . brought logs: Rosenthal in MH, pages 78–79.

p. 121   Colonel Kurovsky and others were named by Friedman, *Pogromchik*, page 11.

p. 121   three-man delegation: Rosenthal in MH, pages 78–79.

p. 121   The forty-three-year-old spiritual leader: The rabbi's birth year, and therefore his age at the time of his murder, was determined after the author saw the entry by Gottlieb, ed., *Ohole-Schem, Biografien und Adressen d. Rabbiners*, page 84.

p. 121   stood near his wooden desk: The Committee of Jewish Delegations, "The Pogroms in the Ukraine Under the Ukrainian Governments 1917–1920," page 241.

p. 122   Velvel, a fourteen-year-old boy: The Committee of Jewish Delegations, "The Pogroms in the Ukraine Under the Ukrainian Governments 1917–1920," page 249, Annex No. 49.

p. 122   along with the rabbi's seven-year-old daughter, Lena: Jerry Cutler, in a correspondence with the author.

p. 122   Some of the peasants arguing the fate of the rabbi can be found in "The Pogroms in the Ukraine Under the Ukrainian Governments 1917–1920," page 241, Annex 49.

p. 122   Velvel escaped: The Committee of Jewish Delegations, "The Pogroms in the Ukraine Under the Ukrainian Governments 1917–1920," Annex No 49.

p. 122   Young Lena feigned death: Jerry Cutler, the great rabbi's grandson and Lena's son, in a correspondence with the author.

p. 122   Author's note: Two of the rabbi's daughters, Lena and Minnie, were initially thought to be the only survivors of his immediate family. After the massacre, they ended up in an orphanage in Kiev. Years later, the sisters eventually immigrated to Toronto, Canada. In a Yiddish newspaper report discovered years later by the author, it appears that one or two other children from the rabbi's large brood may have also survived, probably unbeknownst to Lena and her sister.

p. 122   The majority who escaped the brutal heat of the flames: The Committee of Jewish Delegations, "The Pogroms in the Ukraine Under the Ukrainian Governments 1917–1920," page 242, Annex 50.

p. 122   knew of the great rabbi who had served Tetiev since his youth in 1895: Gottlieb, ed., *Ohole-Schem, Biografien und Adressen d. Rabbiners*, page 84, gives the genealogy of the Tetiev rabbi.

p. 123   Out of six thousand Jews living in Tetiev, only two thousand survived: The Committee of Jewish Delegations, "The Pogroms in the Ukraine Under the Ukrainian Governments 1917–1920," page 242, Annex 50. Please note there are slightly different numbers of residents and victims listed in different sources; these are guesstimates. Friedman, *Pogromchik*, page 12, footnotes the Committee of Jewish Delegations' numbers.

p. 123   The morning after the massacre, Thursday. Rosenthal, Tetiever Khurbn, Part I, #16.

p. 123   fires spread near Tziprivka Street: Rosenthal in MH, pages 78–79.

p. 123   When news of the massacre reached Kiev: Jerry Cutler, in a letter to the author. Jerry learned of this from Ruschel, a then ninety-year-old survivor from Tetiev whom he spoke with many years ago.

p. 124   They sought refuge at a synagogue south of Tetiev: Channa "Anne" Caprove Kravitz, in an interview with the author.

p. 124   commissar sitting *shiva*: Barney Stumacher, on an audio tape.

p. 125   "forged across icy rivers and ponds.": Barbara Stumacher, in "Little Me."

p. 125   when she stepped off a wagon and fell through a thin patch of ice: Barbara Stumacher, in "Little Me."

p. 125   "Spare that man!": Barbara Stumacher, in "Little Me."

p. 125   "Confiscate Court": Channa "Anne" Caprove Kravitz, in an interview with the author.

p. 126   When the group rode through a small town in Podolia Guberniya: Ruby
           Stumacher and Daniel Cutler, in an interview with Abe Stumacher.

CHAPTER SIXTEEN FOOTNOTES

p. 122   Rabbi Gedalia's book: This is mentioned by title in an entry (under Rabbi
           Rabinovitch, a descendant of Rabbi Gedalia) in Gottlieb, ed., *Ohole-Schem,
           Biografien und Adressen d. Rabbiners*, page 84. Joanna Yael Zimmerman
           assisted with the interpretation of the title.

p. 123   The number of four hundred murdered in Pogrebishche, half of them women,
           is confirmed on page 111 by the Committee of Jewish Delegations in "The
           Pogroms in the Ukraine Under the Ukrainian Governments 1917–1920." A
           deposition by Lifschitz, in the same source, pages 91–93, also confirms these
           numbers.

CHAPTER SEVENTEEN: THE PERILOUS CROSSING OF THE DNIESTER RIVER

p. 127   From 1918 to 1940: *Encyclopaedia Britannica*, page 526.

p. 127   in the Carpathian Mountains and flowed in a southeasterly: *Encyclopedia
           Britannica* Online.

p. 127   meanders for about 840 miles: *Encyclopedia Britannica* Online.

p. 127   south of Mogilev-Podolski measures anywhere from five to ten miles:
           Encyclopedia Britannica, page 525.

p. 127   November to January: *Encyclopedia Britannica*, page 525.

p. 128   Barney reluctantly agreed to their outrageous demands: Barney Stumacher,
           on an audiotape.

p. 128   "Then [we] began the climb up the other side": Lessure Mayers, "My Family
           History," page 3.

p. 128   "Our pace [across the mountains] was too slow": Lessure Mayers, "My Family
           History," page 4.

p. 129   Rochela Faynzilberg and her family also faced the unmerciful climb: Rochela
           Faynzilberg (Ruth Feinsilver), "A Mountain Climb," page 2.

CHAPTER SEVENTEEN FOOTNOTES

p. 128   After he arrived in Bucharest: Barney Stumacher, on an audiotape.

p. 128   a hill approximately two miles steep: Bernard Sanders, "A Brief Memoir," page 6.

CHAPTER EIGHTEEN: ADVENTURES IN ROMANIA

p. 131   "Can you believe that there was once a city where no Jew went hungry":
           Malkin, *The Journeys of David Toback*, page 71.

p. 132   This area is physically bordered: Theodore Shabad, *Encyclopedia Americana*,
           page 623.

p. 132   national council . . . appealed to Romania: Wayne S. Vucinich, *Collier's
           Encyclopedia*, page 103.

p. 132   the Treaty of Paris: Wayne S. Vucinich, *Collier's Encyclopedia*, page 103.

p. 133   He had "come into possession": Norman Stumacher, in an interview with the
           author.

p. 133 and announced grandly that he had just bought the café: Norman Stumacher, in an interview with the author.

p. 133 to see his twenty-year-old sister, Bossie: Allan Avery, in a 2004 letter to the author, confirmed that when he asked his cousin Filia Holtzman, she identified Bossie as the sister of Barney (her aunt) who was arrested with him on the train in Bucharest. Barney himself only alluded that it was one of his three sisters who still lived in Europe, but did not identify which one. Other family members also identified the sister as being Bossie.

p. 134 a glamorous singer with the Kiev Opera Company: Blossom Linder, in an interview with the author.

p. 134 Her husband, Boris Weinschel: Blossom Linder, in an interview with the author.

p. 134 took the twenty passports and hid them: Much of the information and dialogue about Bossie and Barney's meeting and subsequent arrest, jailing, and court hearing was based on Barney Stumacher's story. The quotes in this section are attributed to Barney Stumacher, on an audiotape.

CHAPTER EIGHTEEN FOOTNOTES

p. 136 Barney's parents met privately with the vice counselor: Barney Stumacher, on an audiotape.

p. 137 Frieda's sons soon rushed her to a New York City ophthalmologist: Barney Stumacher, on an audiotape. Other relatives also confirmed that Frieda had a cataract operation, and her vision was partially restored; she is even seen wearing eyeglasses in photos of her taken in America.

CHAPTER NINETEEN: LIFE IN KISHINEV

p. 139 from any given country to only 3 percent of the people: Tifft, *Ellis Island,* page 116.

p. 139 The total number of immigrants that the United States was allowing into the country in 1922: Tifft, *Ellis Island,* page 117.

p. 139 The limits for Russia and Romania can be found in Tifft, *Ellis Island,* 117. (Note: Tifft's book was published in 1990, before Ukraine's independence in 1991. There are no figures given separately for Ukraine in the table found on page 117.)

p. 139 was found murdered by the Dniester River, false rumors: Judge, *Easter in Kishinev,* page 40.

p. 140 encouraged by rumors published in *Bessarabets*: Judge, *Easter in Kishinev,* pages 43–45.

p. 140 attacks left forty-nine Jews dead: Jewish Virtual Library (see URL in Bibliography).

p. 141 She was a Romanian general's daughter: Bercovici, *That Royal Lover,* page 99.

p. 141 and an indirect descendant of: Bercovici, *That Royal Lover,* pages 70–71.

p. 141 Queen Marie forced her son to annul the marriage: Bercovici, *That Royal Lover,* page 95.

p. 141 Prince Carol married Princess Helen of Greece: Bercovici, *That Royal Lover,* page 98, and NYT, March 11, 1921, page 20.

p. 142   Queen Marie then handpicked a "suitable" bride: Bercovici, *That Royal Lover,*
            pages 76 and 95.

p. 142   It was the second union between members of these royal families: NYT,
            March 11, 1921, page 20.

p. 142   The couple was married in a civil ceremony held in the Grecian palace: NYT,
            March 11, 1921, page 20.

p. 142   Princess Helen was wearing a white satin gown trimmed in gold : NYT,
            March 11, 1921, page 20.

p. 143   Until 1856, most Gypsies in Romania were slaves: Fraser, *The Gypsies,* page 59.

p. 144   A huge send-off is the rule rather than the exception: The Patrin Web Journal,
            Romani Customs and Traditions: Death Rituals and Customs, page 3.

p. 145   It was an emotional display: The Patrin Web Journal, Romani Customs and
            Traditions: Death Rituals and Customs, page 2, confirms Channa's account of
            the increasing volume and emotional display of Romani mourners.

p. 145   when just seven months after the wedding of Crown Prince Carol and his
            bride Princess Helen: Bercovici, *That Royal Lover,* page 77.

p. 145   *Or chadash al tzion ta' ir*: This is a Hebrew phrase taken from the morning
            prayers.

p. 145   a branch in Israel would end: Zunser, *Yesterday,* page 2.

p. 147   he would be forced to mark a "CT": International Channel Networks (see
            URL in Bibliography).

p. 149   Constanta was the sight of the ancient city of Tomas: Friends and Partners
            Romania (see URL in Bibliography).

CHAPTER NINETEEN FOOTNOTES

p. 143   In 1897, a census indicated that there were 8,636 Gypsy Rom: Crowe, *A
            History of the Gypsies of Eastern Europe and Russia,* page 170.

p. 143   Elemer Illyes estimated that there were 133,000 gypsies in all of Romania:
            Crowe, *A History of the Gypsies of Eastern Europe and Russia,* page 127.

CHAPTER TWENTY: JOURNEY ON THE SS *BRAGA*

p. 150   "Prayer During a Storm at Sea": Mayer (trans.), *Hours of Devotion,* page 93.

p. 152   capable of holding 1,480 passengers: Ellis Island Ship Image for the SS *Braga,*
            which can be found on the Ellis Island website.

p. 153   but it was to remain demilitarized: Columbia Encyclopedia, Sixth Edition,
            Dardanelles, online.

p. 153   In times of peace, the Straits were to remain open to all ships . . . and could
            not hinder the passage of neutral ships: Columbia Encyclopedia, Sixth
            Edition, Dardanelles, online.

p. 154   claimed the lives of between two and three million: Patterson, "Typhus and
            its Control in Russia, 1870–1940," pages 361–62.

CHAPTER TWENTY FOOTNOTES

p. 153   Since the Renaissance, Europeans have called the strait: Walsh, *Encyclopedia
            Americana,* "Dardanelles," page 497.

p. 153   The world formally recognized the country that the Turkish Nationalists:
           Pope and Pope, *Turkey Unveiled,* page 58.

CHAPTER TWENTY-ONE: AMERICA: THE FIRST YEARS

p. 158   "Aliens on Four Ships Too Soon to Enter" and "Most of the 1,896 Who
           Arrived": NYT, September 2, 1923, page 1.

p. 159   An official observer looking through a pair of binoculars: NYT, September 2,
           1923, page 16.

p. 159   "The four steamships which the official observer says": NYT, September 2,
           1923, page 1.

p. 159   during a meeting on September 1 with Commissioner of Immigration: NYT,
           September 2, 1923, page 16.

p. 159   insisted that he called out each half minute: NYT, September 2, 1923, page 16.

p. 159   whom the media referred to as picture brides: NYT, September 2, 1923, page 16.

p. 159   He agreed, in conjunction with the decision handed down by the
           Department of Labor, to allow the passengers to enter America: NYT,
           September 6, 1923, page 1.

p. 160   A tremendous fine was imposed on the four steamship companies: NYT,
           September 6, 1923, page 1.

p. 160   important passengers aboard, including Colonel George Harvey: NYT,
           September 8, 1923, page 17.

p. 162   who had suffered a partial hearing loss after the great fire: Jerold Wise, in an
           interview with the author.

p. 162   for their charitable contributions: *Boston Jewish Advocate,* February 8, 1949,
           page 2.

CHAPTER TWENTY-ONE FOOTNOTE

p. 160   The vigilante murders of approximately six thousand: The People's Korea (see
           URL in Bibliography).

CHAPTER TWENTY-TWO: STRUGGLING IN THE GOLDEN LAND

p. 170   she walked by rows of wooden cages crammed with live chickens: Marcy
           Kravitz Brahin, in an interview with the author.

p. 170   he playfully coupled any English words: Bobby Usatch Katz, in an interview
           with the author.

pp. 170–71 she would surprise him with a small slice of *kapchonka:* Bobby Usatch Katz, in
           an interview with the author.

p. 171   Sunny was hungry and had helped herself to the luscious fruit: Bobby Usatch
           Katz, in an interview with the author.

CHAPTER TWENTY-THREE: THE STORY OF ANNE AND BEN

Much of this chapter was recalled by Channa "Anne" Caprove Kravitz and Ben Kravitz in
an interview with the author.

p. 179   Hersh devoted himself to the people of the shtetl: Saltz in PYB, pages
           244–47.

p. 179   He smuggled goods: Saltz in PYB, pages 241–43.

p. 180   "I decided to write her a letter and give her an ultimatum": Ben Kravitz, in an
            interview with the author, recalling his father's ultimatum to his mother.

CHAPTER TWENTY-THREE FOOTNOTES

p. 176   Ed had married and became a Trenton police officer: This information was
            confirmed by Sharon Silverglade, in a letter to the author. Rebecca had heard
            that he married and became a police officer; the remaining information about
            Ed's life was confirmed by S. Silverglade.

p. 179   Hersh was a member of Pochayev's Chevra Kadisha: Saltz in PYB, pages 244–47.

p. 179   who was stationed in Pochayev: Saltz in PYB, pages 271–72.

CHAPTER TWENTY-FOUR: WHEN SUNNY MET HARRY

Notation: The quotes credited to Sunny regarding her initial impressions of Harry
are remembered by her daughter, Bobby, who read her mother's (now lost) diary many
decades ago.

Much of the information about Sunny, Harry, Anna, and David in this chapter is from
an interview with their daughter and granddaughter, Bobby Usatch Katz.

p. 185   "Stop calling her," he advised: A story told to the author by Ben Kravitz.

p. 186   signed the government document as a single man with no dependents: WWI
            draft registration card of David Usatch, signed by him in Philadelphia on
            June 5, 1917 (roll 1907610, draft board 8).

CHAPTER TWENTY-FIVE: BERYL

Some of the information from this chapter is from an interview with Bobby Usatch Katz.

Some of the information from this chapter is from an interview with Channa "Anne"
Caprove Kravitz and Ben Kravitz.

p. 190   Anne read his death certificate: Commonwealth of Pennsylvania Certificate
            of Death of Benjamin Caprove, filed January 24, 1940, File 306, Registered
            No 1925, signed by Dr. Garfield G. Duncan.

CHAPTER TWENTY-FIVE FOOTNOTES

p. 188   losing fifteen thousand games to the Harlem Globetrotters: Lidz, "The
            Biggest Loser."

p. 191   Even many of the physicians and nurses: University of Pennsylvania Hospital,
            Wartime Service Archives, Image Gallery.

p. 191   The young doctor who signed Beryl's death certificate: 24th Infantry Division
            Corps, online story (see URL in Bibliography. It is from a caption under a photo.)

CHAPTER TWENTY-SIX: RABBI PITSIE AVRAM IN THE BRONX

p. 195   "While a child is still in the womb": Babylonian Talmud, Niddah 30B.

p. 196   but his late father was Rabbi Aryeh Judah Spector: Gottlieb, *Ohole-Schem,
            Biografien und Adressen d. Rabbiners*, pages 361–62.

p. 196   Laizer wrote a story in a careful Hebrew script: Rabbi Laizer Spector, "A
            Composition in Hebrew."

p. 197   she and her daughter (Laizer's sister) Nina traveled : according to Libby's Russian passport, which was shared with the author by her granddaughter Patricia Ricardo Bezalel.

p. 197   "the family had lost contact for many years and according to Laizer": Shirley Landau, in a letter to the author.

p. 198   Rabbi Pitsie Avram and Sara made the long pilgrimage: Ellis Island passenger records.

p. 198   favored his grandson: Max Zaslawsky, in an interview with the author.

p. 199   The story of "Little Moshe" mimicking his grandfather, the rabbi, at prayer: Max Zaslawsky, in an interview with the author.

p. 200   The day that he died, his daughter, Havah, went into hysterics: Max Zaslawsky, in an interview with the author.

p. 200   director of France's National Center of Scientific Research: *Rossiyskaya Evreiskaya Entsiclopediya*, entry 1354.

p. 200   wanted to bring his young cousin: Max Zaslawsky, in an interview with the author.

p. 200   He worked at Livermore, Los Alamos: Max Zaslawsky, in a letter to the author.

p. 202   gathered his shaken community that was seeking refuge: *Reshumot*, volume 3, pages 380–82 on Vinograd.

CHAPTER TWENTY-SIX FOOTNOTES

p. 196   Pitsie Avram's only son: Gottlieb, *Ohole-Schem, Biografien und Adressen d. Rabbiners*, pages 361–62.

p. 196   Earned a PhD in chemistry: *Rossiyskaya Evreiskaya Entsiclopediya*, entry 1354.

p. 203   This was an early pogrom in Stavishche: *Reshumot*, volume 3, 1923, pages 380–82 on Vinograd.

CHAPTER TWENTY-SEVEN: THE EVENTS THAT DEFINED THEIR LIVES IN THE NEW WORLD

p. 206   Letter dated January 31, 1948, was written in Russian by Sophia, Pollya's daughter, to Rebecca and Isaac Caprove and family, and translated by David Goldman, MA.

p. 208   Anne's eleven-year-old daughter, Marcy, hesitated: Marcy Kravitz Brahin, in an interview with the author.

p. 208   Sunny rushed over in a taxicab: Bobby Usatch Katz, in an interview with the author.

pp. 208–09 "Kaddish to be repeated by the sons during": *The Form of Daily Prayers*, page 647.

CHAPTER TWENTY-EIGHT: RAINBOWS

p. 212   he'd jumped to his death: This was sadly confirmed by family stories and by the 1944 New York City (Brooklyn) death certificate of Jacob Cutler #24428.

CHAPTER TWENTY-EIGHT FOOTNOTE

p. 211   Jonathan Cutler shared with the author: Jonathan Cutler, in a letter to the
            author.

**APPENDIX A: THE COLORFUL HISTORY OF BRANICKI PALACE AND THE
SECRET IDENTITY OF ITS FIRST COUNTESS**

p. 217   four centuries to 1622: Rulikowski, *Slownik Geograficzny: Stawiszcze*,
            page 297.

p. 217   "The settlement of Lubomir and Pasieczna": Rulikowski, *Slownik
            Geograficzny: Stawiszcze*, page 297.

p. 218   In 1774, Poland's last king: Rulikowski, *Slownik Geograficzny: Stawiszcze*,
            page 299.

p. 218   was rumored to have been the biological daughter of the world's most
            famous empress: Miller, *Arystokracja*, page 221, and Moscicki, *Polski
            Slownik Biograficzny*, page 393. In addition, Count Ladislas Tarnowski
            writes in his family history that Alexandra was the natural born
            daughter of Empress Catherine II. "Stawiszcze and the Branicki
            Family," page 1.

p. 219   Rumors, passed down: Anna Wolska discusses this in Miller, *Arystokracja*,
            pages 11–12; Count Ladislas Tarnowski openly writes that Aleksandra was
            Catherine's natural-born daughter in his family history, "Stawiszcze and the
            Branicki Family," page 1.

p. 219   the first biological child of Grand Duchess Catherine: Moscicki, *Polski
            Slownik Biograficzny*, pages 393–95.

p. 219   completely enamored with Grigory Potemkin: Moscicki, *Polski Slownik
            Biograficzny*, pages 393–95.

p. 219   Gavrila Romanovitch Derzhavin: Moscicki, *Polski Slownik Biograficzny*,
            pages 393–95.

p. 219   interviewed Anna Wolska: Miller, *Arystokracja*, pages 11–12 (in Polish). For
            more on this story, see Miller's book.

**APPENDIX B: FUNERAL SPEECH FOR COUNT WLADYSLAW BRANICKI,
LAST NOBLEMAN OF STAVISHCHE**

p. 221   whose own mother was baptized in the church: Iwaszkiewicz, *Ksiazka Moich
            Wspomnien*, pages 134–35.

p. 221   that he was the subject of many legends: Iwaszkiewicz, *Ksiazka Moich
            Wspomnien*, pages 134–35.

p. 221   In 1922, the remains of Count Wladyslaw Branicki and his wife, Countess
            Julia (née Potocka), were brought back to Poland: Count Paul Potocki, in a
            letter to the author.

p. 221   Sucha . . . originally purchased in 1846: Tarnowski, "Stawiszcze and the
            Branicki Family," page 2.

p. 222   gifted the estate to his daughter, Countess Anna Tarnowska: Tarnowski,
            "Stawiszcze and the Branicki Family," page 2, and Count Paul Potocki, in a
            letter to the author.

p. 222   Funeral Speech of Wladyslaw Branicki ("Adzio") written and eulogized by
            M. Mazaraki in Polish on September 21, 1922, in Sucha, Poland. Translation
            by Monika Hendry. Courtesy of and special thanks to Countess Rey of
            Montresor. Special thanks to Count Paul Potocki for his assistance.

APPENDIX B FOOTNOTE

p. 222   willed his vast and beloved estate in Stavishche to his third-born daughter,
            Countess Julia Potocka: Tarnowski, "Stawiszcze and the Branicki Family,"
            page 2, and in Kiev Guberniya Notebook (1915), mentioned in a letter from
            Mrs. O. Polozova, states that Wladyslaw Branicki's daughter Julia was the
            new landowner of Stavishche.

APPENDIX C: THE STAVISHCHE POGROM TOMBSTONE LIST (PARTIAL), 1918–1920

pp. 225–27 Source: Tcherikower Archive, File 21642, second page, part IV. Date appears
            to be April 6, 1921.

APPENDIX D: PARTIAL LIST OF STAVISHCHE RESIDENTS MURDERED BY GRIGORIEV'S BAND, HEADED BY ZHELEZNIAK, JUNE 1919

pp. 228–29 Source: Rosenthal in MH, page 2.

APPENDIX E: A PARTIAL POGROM MEMORIAL LIST, 1920

pp. 230–34 Original Source: The Forverts (The Forward); Credit: The Forward
            Association, December 30, 1920, page 1. This list also later appeared in SYB,
            pages 239–44.

APPENDIX F: DEATH LIST(PARTIAL): STAVISHCHE

pp. 235–36 Handwritten list of those killed in Stavishcha (Yiddish name for
            Stavishche) in Tarashcha Uyezd. Source: From the State Archive of
            Kyiv Oblast, Fond P-3050 inventory 1 Case 43. Language: Yiddish. This
            appears in a book by the Kiev Regional Commission of the Jewish Public
            Committee for Assistance to Victims of Pogroms, Information Department,
            with the lists of victims of pogroms, refugees, and children of murdered
            parents in Tarashcha Uyezd, Kiev Guberniya, written between 1920 and
            1921. 199 sheets; this is one page, with a handwritten page number at top as
            196; it appears digitalized as page 213.

APPENDIX G: THE POGROM SURVIVORS: STAVISHCHE, 1923

p. 237   "The 1917–1921 pogroms were the worst and most violent acts against
            the Jews . . .": Chapin and Weinstock, *The Road From Letichev*, volume 2,
            page 499.

p. 238   The June 1923 Report on Stavishche, Kiev Guberniya and the Letter
            of Thanks for Help Rendered: JDC Division, June 1923: Source: The
            American Jewish Joint Distribution Committee Archives, collection
            #21/32, file #504.

APPENDIX H: FATES OF THE VILLAGERS

p. 241   Philip (Phillip) Postrel's letter: This was included as a part of the passport
              application of Philip Postrel, dated February 10, 1921, and issued on
              February 15, 1921, National Archives Microfilm Publication, M1490,
              Certificate Number 141819.

pp. 242–43 Shika de Potch: Dr. Murry Rich, in letters to the author.

pp. 243–44 Sol Moser: Vivian Flamm, in letters to and in an interview with the author.

pp. 244–46 Chiah Sura Spivack: Emily Bayard, in letters to the author.

pp. 246–47 Sarah Cutler: Rita L. Antanir Posin, in an interview with the author.

APPENDIX H FOOTNOTE

p. 242   Some important early visitors: Rulikowski, *Slownik Geograficzny: Stawiszcze*
              pages 297–99.

APPENDIX I: FAMINE, FASCISTS, AND THE HOLOCAUST: STAVISHCHE

p. 248   "At the time, I lived close to the [Stavishche] hospital": Webber, US
              Commission on the Ukraine Famine, Report to Congress, pages 385–93.

p. 248   ". . . Enormous open pits were dug . . .": Webber, US Commission on the
              Ukraine Famine, Report to Congress, pages 385–93.

p. 249   The story of Raisa Bershadskaya's eyewitness account of the Holocaust in
              Stavishche: Faina Avratiner, in an interview with the author.

p. 249   ". . . Then the Gestapo came to the village . . .": Yad Vashem the Holocaust
              Martyrs' and Heroes Remembrance Authority, Signature member in the Yad
              Vashem Archives is YVA M.52/235, frame 2045–51.

p. 250   "Three hundred forty-four people . . .": Yad Vashem the Holocaust Martyrs'
              and Heroes Remembrance Authority, Signature member in the Yad Vashem
              Archives is YVA M.52/235, frame 2045–51.

p. 250   "Every week many people were caught and sent to hard labor": Yad Vashem
              the Holocaust Martyrs' and Heroes Remembrance Authority, Signature
              member in the Yad Vashem Archives is YVA M.52/235, frame 2045–51.

p. 250   After the war ended in 1945, ten Jewish families: Faina Avratiner, in an
              interview with the author.

p. 250   To the group's surprise, their loved ones' bodies: Faina Avratiner, in an
              interview with the author.

p. 250   exhuming the bodies: F. Avratiner, in an interview with the author, and Wolf,
              "Russian Odyssey-Richs' Visit Shtetl Roots," page 9.

p. 251   Michael Mailin: F. Avratiner, in an interview with the author.

p. 251   reveals that in 1939: Spector, ed., *The Encyclopedia of Jewish Life Before and
              During the Holocaust*, volume III, page 1240.

APPENDIX I FOOTNOTE

p. 251   grass covered the raised mounds: Wolf, "Russian Odyssey-Richs' Visit Shtetl
              Roots," page 9.

APPENDIX J: SEARCHING FOR A HISTORICAL TREASURE: THE *MEGILAT HA-TEVAH*

p. 254   felt compelled to leave a written testimony: From the publishers of the first volume of E. D. Rosenthal's (editor) *Megilat Ha-tevah*, in an introduction, probably written by Bialik.

p. 254   who was seriously ill while struggling to complete his work: From the publishers of the first volume of E. D. Rosenthal's (editor) *Megilat Ha-tevah*, in an introduction, probably written by Bialik.

p. 254   Emma Goldman: Goldman writes of a chance encounter in Odessa with Bialik and a "literary investigator" on the pogroms in her own book, *My Further Disillusionment in Russia*, page 10.

APPENDIX K: THE STUNNING DISCOVERY OF THE STAVISHCHE TORAH CROWN

pp. 258–60 Ida Selavan Schwarcz is credited with translating the names on the bells hanging from the Torah crown. The *NJJN* article by the author was included here with permission.

BIBLIOGRAPHY

ORAL HISTORIES
This book is based mostly on the early life of my grandmother Channa "Anne" Caprove Kravitz and her family. I would like to thank and acknowledge the many others and their families listed herewith who shared their stories with me in the hopes that our ancestors and this time period in Jewish history will never be forgotten.

AUDIO RECORDINGS
Channa "Anne" Caprove Kravitz, 1978–1979, four audio tapes recorded by the author. Oral histories passed on to the author from Anne (not included on the tapes) were also used throughout the book.

Barney Stumacher, 1963, audio tape recorded by Phillip Silverman. Courtesy of and special thanks to both Phillip Silverman and Norman Stumacher

Ruby Stumacher, Kolman Stumacher, and Daniel Cutler, February 5, 1972, audio tape recorded by Abe Stumacher. Courtesy of Audrey Stumacher. Special thanks to and courtesy of David Stumacher.

WRITTEN FAMILY HISTORIES, STORIES, AND SPEECHES
Bayard, Emily. "Yasha Kainer's Stories About Russia," 1987. Courtesy of and special thanks to Emily Bayard and special thanks to Yasha Kainer and his family.

Dayan, Yehoshua. "Bayit Be-Yisreal:Eliyahu ve-Batya Dayan," circa 1970s. Translated by Dr. Ida Selavan Schwarcz. Believed to be published privately.

Einbinder Goodman, Betty. "The Sudden Call," a composition written on May 14, 1926.

Feinsilver, Ruth (Rochela Feinzilberg). "An Adventure," 1926. Courtesy of Dr. Abraham Davidson.

Feinsilver, Ruth (Rochela Feinzilberg). "A Mountain Climb," 1926. Courtesy of Dr. Abraham Davidson.

Kaminsky, Alan. "The Stepansky Family Story," 1998. Courtesy of Alan Kaminsky.

Kravitz, Channa "Anne" Caprove. "The Story of My Life," a long letter written to her granddaughter, the author, December 8, 1990.

Mayers, Rose Lessure (Lechtzer/Lichtzer). "My Family History," 1928. Courtesy of Rose Mayers and Ellen Ginsberg-Caplan.

Mazaraki, M. Funeral Speech for Count Wladyslaw Branicki, September 21, 1922, in Sucha, Poland, written for and spoken at his funeral. Translated by Monika Hendry. Obtained by Count Paul Potocki; Courtesy of Countess M. Rey. Housed in the library and archives of Montresor, the private property of Countess Rey.

Sanders, Bernard. "A Brief Memoir," 1984.

Spector, Rabbi Laizer. "The Adventures of My Life," July 28, 1925. Courtesy of Judy Spector Hammond.

Spector, Rabbi Laizer. "A Composition in Hebrew," 1925. Courtesy of Judy Spector Hammond.

Spevack, David. "Recalling My Youth [in Tetiev]." Story appears on Jewishgen.org's kehila links pages on Tetiev and was from "This I remembered," Jewish Federation of Cleveland, 1985.

Stumacher, Barbara. "Little Me," a composition written about her grandparents Itzie and Molly Cutler Stumacher, circa 1968. Also read by Abe Stumacher on the audiotape mentioned already from February 5, 1972. Courtesy of Audrey Stumacher. Special thanks to and Courtesy of David Stumacher.

Tarnowski, Count Ladislas. "Stawiszcze and the Branicki Family," February 2005. Translated by Sophie-Caroline de Margerie. Courtesy of Count Tarnowski and Sophie-Caroline de Margerie. Count Tarnowski referenced the following works in his family history:

———*Materialy do Dziejow Rezydencji* by Roman Aftanazy. Published by the Polish Academy of Sciences, 1987.

———*Almanach Blekitny* by Count Georges (Jerzy) Dunin-Borkowski. Warsaw & Lvov: Nakl. Ksieg. H. Altenberga: 1908.

———*Armorial de la Noblesse Polonaise Titrée* by Simon Konarski. Published by the author, 1958.

GROUP INTERVIEW

Daniel Cutler and Sol Moser, May 25, 1987, interview by the author.

Ben Gold (Golditch), Dora Golditch Rich, and Abe Rich, 1984, interviewed by and courtesy of Dr. Murry Rich.

Ben Kravitz and Anne Caprove Kravitz, 2000, interview by the author.

TELEPHONE AND IN-PERSON INTERVIEWS AND WRITTEN CORRESPONDENCES WITH THE AUTHOR

A special thank you to:

Avery, Allan: great-grandson of Frieda Ravicher

Avratiner, Faina: daughter of Raisa Bershadskaya

Barret, Herb: 2013 president of the First Stavishter Benevolent Association

Bayard, Emily: great-granddaughter of Chiah Sura Postrelka Spivack and cousin of Dr. Yasha Kainer

Beaver, Mindi: granddaughter of Channa Caprove

Bezalel, Patricia Ricardo: granddaughter of Liba Gaisinsky Spector

Brahin, Marcy Kravitz: daughter of Channa Caprove and Ben Kravitz

Cutler, Charles: son of Avrum Cutler and Slova Ova Denka

Cutler, Daniel: son of Yunkel Cutler and Esther Moser

Cutler, Jerry: grandson of Rabbi Simon Rabinovitch (Shimon Rabinowitz) of Tetiev

Cutler, Jonathan: grandson of Avrum Cutler and Slova Ova Denka

Danziger, Lisa Linder: granddaughter of Bossie Stumacher and daughter of Blossom Batt Linder

Flamm, Vivian: daughter of Sol Moser and granddaughter of Haika Stepansky and Itzie Moser

Golditch, Dora: interview performed by Dr. Murry Rich in 1988

Grossman, Esther Goldman: daughter of Eva Haissinsky Goldman

Hammond, Judy Spector: daughter of Rabbi Laizer Spector

Katz, Barbara (Bobby) Usatch: daughter of Sunny Caprove and Harry Usatch

Kravitz, Ben: husband of Channa Caprove

Landau, Shirley: daughter of Rabbi Laizer Spector

Lidz, Sheila Kraidin: daughter of Alexander Kraidin

Linder, Blossom Batt: daughter of Bossie Stumacher

de Margerie, Sophie-Caroline Tarnowska: great-great-granddaughter of Count Wladyslaw Branicki

Moser, Elise: granddaughter of Sol Moser

Moser, Sol: son of Itzie Moser and Haika Stepansky

Muler de Fidel, Elba: granddaughter of Elek Stepansky and Sheindel Bershadsky and great-granddaughter of Yoske Stepansky

Picheny, Michael: grandson of Freada Stumacher and David Picheny

Polozova, Mrs. O., and Olga Muzychuk: directors of archives, the Ukraine Government Archives in Kiev, in a 2004 letter to the author in Ukrainian, translated by Alexander Sharon

Posin, Rita L. Antanir: daughter of Sarah Cutler, granddaughter of Yunkel Cutler and Esther Moser, and great-granddaughter of Cantor David-Yosel Moser

Potocki, Count Paul: great-grandson of Count Wladyslaw Branicki

Rich, Dr. Murry: son of Dvora (Dora Gold) Golditch and grandson of Shika de Potch (Yehoshua Golditch)

Senders, Harry: son of Israel Senderowitz

Silverglade, Bruce: son of Ed Silverglade

Silverglade, Sharon: daughter-in-law of Ed Silverglade

Silverman, Phillip: son-in-law of Barney Stumacher

Stumacher, Norman: son of Barney Stumacher

Wise, Jerold: son of Robert Wise and grandson of Harry Wise and Ida Fastofsky

Zaslawsky, Max (Moshe): grandson of Rabbi Yitzhak Avraham Gaisinsky (Pitsie Avram) and son of Havah (Eva) Gaisinsky and David Zaslawsky

A special thanks to: Marcy Brahin, Stephen Kravitz, Mindi Beaver, Karen Gray, Sussie W., Diana Lang, Ericka Lutz, Anne Eckley, Ed Moser, Marsha Kaufman, Alex Krakovsky, Peter Cutler, Vladimir Oksman, Michael Picheny, and Geri Benedetto for assisting in other ways.

SOURCES

Aftanazy, Roman. *Dzieje Rezydencji Na Dawnych Kresach Rzeczypospolitej* (Annals of Residences From the Eastern Borderlands of the Polish-Lithuanian Commonweath) Vol. 11. Translated by Monika Hendry. Wroclaw, 1991–1997.

American Jewish Joint Distribution Committee (AJJDC) Archives, Collection #21/32, File #504, June 1923.

Bercovici, Konrad. *That Royal Lover.* New York: Brewer and Warren, 1931.

Chapin, David A., and Ben Weinstock. *The Road from Letichev, Volume 2: The History and Culture of a Forgotten Jewish Community in Eastern Europe.* Lincoln, Nebraska: Writer's Showcase Press, 2000.

Children of Kibbutz Mashabei-Sadeh. "Ustingrad Sokoliveka, a Town That Was Destroyed." From a working manuscript, a composition that the children of the kibbutz wrote to perpetuate the memory of the town, believed to be eventually published by the kibbutz with the help of survivors of the community, in Israel, 5732.

Chlopicki, A. *Wedrowki Po Guberni Kijowskiej* (Wanderers Around the Kiev District). Warsaw: Tygodnik Illustrowany, 1881.

Columbia Electronic Encyclopedia. 6th ed. "Lausanne, Treaty of." http://www.infoplease.com /ce6/history/A0829043.html.

Committee of Jewish Delegations. "The Pogroms in the Ukraine Under the Ukrainian Governments 1917–1920." Historical Survey with Documents and Photographs. Bale & Danielsson, London: 1927.

Crowe, David M. *A History of the Gypsies of Eastern Europe and Russia.* New York: St. Martin's Press, 1994.

Draznin, Yaffa. *It Began with Zade Usher: The history and record of the families Bernstein-Loyev /Lewis-Mazur.* Los Angeles: Jamy, 1972.

Encyclopaedia Britannica. "Dniester." William Benton: 1973.

Encyclopedia Britannica Online. 2013. "Dniester River." http://www.britannica.com /EBchecked/topic/167210/Dniester-River.

Encyclopaedia Judaica, volume 4. "Belaya Tserkov." Jerusalem: Keter Publishing House, no date given.

The Form of Daily Prayers, L.D. Hirschler, Vienna: 1922.

Fraser, Angus. *The Gypsies.* Oxford, UK, and Cambridge, US: Blackwell, 1992.

Freeze, ChaeRan Y. *Jewish Marriage and Divorce in Imperial Russia.* Waltham, MA: Brandeis University Press, 2002.

Friedman, Saul S. *Pogromchik: The Assassination of Simon Petlura.* New York: Hart, 1976.

Friends and Partners of Romania, 1997, http://www.friends-partners.org/fpromania /counties/constanta.html (accessed 2003).

Gannes, Abraham P. *Childhood in a Shtetl.* Cupertino, California: Ganton Books (in Cooperation with Professional Press of Chapel Hill, NC): 1993. Courtesy of Howard Gannes.

Gelernt, H., ed. *Pitchayever Yizkor Bukh.* Philadelphia: Wohliner Aid Society, 1960.
   PYB Chapters Cited:
   "A Rabbi For Pitchayev and the Czar on the Attic," by Charles Saltz (translated by Eli Epstein), pages 241–43.
   "Hersh Mindes," by Charles Saltz (translated by Paula Parsky), pages 244–50.

"Pitchayev in America: Israel Kravitz," by Charles Saltz (translated by Eli Epstein), pages 271–72.

Gillman, Joseph M., in collaboration with Etta C. Gillman. *The B'Nai Khaim in America: A Study of Cultural Change in a Jewish Group.* Philadelphia: Dorrance, 1969.

Goldman, Emma. *My Further Disillusionment in Russia.* Garden City, NY: Doubleday, Page, 1924.

Gottlieb, S. N. *Ohole-Schem, Biografien und Adressen d. Rabbiners.* Translated by Yale J. Reisner. Pinsk: MM Glouberman, 1912.

Hachovesh (Believed to be a pseudonym for an unnamed reporter). *Hazefirah* (Newspaper). Warsaw, Russian Poland. Translated by Yale J. Reisner. February 9, 1887, page 2.

Heifetz, Elias. *The Slaughter of the Jews in the Ukraine in 1919.* New York: Thomas Seltzer, 1921.

Holtzman, Elizabeth, with Cynthia L. Cooper. *Who Said It Would Be Easy? One Woman's Life in the Political Arena.* New York: Arcade, 1996.

International Channel Networks, "Ellis Island Medical Inspection," http://www.i-channel.com/education/ellis/medical.html (accessed TKTK).

Iwaszkiewicz, Jaroslaw. *Ksiazka Moich Wspomnien* (The Book of My Memories). Translated by Monika Hendry. Krakow: Wydawnictwo Literackie, 1957.

The Jewish Advocate. "This Week's Award: Harry Wise." February 8, 1949, page 2.

Jewish Virtual Library; American Jewish Historical Society; American Jewish Desk Reference: The Philip Leff Group, Inc. 1999) page 15. https://www.jewishvirtuallibrary.org/the-kishinev-massacre-judaic-treasures.

Judge, Edward H. *Easter in Kishinev: Anatomy of a Pogrom.* New York and London: New York University Press, 1992.

Kushnir, Shimon. *The Village Builder: A Biography of Abraham Harzfeld.* Translated by Abraham Regelson and Gertrude Hirschler. New York: Herzl Press, 1967.

Lidz, Franz. "Biggest Loser." *Endgame,* March 16, 2006.

Malkin, Carole. *The Journeys of David Toback (as retold by his granddaughter).* New York: Schocken Books, 1981. Courtesy of Richard Malkin.

Mayer, Rabbi Moritz (trans.); believed to be from an earlier German work by Fanny Neuda. *Hours of Devotion.* New York: Hebrew Publishing, 1866.

Miller, Leo, and Diana F. Miller, eds. *Sokolievka/Justingrad: A Century of Struggle and Suffering in a Ukrainian Shtetl.* New York: Lowenthal, 1983.

Miller, Marek. *Arystokracja.* Translated Monika Hendry. Warszawa: Proszynski i S-ka, 1998.

Moscicki, Henryk. *Polski Slownik Biograficzny: Alexandra Engelhardt* volume II. Translated by Yale J. Reisner. Krakow: Gebethner and Wolff, 1936.

New York Times. "Aliens on Four Ships Too Soon to Enter." September 2, 1923, pages 1 and 16.

New York Times. "Crown Prince Carol Weds Greek Princess." March 11, 1921.

New York Times. "Fine Ships $600,000 for Surplus Aliens." September 6, 1923, pages 1 and 8.

New York Times, "Harvey Sails Today on the Leviathan," September 8, 1923, page 17.

Patrin Web Journal: Romani Customs and Traditions: Death Rituals and Customs; https://www.oocities.org/~patrin/death.htm.

Patterson, K. David. "Typhus and Its Control in Russia, 1870–1940." *Medical History* 37 (1993): 361–81.

Pope, Nicole, and Hugh Pope. *Turkey Unveiled: A History of Modern Turkey*. Woodstock and New York: Overlook Press, 1997.

Rossiyskaya Evreiskaya Entsiclopediya, first ed. Entry 1354, translated by Vitaly Charny. Moscow: 1995.

Rozental (Rosenthal), Eliezer David (E. D.). *Megilat Ha-tevah: homer le-divre yeme ha-pera'ot veha-tevah ba-Yehudim be-Ukrainah, be-Rusyah ha-gedolah uve-Rusyah ha-Levanah*. Original Manuscript. Translated by Dr. Ida Selavan-Schwarcz (sections on Stavishche, Konela, Sokolovka) and Joanna Yael Zimmerman and Lancy Spalter (Tetiev), and a group of Jewishgen volunteers (Belaya Tserkov). Pages 34–35 are believed to be compiled by Rosenthal who interviewed David Hakman, son of Leyb. Gnazim Archive: Archive of the Hebrew Writers Association, Tel Aviv, Israel.

Rozental (Rosenthal), E. D. *Megilat Ha-tevah: homer le-divre yeme ha-pera'ot veha-tevah ba-Yehudim be-Ukrainah, be-Rusyah ha-gedolah uve-Rusyah ha-Levanah* volume 1. A-B, Havurah: Jerusalem-Tel Aviv, 1927. There are also volumes two and three, believed to be published 1929–1930. Note: The published volume(s) do not include the town of Stavishche—they only include the first part of the Hebrew alphabet. The introduction and just a few of the pages on Tetiev are the only pages referred to from the published source. The other references to MH were seen on its original pages.

Rozental (Rosenthal), E. D. *Reshumot* volume 3. Translated by Dr. Ida Selavan Schwarcz. Moriah: Berlin, 1923. These were articles on pages 380–82 whose original source were believed to be from the Rozental collection. These pages were under "Vinograd," with a mention of Stavishche in both the text and in an editorial footnote; the actual Stavishche pages were not included in *Reshumot*.

Rozental (Rosenthal), E. D. *Tetiever Khurbn*. Translated by Dr. Ida Cohen Selavan-Schwarcz. Commissioned by the Odessa Committee of Idgezkom. American Representatives of the All-Russian Jewish Social Committee (Idgezkom): New York, 1922.

Rousselot, L. M., et al. "The Evolution of the Physician's Assistant." *The Bulletin of the New York Academy of Medicine* 47, no. 12 (December 1971).

Rulikowski, Edward. *Slownik Geograficzny: Stawiszcze*. Translated by Monika Hendry. Poland: Publisher unknown, 1890, pages 297–99.

Shabad, Theodore. "Bessarabia." In *Encyclopedia Americana* volume 3, 1981.

Spector, Shmuel, ed. *The Encyclopedia of Jewish Life Before and During the Holocaust* volume III. New York: New York University Press, 2001.

Stavishcha Relief Organization in Kishinev. "The Destroyed City of Stavishcha (Kiev Region)." Document written July 3, 1922, translated from the Yiddish by Rabbi Shawn B. Zell. Unclear if written by or received by Y. Kligar & Y. Schechtman (YIVO, Files 21264–21268).

Tcherikower Archive, File 234, pages 21641–21643, YIVO. Translated David Goldman, MA.

Tcherikower, Elias. *Di Ukrainer Pogromen in Yor 1919*. Translated by Janie Respitz. New York: YIVO Institute for Jewish Research, 1965.

Tifft, Wilton S. *Ellis Island*. Chicago: Contemporary Books, 1990.

"Twenty-fourth Infantry Division, I Corps, US Army, 'The Victory Division' in Australia During WW2." Australia at War. http://www.ozatwar.com/usarmy/24thinfantrydivision .htm (accessed 2022).

Vladimirsky, Dr. Irena. "The Jewish Settlement in Siberia." The Database of Jewish Communities in the Museum of the Jewish People. http://www.bh.org.il/Communities /Archive/Siberia.asp (accessed 2022).

Vucinich, Wayne S. "Bessarabia." In *Collier's Encyclopedia*, volume 4, 1982.

"Wartime Service." University of Pennsylvania Hospital Archives. http:www.uphs.upenn .edu/paharc/collections/gallery/wartime/Duncan.html (accessed 2022).

Webber, Sue Ellen. "U.S. Commission on the Ukraine Famine, Report to Congress." Case History SW34, pages 385–93. Translated by Darian Diachok. Washington: US Government Printing Office, 1988. http://www.faminegenocide.com/mace_ch3.html (accessed 2004).

Weissman, Aaron, ed. *Stavishche (Stavisht) Yizkor Bukh*. Translated by Dr. Ida Selavan Schwarcz with permission of Dr. Schwarcz and Dr. Robert Barnes, Vered Press, Tel Aviv, Israel, funded and published by the Stavisht Society: 1961.

SYB Chapters Cited:

"Days of Pogroms," by Yisrael Senderowitz, pages 155–57.

"Episodes," by A. Ben-Hayim, pages 179–82.

"From My Childhood," by Yosl Golub, pages 95–18.

"From Stavishche to America," by Moshe Galant, pages 77–84.

"The Last Three years in Stavishche," by Issac Golub, pages 119–29.

"A Letter of Alarm from the Rabbi of Stavishche to the Rabbi of Kiev," by Rabbi Yitzhak Avraham Gaisinsky, et al., pages 235–38.

"Memories," by Havah (Eva) Zaslawsky, pages 189–94.

"My Grandfather, the Rabbi of Stavishche," by Havah (Eva) Goldman, pages 55–59.

"Of Bygone Days," by Rabbi M. HaLevi, pages 41–45.

"Pogrom Happenings in Stavishche" (Document by the former member of the Stavishche Town Authority), by Khlavna Kohen (Kagan), pages 221–34.

"What I Remember About Stavishche," by Meyer Spector, pages 85–94.

"Yitzhak Shadkhen," by Berl Rubin, pages 159–61.

Walsh, John R. "Dardanelles." In *Encyclopedia Americana*. Danbury, CT: Grolier Inc, 1997.

Wolf, Barbara. "Russian Odyssey-Richs' Visit Shtetl Roots." *Jewish Journal North of Boston*. September 22, 1988.

Yad Vashem the Holocaust Martyrs' and Heroes Remembrance Authority. Yad Vashem Archives, YVA M.52/235, frame 2045–2051. "Chronological Records about Temporary Fascist Occupation of the Villages of Stavyshche District and Their Liberation by the Red Army." 1941–1944. KRA #4758 OP#2 SH#43. Translated by Anna Royzner.

Yaroshevich, A. I., ed. *All South-Western Region Information and Address Book of Kiev, Podolia and Volyn Districts*. Translated by Yana Golodnaya Goodstein. Russia: Publisher unknown, 1913.

Zunser, Miriam Shomer. *Yesterday: A Memoir of a Russian Jewish Family*. New York: Harper & Row, 1978 (reprint from 1939). Edited by her granddaughter, Emily Wortis Leider.